RIKI SPRINGWELL

Women Are The Best Preppers

Revolutionizing Emergency Preparedness in 2025 and Beyond

First published by Winters Here Press 2025

Copyright © 2025 by Riki Springwell

All rights reserved. No part of this publication may be reproduced, stored or transmitted in any form or by any means, electronic, mechanical, photocopying, recording, scanning, or otherwise without written permission from the publisher. It is illegal to copy this book, post it to a website, or distribute it by any other means without permission.

First edition

This book was professionally typeset on Reedsy.
Find out more at reedsy.com

For all the women preppers who persevered for centuries before me

Contents

Foreword		ii
Preface		iii
Acknowledgments		iv
1	The Quiet Revolutionaries of Preparedness	1
2	The Evolutionary Edge	10
3	The Pantry is Political	24
4	First Aid Without the Drama	40
5	The Psychology of Survival	55
6	Resource Management: Beyond Hoarding	72
7	The Shelter Mindset	89
8	Community Building: The Real Security System	107
9	The Practical Wardrobe	124
10	Water Wisdom	142
11	The Mobile Survival Strategy	164
12	Tools of the Trade	184
13	The Information Economy	209
14	What About the Children?	267
15	Beyond Survival by Creating the World We Want	287
16	Conclusion: The Preparedness Partnership	315
About the Author		336

Foreword

This is my first book and I thank Winters Here Press for all of their guidance. I was inspired by reading a pre-publication copy of their book THE PROGRESSIVE'S 2025 GUIDE TO PREPPING. You can reach me or Winters Here Press at this email: wintersherepress@gmail.com.

Preface

There is only one purpose in this book: to be prepared.

Acknowledgments

I'd like to acknowledge the work of community members keeping us prepared and those who contributed in any way to the knowledge set down in this book. You are all appreciated. I've never done anything alone. Never will.

1

The Quiet Revolutionaries of Preparedness

The first time I met a self-proclaimed "serious prepper," I nearly choked on my homemade elderberry wine. It was at my neighbor Earl's annual summer barbecue, where the mosquitoes and black flies are thick as molasses and the talk inevitably turns to how much snow we'll get come January. A man named Rick—Earl's cousin from New Hampshire—cornered me by the potato salad to show me pictures of his underground bunker.

"Got eight months of MREs, tactical gear rated for Arctic conditions, and enough ammo to hold off a small army," he boasted, swiping through photos on his phone while adjusting his camo-print baseball cap. "What's your setup like?"

I glanced down at my sensible gardening clogs, still muddy from harvesting the last of my winter squash that morning, and smiled. "Well, I've got three freezers of food I grew myself, enough firewood to last two Maine winters, a gravity-fed water system that works when the power's out, and fifteen different ways to preserve food without electricity. Oh, and I taught the ladies' circle at church how to make antibacterial salves from the plants growing in their backyards."

Rick blinked at me. "But what about protection? Defense systems?"

"I've got Mabel," I said, referring to my ancient shotgun that's run off many a predator from my chicken coop. "And more importantly, I've got seventeen neighbors within shouting distance who all owe me for either childcare, medical help, or food preservation lessons. If things go sideways, I'm calling in those favors."

He looked genuinely puzzled, and that's when it hit me: we were speaking entirely different languages of preparedness.

* * *

Welcome to the wild, practical, and often misunderstood world of women preppers. If you picked up this book expecting tactical gear reviews or instructions for building a bulletproof panic room, you might want to adjust your expectations—though I promise what you'll find here is infinitely more useful for actual survival. With sides of Maine humor and memoir thrown in.

My name is Riki Springwell. I've lived in the northernmost reaches of Maine for thirty-seven years, where the Canadian border is just a stone's throw away and winter isn't a season so much as a way of life. Up here, being unprepared isn't just inconvenient—it can be deadly. When the nearest grocery store is an hour away on a good day and impassable during the frequent blizzards, you learn to think ahead or you don't last long.

I didn't set out to become what people now fashionably call a "prepper." For most of my life, I just called it "getting by" or "common sense." It wasn't until the prepper movement gained mainstream attention that I realized there was a name for what generations of women in my family had been quietly doing all along.

The irony wasn't lost on me: men were discovering (and commercializing) survival skills that women have been practicing since time immemorial. While guys like Rick were buying expensive freeze-dried meals and tactical flashlights, my grandmother had taught me how to preserve a year's worth of vegetables, mix herbal remedies, and maintain essential household supplies through any disruption—skills she learned from her mother, who learned from hers.

Don't get me wrong—I'm not here to bash the boys and their toys. *Boy*, they love their damn toys. Some of that gear is genuinely useful (I'll admit I've invested in a few choice pieces myself). But there's a particular brand of male prepper that has always amused me: the kind who can tell you the ballistic rating of various body armors but can't cook a meal without a microwave or treat an infected wound without a fully-stocked pharmacy.

These are often the same fellows who've spent thousands on guns and ammunition but haven't bothered to meet their neighbors or learn which local plants can serve as food or medicine. They're preparing for dramatic firefights while overlooking the much more likely scenarios of power outages, supply chain disruptions, or medical emergencies—the bread and butter of real-world preparedness that women have traditionally managed.

* * *

The truth is, women have been the original preppers since humans first organized into social groups. Historically, while men have generally focused on immediate protection and provision (hunting, warfare), women have developed the skills of long-term survival: food preservation, medical care, resource management, and community building. Women are keepers of the knowledge base. These less flashy but absolutely essential aspects of preparedness have been largely overlooked in modern prepper culture, which tends to glorify the more dramatic elements of survival.

This gender divide in preparedness approaches isn't just anecdotal. Research consistently shows that women-led households display greater resilience during prolonged crises. After Hurricane Katrina, a study by the Institute for Women's Policy Research found that female-headed households recovered more quickly and reported better adaptation to changed circumstances than their male-headed counterparts. Similarly, UN data from refugee situations worldwide indicates that when women control resource distribution, overall family welfare improves more significantly.

Why? The answer lies partly in approach. In my experience (and backed by research), women tend to prepare with community in mind rather than focusing solely on individual or single-family survival. We're more likely to establish support networks, share resources and skills, and plan for the needs of vulnerable community members—all critical factors in actual disaster recovery.

Take my own preparedness network here in northern Maine. When I started teaching canning classes at the community center fifteen years ago, I wasn't just sharing a skill—I was building a resilience web. Those students became friends who now exchange preserved foods, creating a diverse stockpile none of us could manage alone. When Dotty from down the road mastered cheese-making, she taught the rest of us. When I perfected my herbal medicine formulas, I made sure every household had access. We've created a system where no one person needs to know or have everything.

Compare this to what I call "lone wolf syndrome"—the unfortunately common male prepper fantasy of single-handedly defending a homestead against marauding bands of unprepared people. Not only is this scenario statistically unlikely, but it's also a deeply flawed survival strategy. Humans survived as a species because we cooperated, not because the strongest individual hoarded all the resources.

* * *

Now, I should clarify something important: this book isn't about declaring women superior to men in all things preparedness. That would be as silly as ignoring women's contributions entirely. There are plenty of men who grasp the community aspect of survival, just as there are women who can field strip a rifle blindfolded. What I'm addressing is the imbalance in prepper culture and literature, which has overwhelmingly prioritized traditionally masculine approaches while undervaluing what some think are traditionally feminine ones.

The science supports this balancing of perspectives. Studies in disaster management consistently show that the most resilient communities employ a blend of immediate tactical response (traditionally associated with masculine approaches) and long-term adaptive strategies (traditionally associated with feminine approaches). Neither is sufficient alone.

For example, during the 1998 ice storm that left parts of the Northeast and Canada without power for weeks, our community's recovery relied equally on the men who cleared roads and repaired power lines and the women who operated warming centers, managed community kitchens, and coordinated resource sharing. Both sets of skills proved essential.

Yet when you browse most prepper websites or books, you'd think survival was all bug-out bags and bunkers, with maybe a token mention of food storage. This lopsided approach doesn't just shortchange women's contributions—it creates dangerous blind spots for anyone serious about preparedness.

* * *

I've seen these blind spots play out in real emergencies. During a particularly brutal winter storm in 2010, my neighbor Tom found himself in serious trouble. He had all the gear—generator, snowmobile, satellite phone, enough ammunition to start a small war—but when his appendix nearly burst, none of that helped him. What saved his life was my rudimentary medical training and the community phone tree that got him to the hospital despite roads being impassable to standard vehicles.

Tom later told me, "I'd spent so much time thinking about dramatic scenarios that I overlooked the basics. I had three different tactical knives but not a single course in first aid."

This is precisely the imbalance I hope to address with this book. By highlighting the what some consider traditionally feminine aspects of preparedness—community building, resource management, health care, psychological resilience, and practical sustainability—I aim to create a more complete picture of what true readiness looks like.

And yes, I plan to have some fun with the more absurd aspects of macho prepper culture along the way. If you can't laugh while preparing for potential disaster, you're doing it wrong. After all, maintaining morale is itself a critical survival skill—one at which women typically excel.

* * *

So who is this book for? It's for women who are already quietly prepping but might not call themselves "preppers." It's for men who recognize the gaps in their preparedness strategy and want a more balanced approach. It's for families looking to build real resilience, not just stockpile gear. And honestly, it's for anyone who suspects that survival might require more than an impressive gun collection.

Throughout these pages, I'll be sharing evidence-based strategies drawn from my own experiences in rural Maine, historical examples of community resilience, and current research in disaster management. You'll find practical advice on everything from food security to community organization, emotional first aid to resource management.

I'll also be puncturing some of the more ridiculous prepper myths along the way. No, you probably don't need a gas mask in your everyday carry bag. Yes, your relationships with neighbors are likely more valuable than your stockpile of gold coins. And contrary to popular prepper belief, the ability to identify edible plants in your region will probably serve you better than mastering exotic tactical shooting positions.

This isn't to say traditional prepper concerns like security aren't important—they absolutely are. But they're only part of a much bigger picture that we'll explore together.

* * *

As we navigate this world of preparedness, I invite you to keep an open mind. Some of what I suggest may challenge conventional prepper wisdom. Good. The best preparation involves questioning assumptions and adapting strategies to reality, not ideology.

Remember my neighbor Rick from the barbecue? Two years later, when another in a series of "perfect storms" swept through our region, knocking out power for three weeks, he showed up at my door looking sheepish. His generator had failed, and his freeze-dried meals required water he couldn't heat.

"I think I might have focused on the wrong things," he

admitted.

That evening, he ate a hot meal from my summer harvest and joined our community's recovery effort. By the end of those three weeks, Rick had completely rethought his approach to preparedness. These days, he's as likely to be found at a community canning workshop as a gun show.

That's my hope for this book: not to replace one narrow view of preparedness with another, but to expand our collective understanding of what it means to be truly ready for whatever comes our way.

So grab a cup of tea (or something stronger—I don't judge), get comfortable, and let's talk about how women have been quietly keeping civilization running through disasters since the dawn of time—and how we can all learn from their example. Most of those disasters caused by men, *am-i-right*? Or is 100 percent?

The apocalypse isn't coming, ladies. We've been handling mini-apocalypses since the beginning. It's just time we got credit for it.

2

The Evolutionary Edge

The winter of 2008 taught me more about gender differences than any academic paper ever could. That January, northern Maine was hit with a deep freeze—three weeks of temperatures that never climbed above negative 15 degrees. The wind produced a deeper "feels like" but I never cite wind chills like all those alarmist big city TV weather people love to scream about. It's the *temperature* not the chill! It'll kill ya.

On day four, when the power went out across three counties, the real education began.

I was hosting my brother-in-law Mark and his family, who had fled north from Massachusetts thinking our wood-heated farmhouse would be safer than their all-electric suburban home. The irony wasn't lost on any of us when the grid failed here too. But what fascinated me was watching our different responses unfold in real-time.

While Mark immediately focused on a single problem—getting the generator running—I found myself simultaneously stoking the wood stove, moving perishables to the coldest room, setting up alternative lighting, checking our water reserves, and mentally recalculating our food supplies while comforting my terrified niece. Multitasking is what I do. We do. It wasn't that Mark's task wasn't important—it absolutely was—but his brain seemed incapable of processing anything else until that one problem was solved. Sole focus.

Later that night, as we sat around the fireplace eating a surprisingly decent meal I'd cobbled together from our limited options, Mark looked at me with genuine confusion.

"How did you think of everything at once?" he asked. "I couldn't focus on anything but that damn generator. If we didn't have that started—"

I didn't have a scientific answer then, but I've found one since: what I experienced wasn't supernatural or even particularly special. It was the female brain operating exactly as evolution designed it to.

Nature's Crisis Managers

The human brain is perhaps our most misunderstood organ, especially when it comes to gender differences. We've all heard the oversimplifications: men are from Mars, women are from Venus; men are logical, women emotional; men focus, women multitask. The reality, as neuroscience is revealing, is both more complex and more fascinating—particularly when viewed through the lens of survival scenarios.

Let's start with the structural differences. The female brain typically has a larger corpus callosum—the bundle of nerve fibers connecting the brain's left and right hemispheres. This enhanced connectivity allows for more efficient information transfer between analytical and intuitive processing centers. Translation: while male brains excel at single-focus problem solving (perfect for hunting or combat), female brains are optimized for maintaining awareness of multiple simultaneous concerns (ideal for protecting vulnerable offspring while managing scarce resources).

This isn't just useful—it's potentially lifesaving in a crisis.

During that power outage, my brother-in-law's laser focus on the generator meant we eventually had limited electricity. My distributed awareness meant we also had heat, food, water, light, and emotional stability for the children. Both were necessary, but neither would have been sufficient alone.

I've witnessed this countless times during community crises. After the flood of 2012 washed out most of our county's bridges, it was predominantly women who created the comprehensive response: coordinating emergency housing, identifying vulnerable community members, establishing communication networks, managing limited food supplies, and providing emotional support—often simultaneously and with limited resources.

The men in our community were invaluable for specific tasks like physical rescue operations and infrastructure repair. But they often needed direction to shift between priorities, while the women moved fluidly between immediate needs and long-term planning without external prompting.

This isn't a value judgment—both approaches have survival value. But in our prepper culture that idolizes the lone wolf tactical expert, we've dangerously undervalued the neural wiring that enables comprehensive crisis management.

The Multitasking Reality Check

Now, I need to address a common misconception: the idea that women are supernatural multitaskers who can effortlessly juggle unlimited responsibilities. This myth does women no favors, especially in preparedness contexts.

The neurological truth is more nuanced. No human brain—male or female—can truly focus on multiple complex tasks simultaneously. What the female brain typically does better is rapid context-switching—moving quickly between different tasks while maintaining awareness of each one's status.

During a crisis, this manifests as an enhanced ability to hold multiple concerns in working memory while addressing the most pressing need of the moment. It's not magic—it's a neurological adaptation with evolutionary roots in caregiving demands.

My friend Sarah, who runs our community emergency response team, describes it as "having multiple browser tabs open in your brain, with notifications that alert you when something needs immediate attention." This capacity isn't unlimited, and exceeding it leads to the same cognitive overload anyone would experience.

The practical implications for preparedness are significant. Crisis situations rarely present singular, isolated problems. More often, they involve cascading failures across multiple systems: power, water, food, shelter, security, medical, and psychological. The ability to maintain awareness of each of these domains while efficiently prioritizing responses can mean the difference between thriving and barely surviving.

This is why, when I teach preparedness classes, I emphasize scenario-based training that exercises this context-switching capability. We practice responding to simulated emergencies where, for example, a medical situation occurs simultaneously with a security concern while food is burning on the stove and a child is having an emotional breakdown. These aren't contrived scenarios—they're Tuesday in any major disaster.

The goal isn't to reinforce gender stereotypes but to recognize and develop valuable cognitive skills that have traditionally been dismissed as "women's intuition" rather than respected as legitimate crisis response capabilities.

Pain: The Ultimate Teacher

Let's talk about something that makes people uncomfortable: pain and suffering. Not exactly dinner table conversation, but absolutely crucial to survival scenarios.

The summer I turned forty, I broke my ankle while hiking alone on my property. The pain was extraordinary, but what I remember most clearly was the calm, almost detached mental assessment that immediately took over: I was two miles from the house, no cell service, thunderstorm approaching. I needed to splint the ankle, create a walking stick, and move to shelter before hypothermia became a risk.

I executed this plan methodically, crawling when necessary, and reached safety before the storm hit. Only after I was secure did I allow myself to acknowledge the full extent of the pain.

This wasn't exceptional bravery—it was a physiological response shaped by my biology. Research consistently shows that women not only experience pain differently than men but also typically demonstrate superior pain adaptation capabilities.

The science is fascinating. Women generally have more pain receptors (which, counterintuitively, allows for more precise pain localization and response), lower pain thresholds (we feel pain sooner), but higher pain tolerance (we can function despite it). Studies of endurance athletes have repeatedly demonstrated that women maintain performance under pain conditions that cause male competitors to abandon their efforts.

Researchers specializing in gender differences in pain response say female physiology has evolved to manage the extraordinary pain of childbirth. This has created neurological pathways allowing women to compartmentalize pain signals in ways male brains typically can't.

This isn't just about childbirth, though. The monthly pain experiences that most women endure from puberty create lifetime training in functioning despite discomfort. By the time the average woman reaches thirty, she's had approximately 180 practice sessions in managing cyclical pain while continuing necessary activities.

The survival implications are profound. In emergency scenarios, pain is inevitable—injuries, extreme temperatures, exhaustion, hunger. The ability to function effectively despite pain signals can determine survival outcomes. This isn't about enduring unnecessary suffering; it's about maintaining cognitive function and practical capabilities when physical comfort isn't an option.

I've seen this difference play out dramatically during wilderness survival courses I've taught. When faced with identical discomforts—freezing water crossings, inadequate shelter, limited food—female participants typically maintain decision-making capabilities and group awareness longer than their male counterparts, who more commonly fixate on their individual discomfort.

One male student, a former military officer, admitted after a particularly grueling training: "I've never respected menstruation before this experience. The idea that women deal with pain monthly but still function in society has completely changed my understanding of endurance."

This pain adaptation advantage doesn't make women invincible, but it does create a meaningful edge in scenarios where comfort isn't an option and decisions must be made despite physical distress.

The Social Survival Network

Perhaps the most underrated survival skill in conventional prepper literature is social intelligence—the ability to accurately read other humans, build functional alliances, and navigate group dynamics. Yet in actual collapse scenarios throughout history, from war zones to natural disasters, social capital has repeatedly proven more valuable than almost any physical resource. Being able to read zombies, not so much.

The neurological roots of women's documented advantages in this domain are clear: female brains typically devote more neural real estate to processing nonverbal cues, emotional states, and relationship dynamics. The female brain's enhanced connectivity between analytical and emotional centers creates more integrated social information processing.

These aren't trivial differences. In one striking study from UCLA, female participants correctly identified genuine versus fake emotional expressions 87% of the time, while male participants averaged only 42% accuracy—barely better than random guessing.

I witnessed the survival value of this skill difference during the aftermath of a devastating ice storm. Our community had established a central warming shelter in the town hall, bringing together families from widely different socioeconomic backgrounds, political beliefs, and temperaments—a potential powder keg under stress conditions.

The designated shelter manager, a retired military officer with extensive tactical training, struggled to maintain order as tensions rose. Within two days, he'd created rigid rules, established a dominance hierarchy, and alienated several families who chose to risk freezing rather than remain under his command.

When Marian, a sixty-something retired teacher, stepped in to help, the transformation was remarkable. Without formal authority, she quickly identified the social alliances and friction points among the group. She strategically seated compatible families together, gave agitated individuals meaningful tasks that physically separated them from their triggers, and created flexible systems that allowed for both structure and autonomy.

Within hours, the atmosphere changed completely. Resources were shared more willingly, children were cared for collectively, and genuine cooperation emerged. Marian hadn't provided any additional physical resources—she had simply applied advanced social intelligence to optimize the human elements of the situation.

This isn't a skill limited to women, but the neurobiological evidence for female advantage in this domain is substantial. From infancy, female brains show enhanced response to facial expressions and vocal tone variations. By adulthood, women typically demonstrate measurably superior capabilities in what psychologists call "theory of mind"—the ability to accurately model others' thoughts, beliefs, and intentions.

In survival contexts, this translates to critical advantages: more accurate assessment of whether strangers pose genuine threats, better detection of deception, more effective alliance building, and more sophisticated conflict resolution capabilities. When resources are limited and cooperation essential, these social navigation skills become as important as any physical preparation.

Yet traditional prepper literature often reduces human interaction to simplistic categories: allies versus threats, with an overwhelming emphasis on threat neutralization rather than alliance optimization. This reflects a primarily masculine lens that misses the complex social reality of actual disaster scenarios.

While He's Cleaning His Gun Collection (Again), She's...

Let me paint you a picture I've witnessed countless times in prepper communities. While Dave is methodically cleaning his seventh firearm of the day—a task he's performed weekly for years despite no practical necessity—his wife Jennifer is:

* *Testing and rotating their water storage to prevent contamination*
* *Teaching their children to identify wild edibles in the backyard*
* *Maintaining relationships with neighbors who have complementary skills*
* *Preserving the garden surplus using three different methods for redundancy*
* *Updating their medical supplies based on the family's changing health needs*
* *Modifying recipes to work with their stored food supplies*
* *Creating systems to track resource usage rates for more accurate planning*

Both Dave and Jennifer identify as preppers, but they're preparing for fundamentally different scenarios. Dave is focused on the dramatic, acute threat—the mythical marauding hordes that rarely materialize in actual disasters. Jennifer is addressing the chronic challenges that actually kill people in crisis situations: waterborne illness, malnutrition, preventable medical complications, resource depletion, and social isolation.

I've lost count of the prepper gathering "show and tell" sessions where men proudly display tactical gear they've never used while women exchange practical innovations that have already been field-tested in daily life. At one memorable meeting, while the men compared ammunition stockpiles, I watched two women exchange hand-drawn guides: one for optimizing small-space vegetable production, the other for improvising feminine hygiene supplies when commercial products are unavailable.

The contrast isn't universal—I know men who are extraordinarily practical in their preparedness approach and women who get distracted by tactical fantasies. But the pattern is consistent enough to merit examination.

This difference extends to training priorities as well. In my observation, male preppers disproportionately invest in tactical training (weapons handling, combat techniques, security systems) while often neglecting fundamental skills with higher practical utility: wilderness first aid, conflict de-escalation, water purification, improvisational cooking, basic mechanical repairs, and preventative health maintenance.

Again, the evolutionary logic is clear. Male biology evolved to address acute, high-intensity threats through direct action. Female biology developed to manage chronic, complex challenges through systems thinking and preventative measures. Both are necessary in a comprehensive preparedness strategy, but our cultural prepper narrative has dramatically overemphasized the former at the expense of the latter.

For a practical example, consider home defense, a cornerstone of prepper concerns. The stereotypical male approach often prioritizes firearm acquisition, tactical entry training, and security hardening—all potentially valuable components. The stereotypical female approach considers defensive layers that address a broader threat spectrum: know your neighbors so strangers are immediately obvious; maintain relationships so community members check on each other; design landscapes that provide both food and natural access control; create safe rooms that include water, communication tools, and medical supplies.

The comprehensive approach doesn't exclude tactical elements but places them within a broader context that addresses more probable scenarios and longer timeframes.

Bringing Balance to Preparedness

To be absolutely clear: I'm not suggesting women are inherently superior preppers or that traditionally masculine skills have no place in preparedness. Quite the opposite. Complete preparedness requires the full spectrum of capabilities, from tactical proficiency to social cohesion, from immediate threat response to long-term sustainability.

What I am arguing is that our current prepper culture has developed a profound imbalance, overvaluing acute tactical response while undervaluing chronic resilience building. This imbalance doesn't just shortchange women's contributions—it creates dangerous blind spots for anyone serious about survival. It's same as the blind spots among right-wing and on the other end, left-wing, preppers.

My brother-in-law Mark learned this during our extended power outage. His generator expertise was invaluable, but insufficient. By the fifth day, as he helped me inventory our remaining supplies and modify our cooking methods to conserve fuel, he had a revelation that he later described as "completely reshaping" his understanding of preparedness.

"I realized I'd been preparing for a movie scenario—dramatic, acute, over quickly," he told me. "You were preparing for reality—messy, prolonged, and more about resources than action."

The biological and neurological differences I've outlined offer women certain advantages in crisis situations, but the goal isn't to establish a preparedness matriarchy. The goal is to recognize, value, and develop the full spectrum of survival capabilities, regardless of which gender tends to express them more naturally.

In my own preparedness journey, I've worked deliberately to develop skills that don't come naturally to me: marksmanship, mechanical repairs, rapid tactical assessment. Similarly, I've watched men in my community intentionally cultivate capabilities in emotional management, resource conservation, and social network building that their biology hadn't automatically optimized.

The most prepared individual isn't the one who leans hardest into their biological predispositions—it's the one who complements their natural strengths by developing compensatory skills in their areas of weakness.

The same applies at the community level. The most resilient groups I've encountered maintain a balance of tactical and strategic capabilities, immediate response and long-term planning, resource acquisition and resource management, individual skill development and community coordination.

A Challenge

So here's my challenge to you, regardless of your gender: audit your preparedness strategy for biological bias. Are you investing disproportionately in capabilities that align with your evolutionary programming while neglecting equally important domains that feel less natural?

If you find yourself cleaning weapons that haven't been fired while neglecting food storage rotation...
If you're stockpiling ammunition but can't treat a badly infected wound...
If you can recite ballistic statistics but don't know which local plants have medicinal properties...
If you've invested thousands in security hardware but haven't met your neighbors...
...then you may be allowing biological predispositions to create dangerous gaps in your preparedness strategy.

Conversely, if you've developed robust social networks but neglected personal security training, or if you can preserve food seventeen ways but can't maintain basic tools, you may have the opposite imbalance.

Complete preparedness transcends gender, incorporating the full spectrum of capabilities humans have developed for survival. The most dangerous phrase in preparedness isn't "I don't know how"—it's "That's not my department."

In the chapters that follow, we'll explore specific skill domains where women traditionally excel, not to exclude men from these areas but to highlight capabilities that our male-dominated prepper culture has systematically undervalued. My goal isn't to replace one imbalance with another, but to move toward integrated preparedness that draws on the full range of human capabilities. For everyone.

Because when disaster actually strikes, it won't care about your gender—only about whether you've developed the comprehensive skill set necessary for survival.

3

The Pantry is Political

My grandmother Eleanor—we called her Nana El—lived through the Great Depression as a young wife and mother in rural Vermont. Until the day she died at 94, she never threw away a glass jar, kept a garden that could feed a small army, and maintained a pantry that would make modern preppers weep with envy. When I was about twelve, I asked her why she still canned enough food to survive nuclear winter, despite having a perfectly good grocery store twenty minutes away.

She looked at me with those sharp blue eyes that had witnessed nearly a century of history and said, "Riki, there are two types of security in this world: the kind men create with weapons, which can disappear in an instant, and the kind women create with food, which endures through anything."

It took me decades to fully understand what she meant, but now, watching the fragile supply chains of our modern world stretch and occasionally snap, her wisdom feels prophetic. In prepper communities fixated on tactical gear and ammunition stockpiles, I often find myself channeling Nana El: "That's all well and good, but what are you going to eat in month three?"

The blank stares I receive tell me everything.

The Foundation of All Survival

Let's start with an uncomfortable truth: in any prolonged crisis, from economic collapse to environmental disaster, the leading cause of death isn't violence—it's malnutrition and related illness. History has demonstrated this pattern repeatedly, from the Irish Potato Famine to the Holodomor in Ukraine, from the Siege of Leningrad to more recent famines in various parts of the world. When systems break down, food access becomes the primary determinant of survival.

This reality conflicts with the popular prepper narrative, which often prioritizes defense against human threats while treating food as a secondary consideration—something to be addressed by stockpiling freeze-dried meals or MREs. This approach reflects a fundamentally masculine lens on preparedness that focuses on acute threats rather than chronic necessities.

The women in my family have always understood that a reliable food supply isn't just about avoiding starvation—it's the foundation upon which all other aspects of survival rest. Without adequate nutrition, your immune system falters, your cognitive function declines, your emotional resilience deteriorates, and your physical capabilities diminish. The most sophisticated security system means nothing if its operators are too malnourished to maintain alertness.

During the ice storm of 1998 that left much of the Northeast without power for weeks during the coldest part of winter, I watched this dynamic play out in our community. Families with deep pantries and food preservation knowledge maintained not just physical health but also emotional stability and social cohesion. Meanwhile, households dependent on modern food systems experienced increasing stress, conflict, and eventually dangerous risk-taking behaviors as hunger took hold.

By week three, people were making objectively irrational decisions: attempting hazardous travel on ice-covered roads, using unsafe heating methods that led to house fires, and in some cases, abandoning security measures out of desperation for supplies. These weren't bad people or poor planners by conventional standards—they simply hadn't recognized that food security is the cornerstone upon which all other aspects of resilience depend.

As my friend Diane, who runs the county emergency management office, succinctly puts it: "All emergency scenarios eventually become food emergencies if they last long enough."

Women as Resource Managers: Historical Lessons

Throughout history, women have served as the primary managers of household resources, particularly food. This isn't merely a social construct—though gender roles have certainly reinforced it—but a practical development that emerged across virtually all human cultures. While men typically focused on resource acquisition (hunting, warfare, later wage-earning), women developed sophisticated systems for resource optimization, preservation, and allocation.

During World War II, when rationing transformed American food systems overnight, it was predominantly women who created and implemented the household strategies that kept families nourished despite severe restrictions. The government recognized this reality, directly targeting women with rationing education and recruiting them as neighborhood leaders in food conservation efforts.

The Victory Garden movement—which eventually produced 40% of America's vegetables during the war—was largely organized and maintained by women. My grandmother's diaries from this period, which I still have, detail the complex community networks women established to share knowledge, labor, and resources. They coordinated planting schedules to maximize variety, organized canning parties to process harvests efficiently, and developed creative recipes to maintain nutrition and morale with limited ingredients.

Similar patterns emerged during the Great Depression. Women transformed household food management from a domestic routine into a sophisticated survival strategy. They developed methods to stretch ingredients to their absolute limits, created preservation techniques to minimize waste, and established informal exchange systems that distributed resources throughout their communities.

What's particularly noteworthy about these historical examples isn't just that women managed scarce resources effectively—it's that they did so while simultaneously maintaining the social fabric of their communities. They understood intuitively what modern disaster research confirms: individual survival in prolonged crises depends heavily on community resilience.

The women running Depression-era households didn't just feed their families—they organized community meals, taught preservation skills to neighbors, and created systems for identifying and supporting vulnerable community members. They recognized that collective food security enhanced individual food security, rather than threatening it.

This community-oriented approach contrasts sharply with

many modern prepper philosophies that emphasize guarding personal resources against others—a primarily masculine framework that treats community as a threat rather than an asset. Historical evidence suggests this individualistic approach is not only socially problematic but practically inefficient.

During the Siege of Leningrad—one of history's most extreme food crises—research indicates that survival rates were highest among those who maintained social connections and resource-sharing systems, despite the severe privation that claimed nearly a million lives. Individuals who attempted to hoard resources and isolate themselves experienced higher mortality, even when they began with greater material advantages.

The women who have navigated history's hardest times have consistently demonstrated that effective food security isn't just about having supplies—it's about having systems, knowledge, and communities.

The Science of Staying Fed

My first serious introduction to food preservation came when I was eight years old. Nana El sat me down with an alarming mountain of green beans and demonstrated how to prepare them for canning. As we worked, she explained the chemistry of botulism, the physics of creating proper seals, and the biology of competing microorganisms in preserved foods. By age ten, I could safely pressure-can vegetables and water-bath-can fruits without supervision.

This wasn't just a quaint traditional skill being passed down—it was a science education disguised as domestic training. Modern food preservation technologies haven't fundamentally changed the biological and chemical principles that my grandmother understood through practical experience. What has changed is our cultural relationship to this knowledge.

In contemporary prepper communities, I frequently encounter individuals—usually men—who have purchased expensive food storage systems without understanding the basic science of nutrition, preservation, or food safety. They can tell you the shelf life of their freeze-dried supplies but not the caloric requirements for different activity levels or the symptoms of specific nutrient deficiencies.

This knowledge gap creates dangerous vulnerabilities. During a workshop I conducted on long-term food planning, a participant proudly described his year's supply of stored food—an impressive quantity that would have led to severe malnutrition within months due to protein imbalance and vitamin deficiencies. His stockpile reflected marketing rather than nutritional science.

Effective food preparedness requires understanding several domains of scientific knowledge:

1. *Nutritional requirements*: Different age groups, activity levels, and health conditions require specific macro and micronutrient profiles. In crisis situations, these requirements often increase due to stress and environmental challenges.
2. *Preservation chemistry*: Each preservation method—canning, dehydrating, fermenting, smoking, salting—creates different chemical environments that inhibit microbial growth through specific mechanisms. Understanding these principles allows for troubleshooting and adaptation when ideal conditions aren't available.

3. *Storage physics*: Temperature, humidity, light exposure, and oxygen levels all affect food deterioration through distinct physical processes. Managing these variables can dramatically extend storage viability.

4. *Culinary biochemistry*: Cooking methods significantly impact both nutrient availability and energy efficiency. In resource-limited scenarios, understanding how different preparations affect nutritional outcomes becomes crucial.

5. *Agricultural biology*: Growing food requires practical knowledge of soil science, plant physiology, pest management, and seasonal cycles—complex biological systems that can't be mastered through crisis-time crash courses.

The depth of knowledge required in each of these domains helps explain why food preparedness has traditionally been a lifelong female specialization rather than a hobby or secondary skill. Historically, women began learning these complex systems in childhood and continued developing expertise throughout their lives, creating a community knowledge base maintained across generations.

When this intergenerational knowledge transfer was disrupted by modernization, much was lost. The convenience of contemporary food systems allowed us to outsource this expertise, and many families no longer maintain these traditional skills. In prepper communities, this has created a dangerous knowledge vacuum often filled by commercial products rather than practical capability.

The solution isn't necessarily returning to strictly traditional gender roles, but rather recognizing the depth of expertise required for true food security and recommitting to developing these skills regardless of gender. The science hasn't changed—only our relationship to it.

Nourishment Beyond Nutrition

During the fourth day of a winter power outage some years back, I watched my usually stoic neighbor Tom nearly break down in tears—not over the cold, the darkness, or even basic hunger, but because he was eating his tenth consecutive meal of cold baked beans straight from the can. "I never thought food would matter this much," he confessed.

This moment crystallized something I'd observed repeatedly in emergency situations: food isn't just biological fuel. It serves essential psychological, social, and even spiritual functions that become exponentially more important during crises.

Meal planning for disaster scenarios must account for these dimensions—something women have traditionally managed as extensions of their peacetime roles. When I teach wilderness survival courses, I emphasize that the most dangerous deprivation isn't always caloric—it's the loss of food's non-nutritional functions:

1. *Psychological comfort*: Familiar foods provide continuity and normalcy during chaotic situations. This isn't trivial—it's a powerful psychological anchor that can prevent cognitive deterioration.

2. *Social bonding*: Shared meals maintain community cohesion under stress. The ritual of eating together reinforces collaboration precisely when isolation becomes most dangerous.

3. *Temporal structure*: Regular meals provide structure when normal schedules collapse, creating essential psychological scaffolding during prolonged emergencies.

4. *Cultural continuity*: Traditional foods connect people to their identities and histories, providing emotional resilience during disorienting circumstances.

5. *Celebration capacity*: The ability to create special meals, even under constrained conditions, allows for marking important moments and maintaining morale.

My grandmother's Depression-era recipe collection reflects this multidimensional understanding of food's role. Alongside utilitarian instructions for stretching scarce ingredients, she maintained "company recipes" and "celebration meals" that could be created from stored staples. These weren't frivolous—they were strategic tools for maintaining social bonds and psychological health during extended hardship.

This aspect of food preparedness rarely appears in conventional prepper literature, which tends to reduce food to its caloric and nutritional components—an approach that addresses biological survival while neglecting the equally important dimensions of psychological and social survival.

The most effective food preparedness strategies address all these dimensions simultaneously, balancing immediate nutritional needs with longer-term psychological and social requirements. This comprehensive approach has traditionally fallen within women's domain, reflecting a more integrated understanding of human needs during crisis.

Tactical Meal Planning vs. Actually Feeding People

Let me paint you a scene I've witnessed variations of repeatedly at prepper gatherings:

Tactical Tim arrives with his impressive food storage spreadsheets, detailing precisely how many calories of freeze-dried Mountain House meals he's stockpiled. He can tell you exactly how many days his supply will last based on standardized consumption rates and has organized his storage using military-style inventory systems. His meals require only hot water, which he plans to produce using his tactical stove and water purification system. His preparations emphasize efficiency, standardization, and minimized preparation time.

Meanwhile, *Practical Pam* quietly mentions her rotating pantry of home-preserved foods, heirloom seed bank, community garden participation, and collection of wood-fired cooking methods. She produces a jar of last season's peaches, which she opens to share with the group. Rather than focusing on a single catastrophic scenario, her system addresses multiple timeframes simultaneously: this week's meals, this season's preservation, next year's planting. Her approach integrates daily life with emergency preparedness rather than treating them as separate domains.

The contrast in these approaches reveals fundamentally different understandings of what constitutes food security:

Tim's Tactical Approach:
- Emphasizes acquisition over skill development
- Treats food as a static resource to be stockpiled
- Focuses on maximum shelf life over nutritional density
- Assumes individualistic consumption
- Optimizes for simplicity and standardization
- Creates a hard boundary between normal life and emergency scenarios

- Typically requires substantial financial investment

Pam's Practical Approach:
- Emphasizes skill development over acquisition
- Treats food as a renewable resource to be managed
- Balances shelf stability with nutritional quality
- Assumes community-based consumption
- Optimizes for flexibility and adaptability
- Integrates preparation into daily life systems
- Typically requires substantial time investment but lower financial outlay

Both approaches have merits, but most successful historical examples of surviving food system disruptions more closely resemble Pam's model. During the Special Period in Cuba following the Soviet collapse, for instance, communities that rapidly developed local food production and preservation capabilities fared significantly better than those dependent on centralized distribution of stored supplies, which quickly depleted.

The tactical approach relies heavily on technology and supply chains that existed before the crisis—the very systems that may be compromised during an actual emergency. The practical approach develops capabilities that can adapt to changing conditions and regenerate resources rather than merely consuming them.

This isn't to suggest that stored food has no place in preparedness—it absolutely does, especially for bridging immediate gaps. But storage alone, without the skills and systems to eventually replace what's consumed, creates a dangerous vulnerability once supplies deplete.

The distinction often falls along gender lines, reflecting different approaches to resource management. Traditional male approaches often emphasize resource acquisition and protection; traditional female approaches typically emphasize resource optimization and regeneration. Complete food security requires both dimensions.

The Politics of the Pantry

When I use the phrase "the pantry is political," I'm not suggesting that food storage has partisan implications. Rather, I'm pointing to the deeper reality that control over food resources fundamentally shapes power relationships at every level, from households to nations.

Throughout history, those who controlled food controlled everything else. From ancient grain stockpiles that cemented the authority of early empires to the modern corporate concentration of our food system, food has always been the ultimate leverage point in human affairs.

At the household level, this reality has shaped gender dynamics for millennia. Women's traditional control over food preparation and preservation wasn't merely a domestic chore—it represented a critical form of power within family systems. The woman who managed the pantry literally held the family's survival in her hands, creating a counterbalance to male authority in other domains.

This balance has been significantly disrupted by the industrialization of our food system, which transferred food knowledge and control from household managers (primarily women) to corporate entities. The resulting dependency on external systems represents not just a practical vulnerability but a profound shift in power relationships.

The act of reclaiming food production and preservation skills isn't merely practical preparedness—it's a political statement about autonomy and resilience in a world of increasing centralization. When you can feed yourself and your community without corporate overlords, you've reclaimed a fundamental form of power that humans have exercised for most of our existence.

This perspective helps explain why serious food preparedness often meets cultural resistance beyond simple convenience factors. Our industrial food system benefits from dependency, not autonomy. The woman with a productive garden, preservation skills, and community food networks represents a challenge to centralized control of this critical resource.

During World War II, Victory Gardens weren't just practical responses to food shortages—they were political acts that demonstrated citizen capability during national emergencies. The government initially discouraged home gardens, fearing they would reduce dependence on the rationing system that allowed centralized control of resources. Only when their popularity made them unstoppable did officials pivot to presenting them as patriotic initiatives.

Similar dynamics emerged during the COVID-19 pandemic, when unprecedented numbers of Americans attempted to establish gardens and learn food preservation. The surge in demand for seeds, canning supplies, and freezers represented not just practical responses to temporary shortages but growing recognition of the vulnerabilities created by our centralized food systems.

The most politically radical act may be growing a garden, building a pantry, and teaching others to do the same. This isn't survivalist paranoia—it's reclaiming an essential human capability that we've outsourced at our peril.

My grandmother understood this. Her pantry wasn't just food storage—it was her declaration of independence from systems she had seen fail during the Depression. When she taught me to preserve food, she wasn't just passing down recipes—she was transferring power.

The Path Forward

As with most aspects of preparedness, the most effective approach to food security isn't choosing between traditionally male or female perspectives, but integrating them into complementary systems. The tactical and practical must work in concert, not opposition.

In my own household, our food security strategy combines elements from both approaches. *We is the operative word:*

- *We maintain short-term emergency supplies that require minimal preparation, bridging immediate disruptions.*
- *We practice food preservation techniques that extend our garden's productivity throughout the year.*
- *We've developed multiple cooking methods that function without modern infrastructure.*
- *We participate in community food systems that distribute both production and preservation tasks.*
- *We cultivate open-pollinated seeds that can be saved for future growing seasons.*
- *We continuously develop food-related skills rather than relying solely on stored products.*

This integrated approach addresses different timeframes

simultaneously: the immediate emergency, the medium-term adjustment period, and the long-term adaptation that major disruptions might require.

What's notably absent from our strategy is the assumption that we should hoard resources while others go without. Historical evidence consistently shows that communities who share food resources and knowledge demonstrate greater collective survival rates than those who fragment into competing individual units.

The women in my family have always understood that true food security comes not from having what others lack, but from building systems that enhance community resilience. My grandmother's pantry was impressive not just for its contents but for how frequently those contents were shared with neighbors in need—creating reciprocal relationships that benefited everyone during hard times.

This perspective reflects a feminine approach to resource management that prioritizes sustainability and community over hoarding and exclusion. It's not naive altruism—it's practical recognition that no individual can maintain complete self-sufficiency indefinitely.

As you assess your own food preparedness, consider which aspects you've emphasized and which you've neglected. Have you focused on acquisition while neglecting skill development? Have you considered caloric needs but overlooked psychological and social dimensions? Have you developed storage systems without regenerative capacity?

The pantry remains political because it represents a fundamental choice: Will we approach crisis with a mindset of scarcity and competition, or abundance and cooperation? Will we treat food as a weapon to be hoarded, or a tool for building resilient communities?

My grandmother's approach—practical, community-minded, and skill-based—has weathered every crisis from the Depression through modern disruptions. The proof, as they say, is in the pudding—preferably home-preserved and shared with neighbors.

4

First Aid Without the Drama

The day my neighbor Ed nearly sliced off part of his thumb with a chainsaw taught me everything I needed to know about the gender divide in emergency medicine. As blood pulsed from the wound, Ed's brother-in-law Stan—a self-proclaimed "tactical medic" with an expensive kit and weekend training—froze completely. He stared at his specialized equipment like it had suddenly transformed into alien technology while mumbling something about pressure points and tourniquets.

Meanwhile, Ed's wife Donna calmly walked over, elevated the hand, applied direct pressure with a clean dish towel, and told me exactly which supplies to retrieve from her kitchen cabinet. Within minutes, she had cleaned the wound, applied butterfly bandages to close it properly, dressed it with antibiotic ointment, and bandaged it securely. The entire time, she kept up a steady conversation about the summer berry harvest to keep Ed distracted from the pain.

When I complimented her quick response later, she shrugged and said, "Three kids, two decades of farm life, and a mother who was a nurse. You learn to handle blood without hyperventilating."

Stan was still reorganizing his untouched medical kit when we finished, muttering about protocols and assessment algorithms.

This scene captures something I've witnessed repeatedly in emergency situations: the stark difference between theoretical medical knowledge and practical healthcare capability. It's the difference between having expensive equipment you've never really used and having treated dozens of actual injuries with whatever materials were at hand. It's also, frequently, the difference between traditionally male and female approaches to emergency healthcare.

The Original Healthcare Providers

Throughout human history, women have served as the primary healthcare providers for their families and communities. This wasn't a matter of preference but of necessity—someone needed to address the constant stream of illnesses, injuries, births, and deaths that characterize human existence, and this responsibility typically fell to women.

This historical pattern created a distinct approach to medicine that differs significantly from modern institutional healthcare. Traditional female healing practices emphasized:

* *Preventative care integrated into daily routines*
    * *Close observation to detect problems early*
    * *Resourceful use of available materials*
    * *Practical knowledge passed through direct mentorship*
    * *Treatment of the whole person, including emotional needs*

Continuous care rather than episodic intervention

My great-grandmother Mary was the unofficial healer for her rural community in the 1920s and 30s. Without formal medical training, she delivered babies, treated injuries, managed chronic illnesses, and prepared bodies for burial. Her medical reference wasn't Gray's Anatomy but a handwritten journal of observations, folk remedies, and practical techniques refined through direct experience.

While modern medicine has thankfully advanced beyond many of the limitations of traditional healing, something important was lost in the transition to professionalized healthcare: the integration of medical knowledge into ordinary household management. As medicine became the domain of predominantly male doctors in institutional settings, everyday healthcare knowledge was systematically devalued and eventually lost in many families.

This knowledge gap becomes dangerously apparent during emergencies when professional medical care is unavailable. The COVID-19 pandemic offered a stark reminder of this vulnerability as families suddenly found themselves managing illness without access to routine medical support. Those with retained healthcare knowledge adapted more effectively than those who had completely outsourced their medical self-sufficiency.

My own journey into emergency medicine began with the practical traditions passed down through the women in my family, supplemented by formal Wilderness First Responder training and ongoing education. This combination of approaches—the institutional knowledge of modern medicine and the practical wisdom of traditional healing—provides more comprehensive capability than either tradition alone.

The most effective preparedness strategy involves reclaiming this integrated approach to healthcare, recognizing that medical self-sufficiency isn't about stockpiling supplies— it's about developing practical capability that functions under adverse conditions.

Beyond Bandages: The Practical Medical Skills

When I teach emergency preparedness workshops, I often begin the medical section by asking participants to imagine treating a significant injury without their first aid kit. The uncomfortable silence that follows reveals how deeply we've confused having supplies with having capabilities.

True medical preparedness lies not in your equipment but in your skills—particularly in your ability to prevent, assess, and creatively address health issues with whatever resources are available. These capabilities have traditionally fallen within women's domain as family healthcare providers, creating distinct approaches to emergency medicine that deserve recognition.

Prevention represents the most underrated medical skill and has historically been managed through female-dominated household systems: food safety practices, environmental hazard reduction, hygiene protocols, and early intervention in developing problems. These unglamorous routines prevent more suffering than dramatic rescue techniques ever address, yet they receive minimal attention in prepper literature.

During an extended power outage several winters ago, I watched two neighboring families experience dramatically different health outcomes despite similar resource constraints. The Mitchell family, led by a mother with comprehensive household management systems, maintained strict food safety protocols, regular hand hygiene despite limited water, and careful carbon monoxide prevention measures with their alternative heating. The Brady family, lacking these systematic approaches, experienced food poisoning and carbon monoxide exposure that could have been fatal without intervention.

The difference wasn't resources or luck—it was the presence or absence of preventative systems.

Diagnostic capability—the ability to recognize and assess medical problems before they become crises—similarly represents a crucial skill traditionally developed through women's roles as primary observers of family health. This capability involves both technical knowledge and observational sensitivity: recognizing subtle changes in condition, distinguishing serious issues from minor concerns, and accurately tracking symptoms over time.

During wilderness medical training, I've repeatedly noticed that women often detect deteriorating patient conditions earlier than their male counterparts—not due to innate talent, but because of socialized attentiveness to physical and emotional changes in others. This early recognition can dramatically improve outcomes in emergency situations, particularly with conditions like shock or infection where treatment timing directly impacts survival.

Perhaps the most valuable emergency healthcare skill is improvisation—the ability to create functional solutions with available materials when ideal supplies are unavailable. This capability has deep roots in women's historical experience managing household health with limited resources.

My aunt Catherine, who worked as a rural midwife in the

1950s, once stabilized a severe postpartum hemorrhage using only items found in the patient's kitchen. When I asked how she developed this improvisational confidence, she explained: "Necessity and observation. I watched my mother handle family emergencies with whatever was at hand, then practiced thinking about alternative uses for everyday objects until it became second nature."

This improvisational capability contrasts sharply with the protocol-focused training many male preppers pursue, which often assumes that specialized equipment will be available. Both approaches have merit, but in actual emergencies, the ability to adapt and improvise consistently proves more valuable than rigid protocol adherence that depends on specific supplies.

The most effective emergency healthcare providers I've encountered combine these traditionally feminine capabilities—prevention, observation, and improvisation—with the technical knowledge emphasized in formal medical training. This integrated approach creates true medical resilience that functions under adverse conditions.

The Invisible Emergency: Mental Health

Several years ago, during a severe ice storm that left our community without power for nearly two weeks, I witnessed a troubling pattern: as physical conditions stabilized, psychological conditions deteriorated. By day ten, households that had effectively managed their physical needs were experiencing significant mental health challenges: anxiety, depression, conflict, and in some cases, dangerous decision-making driven by psychological distress.

This pattern repeats across disasters worldwide. Once

immediate survival needs are addressed, the psychological impact of disruption often becomes the limiting factor in community resilience. Yet mental health management receives minimal attention in conventional preparedness literature, creating a dangerous blind spot.

Historically, management of family and community mental health has fallen primarily to women, who traditionally maintained the emotional infrastructure of households alongside their physical operations. This gendered division created distinct psychological support capabilities that become crucially important during prolonged emergencies.

During that ice storm, I observed that households with established emotional management systems fared significantly better than those without such structures. These systems weren't complex—they included:

*Regular rhythms of gathering and separation that provide connection and space
 *Deliberate attention to maintaining normalcy through familiar rituals and routines
 *Designated time for expressing concerns and processing emotional responses
 *Recognition and celebration of small victories and positive developments
 *Intentional management of information flow to prevent overwhelming anxiety

These approaches reflect traditional female crisis management strategies that prioritize psychological sustainability alongside physical survival. They recognize that human resilience requires emotional regulation as much as physical safety—particularly during extended emergencies when psychological deterioration can lead to catastrophic decision-making.

My neighbor Ruth, a retired psychiatric nurse who has lived through numerous disasters, puts it succinctly: "In the first days of an emergency, physical needs determine survival. After that, it's all about mental health. The people who break down psychologically make fatal mistakes regardless of their physical preparations."

This perspective rarely appears in conventional prepper literature, which tends to focus on dramatic physical threats while overlooking the subtler but equally dangerous psychological hazards of extended emergencies. This oversight reflects a predominantly masculine approach to preparedness that emphasizes external threats over internal vulnerabilities.

Effective mental health preparedness involves developing specific capabilities before crises occur:

*Creating personal and family practices for managing anxiety
 *Establishing communication routines that allow for authentic emotional expression
 *Developing multiple coping strategies that function under constrained conditions
 *Building awareness of psychological warning signs that require intervention
 *Maintaining mental health supplies (medications) as diligently as first aid supplies

These capabilities should be developed and practiced during normal conditions, creating psychological muscles that can function under stress. Just as physical first aid skills require regular review, mental health management skills need consistent attention to remain effective during emergencies.

The most resilient communities I've observed integrate physical and psychological preparedness rather than treating them as separate domains. They recognize that the human organism doesn't neatly separate these aspects of experience—physical conditions impact mental health, and psychological state directly affects physical capability.

This integrated approach has traditionally been maintained by women serving as family healthcare providers, who understood that treating a child's physical illness required simultaneously addressing their emotional needs. Modern preparedness would benefit from reclaiming this holistic perspective rather than artificially separating physical and psychological resilience.

The Resilience Web: Community Medical Networks

The most dangerous illusion in medical preparedness is the fantasy of complete self-sufficiency—the belief that with enough supplies and training, you can handle any health challenge independently. This misconception appears frequently in prepper communities and reflects a primarily masculine approach to resilience that emphasizes individual capability over community systems.

Historical evidence consistently contradicts this fantasy. Throughout human history, effective healthcare has operated through networks of providers with complementary knowledge and resources, not through isolated individuals. This pattern appears across cultures and time periods because it reflects practical reality: no single person can maintain comprehensive medical capability across all domains.

My own community's medical resilience network evolved organically from traditions established by generations of rural women. The structure is simple but effective.

Sarah, a retired nurse, maintains expertise in wound care and post-surgical support. James, an EMT, handles acute trauma assessment and stabilization. I maintain certifications in wilderness medicine and natural pharmaceuticals. Diane specializes in pediatric issues from her experience as a school nurse. Robert, with a background in mental health, provides psychological first aid. Maria, who cared for elderly parents, has developed expertise in geriatric support

Each of us maintains appropriate supplies and continuing education in our specialty areas while developing basic competency across other domains. We meet quarterly to review protocols, update contact information, and conduct training exchanges that expand our collective capability.

This distributed approach creates redundancy, prevents knowledge gaps, and allows specialized expertise to develop where individual interest and aptitude exist. It's significantly more effective than expecting each household to maintain comprehensive but shallow medical capability across all possible scenarios.

The network's strength lies not just in its technical resources but in its social infrastructure—the relationships and communication channels established before emergencies occur. During actual crises, these pre-existing connections allow rapid resource mobility and information sharing without the friction that develops when strangers attempt to coordinate under stress.

Creating such networks requires skills traditionally associated with women's social roles: relationship building, needs assessment, diplomatic negotiation, and system maintenance through regular communication. The most effective networks I've encountered are typically organized by individuals with these capabilities rather than those with the most impressive technical credentials.

The process begins with simple steps that anyone can initiate:

*Inventory the existing medical knowledge and resources
   *Identify critical gaps in capability that need addressing
   *Establish clear communication protocols for emergency activation
   *Create resource-sharing agreements before they're needed
   *Develop skill-exchanges that build both capability and relationships

This approach reflects a traditionally feminine understanding of resilience that emphasizes interconnection rather than isolation. It recognizes that true security comes not from hoarding resources and skills but from building systems that enhance collective capability.

The resulting medical networks function effectively during actual emergencies because they combine technical capacity with social infrastructure—addressing both the practical and relational dimensions of healthcare delivery. This integrated approach has historically been developed and maintained primarily by women, whose social roles required simultaneous attention to both technical and interpersonal aspects of care.

The $2,000 First Aid Kit vs. What Actually Saves Lives

The medical supply catalog arrived in the mail on the same day as the community health fair—a juxtaposition that perfectly illustrated the disconnect between consumer medical culture and practical healthcare capability.

The catalog featured a "premier survival medical kit" priced at $1,995, containing an impressive array of specialized equipment: surgical instruments, advanced airway devices, prescription antibiotics, and military-grade trauma supplies. The photography was spectacular—all burnished metal instruments and tactical black cases arranged dramatically against stark backgrounds.

Meanwhile, at the community health fair, local nurses were teaching basic lifesaving skills with household items: how to recognize stroke symptoms, when to apply direct pressure versus a tourniquet (hint: almost always direct pressure), how to prevent wound infection with proper cleaning techniques, and how to identify early signs of serious illness.

The contrast was telling: one approach emphasized owning specialized equipment; the other emphasized developing fundamental capabilities.

This dichotomy appears consistently in emergency medical preparedness, often along gender lines. In my observation, male preppers typically prioritize acquiring advanced medical equipment and specialized supplies, while female preppers typically emphasize skill development, preventative measures, and improvisation capabilities.

The equipment-focused approach isn't wrong—specialized medical supplies certainly have value. The problem arises when equipment becomes a substitute for capability rather than an enhancement to existing skills. I've encountered numerous preppers with surgical instruments they don't know how to use, advanced medications they can't safely prescribe, and diagnostic equipment they can't accurately interpret.

During an actual wilderness medical emergency, I watched a well-equipped but under-trained individual frantically search his extensive kit for the "right" supply while a former obstetrical nurse calmly stabilized the patient using a scarf, a water bottle, and branches fashioned into an improvised splint. By the time he located his specialized equipment, the immediate crisis had been managed with available materials.

This scene perfectly captured the reality that experienced emergency responders understand: the vast majority of life-saving interventions involve basic techniques with simple tools, not advanced procedures with specialized equipment.

The statistics on emergency survival confirm this pattern. Across multiple studies of wilderness accidents, mass casualty events, and natural disasters, the interventions that consistently save the most lives are remarkably simple:

*Bleeding control through direct pressure
   *Airway positioning to prevent aspiration
   *Infection prevention through wound cleaning
   *Proper hydration and electrolyte maintenance
   *Basic fracture immobilization
   *Prevention of hypothermia or hyperthermia

None of these critical interventions requires expensive equipment, but all require practical knowledge properly applied. A $2,000 medical kit in untrained hands provides primarily psychological comfort rather than actual capability, while skilled hands can save lives with materials found in any household.

This reality doesn't mean specialized medical supplies have no place in preparedness—they absolutely do. The ideal approach combines appropriate equipment with comprehensive training and practical experience. However, if resources are limited (and they always are), skill development consistently provides better survival outcomes than equipment acquisition.

My own emergency medical kit reflects this balanced approach. It contains some specialized items that enhance my trained capabilities, but its core components are multipurpose supplies that support fundamental interventions: materials for bleeding control, wound cleaning, basic splinting, and comfort care. More importantly, I regularly practice with these supplies so their use is automatic under stress.

The most valuable component of my medical preparedness isn't in my kit at all—it's the accumulated experience of treating actual injuries, illnesses, and psychological crises in field conditions. This practical capability allows adaptation to whatever situation and resources present themselves rather than depending on specific equipment being available.

This experience-based approach has traditionally been developed through women's roles as family healthcare providers, where daily management of everything from minor injuries to serious illnesses created practical wisdom that no course or manual can fully convey. This wisdom encompasses not just technical skills but contextual judgment: knowing when to intervene versus when to wait, recognizing which situations require immediate action versus careful observation, and understanding how to manage limited resources across multiple needs.

As you assess your own medical preparedness, consider which aspect you've emphasized. Have you invested primarily in equipment or in capability? Are you prepared only for scenarios where your specialized supplies are available, or can you effectively improvise with whatever materials present themselves?

Genuine medical resilience emerges from the integration of appropriate supplies, comprehensive training, and practical experience—with the greatest emphasis on developing capabilities that function regardless of equipment availability. This balanced approach has traditionally been exemplified by women serving as family healthcare providers, who rarely had access to specialized supplies but developed remarkable adaptability through daily practice.

The most prepared individual isn't the one with the most impressive medical kit—it's the one who can effectively address health crises with whatever resources are available, while preventing most emergencies from occurring in the first place through sensible precautions and early intervention.

As my wilderness medicine instructor wisely noted: "Your most important medical tool is between your ears, not in your backpack."

5

The Psychology of Survival

The blizzard of 2015 buried our community under nearly four feet of snow in less than twenty-four hours. Roads became impassable, power lines collapsed under the weight of ice, and temperatures plummeted to dangerous levels. As the designated emergency shelter coordinator, I had a front-row seat to one of the most fascinating psychological experiments imaginable: how different personalities respond when modern comforts vanish and survival instincts kick in.

By day three of our communal confinement in the town hall, clear patterns had emerged. Frank, a successful corporate attorney with an impressively equipped bug-out vehicle, had become increasingly agitated, hoarding supplies in his corner and challenging any decisions not made by him personally. Meanwhile, Linda, a kindergarten teacher with minimal formal preparation but decades of experience managing roomfuls of unpredictable small humans, had quietly established systems that kept everyone fed, occupied, and remarkably cooperative despite the stress.

When I asked her later how she'd maintained such calm effectiveness while others deteriorated into territorial anxiety, she laughed. "You think kindergarteners during a lockdown drill are any different from adults during an emergency? People are people. They need clear boundaries, meaningful tasks, regular routines, and occasional reminders that they're doing a good job. Oh, and snacks. Never underestimate the power of snacks!"

That response captures something fundamental about survival that most preparedness literature mysteriously overlooks: the greatest threats in most emergency scenarios aren't external dangers but internal psychological responses that lead to poor decisions. All the tactical gear and survival supplies in the world won't save you if panic, poor judgment, or social conflict undermines your basic functioning.

This psychological dimension of emergency response has traditionally fallen within women's domain as family and community stabilizers. The resulting skills—emotional regulation, social cohesion maintenance, conflict management—represent crucial survival capabilities that deserve recognition alongside more dramatic tactical skills.

The Emotional Command Center

In the hierarchy of survival needs, we typically focus on the physical essentials: air, shelter, water, food. This prioritization makes logical sense for immediate life-threatening emergencies. However, once these basic needs are minimally addressed, a different factor often determines long-term survival outcomes: emotional regulation capability.

The ability to manage your own emotional state—and subsequently make rational decisions despite fear, uncertainty, discomfort, and other distressing feelings—represents perhaps the most critical survival skill. Without this foundational capability, all other preparedness measures can be rendered useless by panic-driven choices or paralysis.

Women typically develop more extensive emotional regulation capabilities through both biological predisposition and social training. From childhood, girls are generally expected to identify, process, and manage emotions—both their own and others'—creating psychological muscles that strengthen through regular use. By adulthood, most women have extensive practice navigating emotional landscapes that many men have been explicitly discouraged from exploring.

During a particularly harrowing wilderness first aid scenario in my training course, I watched this gender difference play out in real time. When confronted with a realistic simulation of a compound fracture complete with theatrical blood and convincing distress from the patient, the predominantly male participants demonstrated an interesting pattern: technically correct interventions delivered with increasing emotional dysregulation. Their hands shook more severely as the scenario progressed, their communication became progressively more fragmented, and their ability to prioritize deteriorated noticeably.

The female participants, while not necessarily more technically proficient, maintained significantly better emotional regulation throughout the scenario. Their hands remained steadier, their communication clearer, and their decision-making more consistent from beginning to end. The difference wasn't skill or courage—it was emotional processing capacity.

This pattern emerges repeatedly in actual emergencies.

Research from disaster response organizations consistently shows that individuals with strong emotional regulation capabilities make better decisions under pressure, maintain longer functional endurance during extended crises, and experience less debilitating psychological aftermath once the emergency passes.

These capabilities aren't exclusively female, but they are nurtured through traditionally feminine social training that teaches emotional awareness rather than emotional suppression. The resulting skills—recognizing emotional states as they emerge, processing feelings without being overwhelmed by them, and maintaining rational function despite emotional distress—create resilience that physical preparation alone cannot provide.

My friend Elena, who survived the devastating 2010 earthquake in Haiti while working as a nurse, describes this capacity perfectly: "Technical medical skills kept people alive initially, but emotional regulation kept me functioning when everyone around me was falling apart. I could feel terror, grief, and exhaustion without being controlled by them. That ability to feel everything but still choose my actions saved more lives than any specific medical intervention."

This emotional intelligence represents a form of preparedness rarely mentioned in conventional survival literature but consistently identified by actual disaster survivors as crucial to their outcomes. The most comprehensive preparedness approach includes deliberate development of these psychological capabilities alongside more tangible preparations.

When Stress Hits: Gender Differences in Crisis Response

The science of stress response reveals fascinating gender

differences with significant implications for emergency situations. While individual variations certainly exist, broad patterns emerge that help explain the different approaches men and women typically bring to crisis management.

Under acute stress, most male physiology defaults to a classic "fight-or-flight" response. This evolutionary adaptation floods the body with adrenaline and cortisol, narrowing focus to immediate threats and suppressing systems unnecessary for immediate survival. This response creates exceptional capabilities for short-term, high-intensity situations but can significantly impair complex decision-making, social awareness, and long-term planning—all crucial components of extended emergency management.

Female stress response typically includes an additional pathway that researchers have dubbed "tend-and-befriend." While women experience the same fight-or-flight activation, they simultaneously produce higher levels of oxytocin, which creates a counterbalancing urge to protect vulnerable group members (tend) and strengthen social connections (befriend). This additional response pathway evolved because isolated females with dependent offspring faced greater survival risks than isolated males.

The practical implications during actual emergencies are significant. The predominant male stress response optimizes for immediate physical threats but can create psychological tunnel vision that misses complex factors and social dynamics. The predominant female stress response maintains broader situational awareness that includes both immediate dangers and longer-term group survival needs.

I observed these differences clearly during a flash flood that struck our county in 2011. As water rose rapidly around a community center where several families had taken shelter, the immediate response divided along predictable gender lines. Most men focused exclusively on the water itself—measuring its rise, securing physical barriers, and preparing for possible evacuation. Most women simultaneously addressed the water threat while organizing the children, identifying individuals needing special assistance, establishing communication systems, and preparing contingency plans.

Both approaches contributed valuable elements to the emergency response. The intensity of masculine focus helped address the immediate water threat, while the broader feminine awareness prevented secondary emergencies from developing among vulnerable group members. The most effective overall management emerged when both response styles were recognized and integrated rather than one dominating the other.

Research on decision-making under stress reveals another important gender difference. Studies consistently show that stress magnifies gender-typical decision patterns: men become more risk-seeking under pressure, while women become more risk-attentive. Again, both tendencies offer survival advantages in different contexts. Risk-seeking can create breakthrough solutions during immediate life-threatening emergencies, while risk-attentiveness prevents cascading failures during extended crisis management.

The key insight isn't that one approach is universally superior, but that comprehensive emergency resilience requires both capabilities working in concert. Communities that integrate these complementary stress responses typically demonstrate better outcomes during actual disasters than those dominated by a single approach.

As you assess your own emergency preparedness, consider which stress response pattern you default to under pressure. Do you narrow focus to immediate threats while losing peripheral awareness? Do you maintain social awareness at the expense of decisive action? Recognizing your typical pattern allows you to develop complementary capabilities or ensure you have team members who naturally provide the balance your own responses might lack.

The most resilient individuals and communities don't rely exclusively on either the fight-or-flight or the tend-and-befriend pathway. They develop the discernment to deploy each response appropriately as different phases of an emergency require different psychological assets.

The Communication Factor: Building Resilience Through Words

During a multi-day power outage in the depths of winter some years back, I watched two neighborhood groups develop dramatically different trajectories despite nearly identical resource limitations. By day five, one group had deteriorated into bickering, hoarding, and isolation, while the other had created remarkably effective systems for sharing heat, food, and support.

The difference wasn't preparedness levels, leadership structure, or resource abundance. It was communication patterns.

The resilient group employed communication styles traditionally associated with feminine social norms: transparent information sharing, explicit verbal acknowledgment of concerns, inclusive decision processes, and regular emotional check-ins. The fragmented group defaulted to communication patterns more commonly found in masculine environments: minimal information sharing on a "need to know" basis, implicit rather than explicit acknowledgment of issues, hierarchical decision processes, and suppression of emotional content.

This observation aligns with research on community resilience during disasters, which consistently identifies communication patterns as critical determinants of group cohesion under stress. Studies from events ranging from Hurricane Katrina to the 2011 Japanese tsunami indicate that communities with more open, explicit, and emotionally inclusive communication demonstrate significantly better collective outcomes regardless of physical resource levels.

Women typically develop more comprehensive communication capabilities through social training that emphasizes relationship maintenance as a primary objective. From early childhood, most girls receive explicit and implicit instruction in communication styles that preserve social bonds: active listening, perspective-taking, conflict de-escalation, and emotional validation. These skills, honed through decades of practice navigating complex social environments, become crucial assets during emergencies when group cohesion directly impacts survival.

In practical terms, these communication differences manifest in several key areas relevant to emergency response. Information distribution tends to follow different patterns along gender lines. Female-led communication systems typically create more comprehensive information sharing with explicit verification of understanding, while male-led systems often distribute information based on perceived relevance to specific roles. During actual emergencies, the more comprehensive approach typically prevents dangerous knowledge gaps that can develop when individuals lack contextual information outside their immediate tasks.

Emotional content receives different treatment in traditionally masculine versus feminine communication styles. In most male-dominated environments, emotional expression is often treated as separate from (and potentially interfering with) operational content. In female-dominated settings, emotional content is more typically integrated as relevant data about group functioning. During extended emergencies, the integrated approach generally prevents the emotional pressure buildup that eventually disrupts operations when feelings are systematically suppressed.

Conflict management follows distinct patterns that impact group stability during stress. Female socialization typically emphasizes maintaining relationship continuity through conflict, while male socialization often focuses on establishing clear outcomes even at the cost of relationship damage. In extended emergency situations, the relationship-preserving approach usually supports better long-term functioning, as fractured social bonds create operational vulnerabilities regardless of how decisively the original conflict was settled.

My friend Catherine, who served as a disaster relief coordinator for over twenty years, notes that communication differences consistently predicted which emergency shelters would develop significant problems: "Whenever I walked into a shelter and heard primarily directive communication with minimal acknowledgment of feelings or concerns, I knew we'd be managing conflict within 48 hours. The shelters that maintained open information flow and regular emotional processing almost never developed the kind of escalating tensions that required intervention."

This observation doesn't suggest that traditionally feminine communication styles are universally superior—directive communication offers real advantages during immediate life-threatening situations requiring rapid coordination. The most effective emergency response systems integrate both approaches, employing directive communication during acute threats while maintaining the relationship-building patterns that sustain group function over time.

As you develop your own emergency preparedness, consider the communication patterns you default to under stress. Are you creating systems that will sustain social cohesion during extended hardship, or approaches that might optimize short-term efficiency at the cost of long-term group stability? The most comprehensive preparation addresses both dimensions rather than treating them as competing priorities.

The Group Crucible: Managing Dynamics Under Pressure

No insight has served me better during emergency management than this simple observation about human dynamics: In virtually every disaster scenario I've either experienced or studied, the initial emergency—whether storm, power loss, or other disruption—ultimately created less suffering than the human responses that followed.

Managing group dynamics during high-stress situations isn't a secondary consideration in emergency preparedness—it's often the primary determinant of outcomes once basic survival needs are addressed. This domain has traditionally fallen within women's responsibilities as family and community caretakers, creating gender-typical skills in group management that become invaluable during extended emergencies.

I witnessed the critical importance of these skills during a severe winter storm that isolated our rural community for nearly two weeks. As designated shelter coordinator, I observed how quickly the initial cooperative atmosphere deteriorated as different personalities, priorities, and coping mechanisms emerged under stress.

By the fourth day, clear factions had developed: a group prioritizing strict resource conservation, another advocating more comfortable conditions to maintain morale, and a third focused on expanding our capacity to bring in additional community members still isolated in their homes. The tension between these perspectives created increasing conflict that threatened our collective functioning more seriously than any external conditions.

Addressing this dynamic challenge required skills I'd developed through decades of managing family gatherings, community organizations, and professional teams—capabilities traditionally cultivated through female social roles:

*Identifying unstated needs driving stated positions
　*Recognizing when resource conflicts masked deeper status or security concerns
　*Creating decision processes that maintained dignity for all participants
　*Establishing emotional safety that allowed authentic expression without escalation
　*Developing role assignments for difficult personalities

These group management capabilities rarely appear in conventional preparedness manuals, yet they consistently emerge as crucial factors in actual disaster response. FEMA's after-action reports repeatedly identify group dynamic management as a critical success factor in emergency shelter operations, noting that technical resource adequacy means little if social cohesion collapses.

Women typically develop these capabilities through social training that emphasizes maintaining group harmony as a measure of personal success. From childhood, most girls receive explicit and implicit instruction in managing interpersonal tensions, anticipating emotional needs, and preserving relationships through conflict—creating psychological skills that strengthen through regular application in family and community contexts.

The resulting capabilities—conflict de-escalation, perspective balancing, emotion regulation within groups—represent sophisticated psychological technologies developed through generations of practical experience. These skills aren't flashy or dramatic, but they consistently prevent the social fragmentation that undermines survival in extended emergency situations.

My friend Robert, who served with an elite military unit before becoming an emergency management professional, notes that these traditionally feminine group management skills often determine mission outcomes more decisively than tactical capabilities: "In twenty years of crisis response, I've never seen a mission fail because people couldn't shoot straight or navigate accurately. I've seen dozens fail because the team couldn't manage internal conflicts or maintain communication under stress."

As you develop your emergency preparedness strategy, consider whether you've invested as much in psychological preparation as physical readiness. Have you developed the skills to maintain group cohesion during extended stress? Can you manage the inevitable personality conflicts that emerge when people with different coping mechanisms face shared threats? These capabilities may ultimately prove more valuable than many of the material preparations that receive more attention in conventional prepper culture.

Lone Wolf vs. Wolf Pack: Why Survival Is Not a Solo Sport
The most persistent and dangerous myth in prepper culture is the fantasy of the self-sufficient lone wolf—the individual who, through superior preparation and skill, thrives independently while society crumbles around him. This seductive narrative appears throughout preparedness literature, particularly in male-oriented content that emphasizes individual capability over community resilience.

It's also completely contradicted by actual survival data.

Throughout human history, from prehistoric survival to modern disasters, the evidence consistently shows that lone individuals experience dramatically higher mortality rates than those embedded in functional groups. This pattern applies regardless of how well-equipped or skilled the individual might be, because human survival has always been a fundamentally cooperative endeavor.

The lone wolf fantasy persists because it's emotionally satisfying in a way that messy, complicated human communities are not. The solo survivor answers to no one, makes clean, uncontested decisions, and heroically overcomes challenges through personal prowess. The reality of group survival—with its necessary compromises, interpersonal tensions, and shared decision-making—lacks this emotional simplicity.

I encountered a particularly stark example of this contrast

during a regional flooding event that isolated numerous households in our county. Those who had invested in community connections before the disaster received assistance with evacuation, resource sharing, and property protection. Those who had cultivated "lone wolf" independence found themselves truly alone when their individual capabilities proved insufficient for the scenario that actually unfolded—which, like most real emergencies, didn't match the specific preparations they had made.

One particularly memorable case involved a self-proclaimed "prepper" who had invested tens of thousands of dollars in his remote property, including elaborate security systems, food storage, and independent utilities. When floodwaters threatened this carefully constructed fortress, he discovered that his individual capabilities couldn't address the scale of the threat. With no community connections to call upon, his options narrowed to watching his investments wash away or risking his life to protect them alone.

Meanwhile, a neighborhood with far fewer material preparations but strong social connections organized a remarkably effective flood response using pooled equipment, coordinated labor, and shared expertise. Their collective capabilities far exceeded what any individual household could have managed independently, allowing them to protect most properties and evacuate vulnerable residents before conditions became life-threatening.

This pattern repeats throughout disaster research: the survival unit is rarely the individual, but rather the small cooperative group. The most effective size typically ranges from 6-15 people—large enough to provide diverse skills and distributed workload, but small enough to maintain cohesive function without complex management structures.

Wolves themselves understand this reality perfectly. Despite the "lone wolf" mythology popular in survival culture, actual wolves are intensely social creatures whose hunting success and territorial defense depend entirely on pack coordination. A genuine lone wolf—one actually separated from its pack—typically experiences a short and difficult existence before either reintegrating into a social group or succumbing to challenges it can't overcome alone.

The same principle applies to human survival. Our species evolved specific adaptations for cooperative living because this strategy proved consistently superior to individual effort across countless generations and environments. These adaptations include not just our capacity for language and coordination, but fundamental psychological needs for connection that influence everything from stress regulation to decision quality.

Research on actual survival situations, from wilderness accidents to natural disasters, consistently shows that psychological isolation creates objective survival disadvantages beyond the obvious practical limitations:

*Isolated individuals demonstrate poorer decision-making under stress
  *Social isolation accelerates cognitive deterioration during sleep deprivation
  *Recovery from injury or illness proceeds more slowly without social support
  *Motivation to persevere through diminishes without social accountability or purpose

Even from a purely tactical perspective, the lone operator model creates critical vulnerabilities that groups naturally mitigate: no capacity for continuous security (everyone needs to sleep), no distribution of expertise across crucial survival domains, no redundancy for injury or illness, and no motivational support during inevitable psychological low points.

The most effective preparedness strategy isn't becoming an island of self-sufficiency, but rather developing what anthropologists call "networks of obligation"—mutual assistance relationships based on reciprocal value creation. These networks characterized human survival throughout our evolutionary history and continue to determine outcomes in modern disasters more reliably than individual preparation levels.

My own preparedness approach prioritizes this social dimension alongside material readiness. I maintain:

*Regular skill exchanges with neighbors that create mutual capability awareness

*Reciprocal assistance patterns can be activated during emergencies

*Intentional role development allows community members to contribute

*Communication systems that function independently of municipal infrastructure

*Decision frameworks for resource sharing under constrained conditions

These social preparations have consistently proven more valuable during actual emergencies than many of my material provisions, creating response capabilities that no individual could maintain regardless of investment level.

This approach reflects a traditionally feminine perspective on security that emphasizes relationship networks rather than hardened boundaries—a view developed through women's historical experience managing family and community survival through cooperative systems rather than individual prowess.

The wolf pack, not the lone wolf, represents the appropriate model for human survival. Our evolutionary success has always depended on our social capabilities, not our individual strength. The most prepared person isn't the one who needs no one, but the one who has established mutual support systems that enhance everyone's resilience.

In the words of my grandmother, who lived through the Depression and numerous personal hardships: "The only thing more dangerous than having no preparations is thinking you can survive alone with the wrong ones."

6

Resource Management: Beyond Hoarding

The first time I visited my neighbor Derek's legendary "prepper bunker," I had to physically restrain myself from laughing out loud. After months of mysterious deliveries and hushed conversations about his "resource security protocol," he finally invited me to witness what he clearly considered the eighth wonder of the survivalist world.

What I found was a shrine to panic buying that would make a doomsday shopping channel proud: seventeen identical tactical flashlights still in their packaging, enough beef jerky to preserve a small cow herd in perpetuity, and a tower of toilet paper that reached the ceiling. The pièce de résistance was an entire wall dedicated to camouflage gear in various patterns, despite the fact that Derek lived in a suburban development where the most threatening wildlife was the occasional aggressive red squirrel.

"What do you think?" he asked, beaming with pride. "I'm set for at least two years."

What I thought but didn't say: "You're set for exactly one type of emergency, assuming it precisely matches your preparations and doesn't require adaptation, creativity, or—heaven forbid—sharing."

What I actually said: "That's quite the collection. Have you practiced using everything under stress conditions?"

His blank stare told me everything I needed to know. Derek had confused accumulation with preparation, a distinction that separates effective resource management from what I call "apocalypse hoarding syndrome."

This confusion isn't entirely Derek's fault. The predominant prepper narrative emphasizes stockpiling over skill building, accumulation over adaptation. This approach reflects a primarily masculine response to uncertainty that focuses on controlling physical resources rather than developing flexible systems for managing whatever resources become available.

Meanwhile, women have been quietly practicing a different approach to resource management for generations—one developed through practical experience stretching limited supplies to meet unlimited needs.

The Art of Resource Stretching

My grandmother lived by a Depression-era saying that's become my resource management mantra: "Use it up, wear it out, make it do, or do without." This wasn't a cute decorative phrase on her kitchen wall—it was a sophisticated resource management philosophy developed through practical necessity.

The female art of stretching resources has historically been dismissed as mere household thrift, but it actually represents a complex adaptive system developed through generations of women managing family survival with inadequate materials. This approach emphasizes:

*Extracting maximum utility from each resource
  *Transforming single-use items into multi-purpose tools
  *Identifying creative substitutions when ideal supplies aren't available
  *Preserving resource quality through proper maintenance
  *Creating regenerative systems rather than consumptive ones

I witnessed the practical value of these skills during a particularly harsh winter when supply deliveries to our rural community were disrupted for nearly three weeks. Households that had stockpiled extensive but narrow resources quickly faced unexpected limitations, while families with fewer supplies but better stretching skills maintained surprisingly comfortable conditions.

My friend Sarah's family demonstrated this contrast perfectly. Despite having a modestly stocked pantry compared to some neighbors, she created remarkably varied and nutritious meals throughout the disruption by:

*Using vegetable trimmings and bones to create stock bases
  *Employing different preparation methods to transform the same ingredients
  *Identifying complementary flavors that created satisfaction with smaller portions
  *Preventing waste through careful storage and creative reuse of leftovers
  *Adapting recipes to substitute available ingredients for

unavailable ones

Meanwhile, better-stocked households complained of "emergency food fatigue" as they consumed their limited repertoire of stored foods with minimal variation or adaptation. By the third week, some were struggling with meal skipping and nutritional gaps despite having objectively more calories available.

This pattern extends beyond food to all resource domains. During that same weather event, I observed similar contrasts in how households managed heating fuel, water, lighting, and entertainment. Those with stretching skills maintained higher quality of life with fewer raw resources than those who had stockpiled extensively but lacked adaptation capabilities.

The practical applications of resource stretching in crisis scenarios are virtually limitless, but several principles consistently prove valuable:

*Viewing each resource as a starting point rather than a fixed-purpose item
  *Identifying the core function an item serves rather than its conventional use
  *Developing detailed knowledge of material properties
  *Maintaining awareness of potential secondary uses while consuming primary ones
  *Creating systems that capture and reuse byproducts rather than discarding them

My personal favorite example comes from a summer storm that knocked out power while I was hosting a workshop on emergency preparedness—a timing so perfect it seemed almost staged. As participants watched, I transformed an ordinary tuna can into an effective oil lamp using cooking oil and a strip of cotton shirt as a wick. The demonstration perfectly illustrated how ordinary items can serve extraordinary purposes when you understand their properties rather than just their conventional uses.

The art of resource stretching isn't merely about making do with less—it's about seeing possibilities beyond the obvious. This capability has traditionally been developed through women's roles as household resource managers, where success was measured not by how much you had but how effectively you used what was available.

Stockpiling vs. Hoarding: The Critical Distinction

Not all resource accumulation is created equal. The line between prudent stockpiling and counterproductive hoarding often proves elusive in prepper communities, where "more is better" frequently becomes an unquestioned mantra.

The distinction isn't about quantity but about intention, organization, and integration into broader preparedness systems. Effective stockpiling represents one component of resource management, while hoarding typically substitutes for more comprehensive preparation.

During a community emergency preparedness assessment I conducted, this distinction became starkly clear. Two households had invested roughly equal amounts in stored supplies, but with dramatically different approaches:

The Robinson family had developed what I call "intentional redundancy"—carefully selected supplies that addressed specific scenarios they'd thoughtfully identified, stored in organized systems they regularly practiced using, with clear rotation protocols that integrated the resources into their normal life.

The Matthews household had accumulated what might be called "anxious excess"—a haphazard collection of items purchased primarily during sales or panic-buying episodes, stored wherever space permitted with minimal organization, rarely if ever practiced with, and largely forgotten until the next accumulation urge struck.

Both families had significant resource investments, but only one had created actual preparedness. The distinction wasn't financial but philosophical—the Robinsons viewed their supplies as tools within systems, while the Matthews treated acquisition itself as the goal.

This difference typically becomes apparent when you ask one simple question: "Can you tell me the scenario where this specific item becomes your limiting factor for survival?"

People engaged in effective stockpiling can generally answer this question clearly. They've thought through specific circumstances where particular resources become critical constraints, and they've acquired those items with intentional redundancy proportional to their importance.

Those caught in hoarding patterns typically respond with vague references to unspecified emergencies or the ubiquitous "better to have it and not need it" justification—revealing that acquisition has become disconnected from concrete preparation objectives.

The most effective resource management approach balances strategic stockpiling with skill development in roughly equal proportion. For each resource category, this balance might include:

Food: *Maintaining reasonable stores of shelf-stable basics while developing preservation skills to process seasonal abundance*
Water: *Installing storage capacity while learning multiple purification methods using improvised materials*
Medicine: *Stockpiling critical supplies while developing knowledge of alternative treatments using available substances*
Energy: *Storing fuel reserves while creating multiple alternative systems for essential functions*
Tools: *Acquiring key equipment while practicing maintenance and improvisation skills*

This balanced approach reflects a primarily feminine perspective on resource security that emphasizes capability over possession. While not exclusively gendered, this viewpoint has traditionally been developed through women's experiences managing household resources under constraints while men focused more on resource acquisition.

The most resilient households I've encountered maintain this balance, recognizing that stored resources without usage skills create brittle preparedness, while skills without basic supplies create unnecessary hardship. Neither stockpiles nor skills alone create true readiness—the integration of both does.

When assessing your own resource management approach, consider whether you've developed proportional capability for each item you've stockpiled. Can you effectively use, maintain, repair, and eventually replace everything you've stored? If not, you may have slipped from strategic stockpiling into the false security of hoarding.

As my grandmother wisely noted: "It's not what you have that saves you—it's what you know how to do with whatever you have."

Flexible Systems for Uncertain Futures

Perhaps the most dangerous illusion in preparedness culture is the fantasy of accurate prediction—the belief that we can anticipate exactly which emergency scenario will emerge and prepare specifically for it. This misconception drives much of the rigid stockpiling I've observed, where people prepare extensively for one particular disaster while remaining vulnerable to countless others.

Reality consistently teaches a different lesson: the emergency you experience is rarely the one you specifically prepared for. This truth demands resource management systems characterized by flexibility and adaptability rather than narrow optimization.

I learned this principle the hard way during an ice storm that left our community without power for eleven days—a scenario I had generally prepared for with alternative heating, lighting, and cooking systems. What I hadn't anticipated was that the extended school closures would bring my sister's three children to stay with me, instantly tripling my household size and transforming all my carefully calculated resource equations.

This experience taught me to design systems with flexibility parameters rather than fixed capacities. For each resource category, I now consider:

Scalability: *Can the system expand or contract to accommodate different group sizes?*

Substitutability: *Can core functions be maintained using different resource inputs?*

Modularity: *Can components be reconfigured for different circumstances?*

Redundancy: *Do critical functions have multiple independent support systems?*

Adaptability: *Can the system be modified quickly as needs change?*

Women have traditionally excelled at creating these flexible systems through their experiences managing households where conditions, needs, and available resources constantly change. The resulting expertise in adaptive resource management becomes particularly valuable during emergencies, when pre-crisis plans inevitably require modification.

My friend Elena demonstrated this capability remarkably during a flash flood that forced her family from their home with minimal warning. While her husband initially despaired over the specific preparations left behind, Elena quickly established alternative systems using available resources in their temporary shelter—creating washing facilities from borrowed buckets, improvising cooking equipment from repurposed containers, and establishing sleep systems from unconventional materials.

Her capacity to rapidly create functional systems independent of specific resources stems from a traditionally feminine approach to household management that emphasizes function over form. Rather than relying on particular items, this approach focuses on meeting underlying needs through whatever means are available.

The most effective emergency resource systems maintain this functional flexibility, focusing less on specific supplies and more on developing adaptable methods to meet core needs.

Instead of just storing specific foods, developing cooking skills that can transform whatever ingredients are available. Rather than relying solely on particular tools, understand the basic principles that allow improvisation of essential implements. Beyond stockpiling specific medications, learn multiple approaches to addressing common health concerns. Instead of depending on dedicated equipment for each function, identify multi-purpose items that serve various needs.

This flexibility-focused approach has historically been developed through women's domestic experiences, where success required adapting to constantly changing family needs, seasonal resource availability, and unexpected circumstances. The resulting skills—creative substitution, system reconfiguration, function-based thinking—create resilience that fixed resource stockpiles alone cannot provide.

As you develop your own preparedness systems, consider whether you're creating rigid structures optimized for specific scenarios or flexible capabilities that can adapt to whatever actually unfolds. The most resilient approach focuses less on having exactly the right supplies and more on developing the ability to create effective solutions with whatever resources become available.

The Real Economy of Crisis

When discussing economic preparedness, conventional wisdom in prepper communities often focuses on stockpiling barterable goods or precious metals based on assumptions about what will hold value during societal disruption. This approach typically reflects more Hollywood apocalypse scenarios than historical reality.

Actual economic patterns during crises consistently demonstrate that value derives not from intrinsic material properties but from immediate utility within specific contexts. The most valuable resources aren't those that were expensive before the crisis, but those that address current limiting factors—which vary dramatically depending on the emergency circumstances.

During an extended power outage in our region, I watched as theoretical value hierarchies quickly collapsed in the face of practical needs. The neighbor with a working generator and willingness to charge devices suddenly possessed more practical "wealth" than those with extensive precious metal collections. The family with extra propane became more economically powerful than those with designer goods. The household with advanced food preservation knowledge gained more community value than those with expensive but idle technological toys.

Women have traditionally understood this context-dependent nature of value through their experiences managing household economies, where practical utility consistently outweighs abstract value metrics. This perspective becomes crucial during disruptions, when conventional economic frameworks deteriorate and are replaced by immediate utility assessments.

The most valuable crisis resources typically share several characteristics regardless of pre-crisis pricing:

*Addressing essential physiological needs (water purification, food preparation)

　*Solving common but critical problems (wound care, sanitation management)

　*Enhancing quality of life (comfort measures, simple pleasures)

*Multiplying value of resources (preservation methods, knowledge sharing)

Perhaps most importantly, genuine value during crises frequently emerges from capabilities rather than possessions—the ability to solve problems, create solutions, and transform available materials into needed resources.

I witnessed this reality during community recovery from a hurricane, when individuals with practical skills—minor medical care, small engine repair, food preservation, emotional support—became the true "wealthy class" regardless of their pre-disaster financial status. Meanwhile, many conventionally wealthy households discovered that their status symbols offered little practical utility in addressing immediate needs.

This pattern reveals an important truth: in genuine emergencies, the most valuable preparation isn't stockpiling historically valuable items, but developing capabilities that create value within whatever circumstances emerge. This approach has traditionally been exemplified by women's focus on practical household skills that maintain family welfare through changing conditions.

When preparing for potential economic disruptions, consider whether you're investing in abstract value that requires specific conditions to be meaningful, or developing capabilities that create practical value across diverse scenarios. The most resilient approach focuses less on accumulating pre-valued items and more on building the skills to generate contextual value regardless of circumstances.

As my grandmother astutely observed: "In hard times, what you can do always outvalues what you have."

101 Uses for His Tactical Gear Collection When the Crisis Is Actually a Flood

After twenty years in the preparedness community, I've encountered enough tactical gear collections to equip a small militia—almost none of which proved useful during the actual emergencies we've experienced. Since humor helps medicine go down, here's my field guide to repurposing all that tactical gear when reality doesn't match the zombie apocalypse fantasy:

The Tactical Vest with 37 Pouches

- Excellent floating device when properly sealed (test BEFORE the flood)
- Hanging garden for small herbs when suspended from rafters
- Organizational system for medical supplies if you remove the ammo holders
- Halloween costume for years to come ("I'm dressed as wishful thinking")
- Visual reminder of financial choices that could have bought an actual boat

The Collection of Tactical Flashlights

- Waterproof containers for matches and small valuables
- Surprisingly effective hammers when batteries are installed
- Impromptu lane markers for evacuation routes
- Trade fodder (everyone needs light)
- Marriage counseling tool: "See, honey? I told you we'd need these!"

Military-Grade Paracord (872 feet of it)
- Actually useful! Congratulations on the one practical purchase
  - Clothesline for drying everything that got soaked
  - Impromptu animal leashes for evacuating pets
  - Guy lines for tarps covering damaged roofs
  - Measuring tool when you tie knots at regular intervals

Night Vision Goggles (used exactly once)
- Waterproof container for documents when sealed in their case
- Barter item for someone who prepared for the wrong disaster too
- Entertaining distraction for bored children
- Paperweight for wind-blown evacuation instructions
- Conversation piece: "This is why we have separate bank accounts"

Tactical Knife Collection
- Actually useful for cutting damaged materials
- Makeshift screwdrivers (the fancy handles, not the blades!)
- Signaling mirrors if they're shiny enough
- Trading items for people who prepared for zombie scenarios
- Family heirlooms: "This is the knife great-grandpa never needed"

Combat Boots (multiple pairs)
- Actually useful in flood conditions if they're waterproof
- Planters for emergency vegetable starts

- Water scoops in desperate situations
- Doorstops to prevent floodwater from entering rooms
- Conversation starter with emergency responders

Ghillie Suit
- Emergency mop for flood cleanup
- Impromptu water filter (not for drinking water!)
- "Coming home" present for the family dog
- Insulation material when dried thoroughly
- Halloween decoration for the next five years

Tactical Backpacks (one for each family member and several spares)
- Actually useful for evacuation if not overloaded
- Sandbags when filled with soil or sand
- Waterproof storage when properly closed
- Cushions when inflated with air and sealed
- Visual aids for the "preparedness versus practicality" family discussion

MREs (enough to feed a platoon)
- Surprisingly buoyant when sealed in their packaging
- High shelves and platforms when stacked in plastic bins
- Actually useful for short-term feeding if you don't mind the constipation
- Trade goods for fresh food (one MRE = psychological value of three fresh meals)
- Science experiment: "How long until we'd rather go hungry?"

Gas Masks and Filters

- Impromptu water containers when properly cleaned
- Conversation piece with emergency responders
- Halloween costumes for the next decade
- Tangible reminder that preparation requires scenario flexibility
- Marriage counseling exhibits: "This is why we need to discuss major purchases"

Ammunition Stockpile
- Keep this high, dry, and properly stored! Wet ammunition is dangerous waste
- Heavy weights for anchoring items that might float away
- Trade items for people preparing for different disasters
- College fund after the emergency passes if properly preserved
- Relationship test: count how many eyerolls when mentioned during evacuation

Tactical First Aid Kit (with items you can't identify)
- Actually useful if you've trained with the components
- Status symbol in emergency shelters: "That person has a tourniquet!"
- Trading opportunity with actual medical personnel
- Educational: "Let me explain why this needle isn't helpful for flood-related injuries..."
- Entertainment: challenge family members to identify the mysterious medical devices

The point of this list isn't to mock preparation—it's to highlight the importance of flexible readiness rather than rigid scenario fixation. The most resilient approach balances specific preparations with adaptable capabilities, recognizing that our predictive abilities are imperfect at best.

The next time you're considering a specialized preparation purchase, ask yourself: "How would this serve me if a completely different emergency occurs?" If the answer involves creative repurposing rather than direct utility, consider whether your resources might be better invested in more flexible capabilities.

As I remind the tactical enthusiasts in my community: "The best gear for an emergency is the gear that's useful in the emergency you actually have—not the one you fantasized about."

7

The Shelter Mindset

The most revealing moment in my prepper education came during a tour of what my neighbor Carl proudly called his "ultimate survival shelter." After months of secretive construction and mysterious deliveries, he had invited a select few to witness the underground bunker he'd installed at considerable expense beneath his garage.

As we descended into his subterranean fortress, Carl pointed out the reinforced walls, air filtration system, EMP hardening, and impressive array of supplies meticulously organized on industrial shelving. "I can seal myself in here for six months if necessary," he announced with unmistakable pride. "Completely self-contained and secure from any external threats."

When the tour concluded, I asked the question no one else seemed willing to voice: "Carl, it's impressive, but what happens in month seven?"

His expression shifted from pride to confusion. "What do you mean?"

"I mean, what's your transition plan for emerging? How will you reintegrate with whatever community remains? Have you developed skills to rebuild rather than just hunker down?"

The uncomfortable silence that followed revealed everything about the fundamental flaw in the bunker mentality: it prepares for survival in isolation but not for living in the aftermath. Carl had created an impressive tomb, not a functional transition space for navigating changing circumstances.

This encounter crystallized for me the critical distinction between the fortress approach to preparedness—focused on sealing oneself away from threats—and what I call the shelter mindset—creating adaptive spaces that support both immediate safety and longer-term resilience. This distinction often falls along gender lines, reflecting different approaches to security that have profound implications for genuine preparedness.

Creating Living Spaces Within Crisis

When my region experienced devastating ice storms that left many communities without power for weeks during the coldest part of winter, I observed a fascinating pattern in emergency shelter adaptations. Households led by individuals with traditional homemaking experience—predominantly but not exclusively women—transformed their spaces with remarkable effectiveness despite severe constraints.

These adaptations went far beyond basic survival measures to create functional living environments that maintained essential activities despite infrastructure failures. Rather than merely establishing minimal conditions for biological survival, these households developed comprehensive systems that supported continued family functioning across multiple domains.

My friend Rebecca consolidated her family's living area into their small sunroom, using furniture to create defined spaces for sleeping, cooking, eating, and recreation within the single heat-able room. Rather than treating this as a temporary survival measure, she thoughtfully arranged the space to maintain normal family routines and relationships despite the constrained conditions.

Across town, Jennifer transformed her living room into what she called a "winter camp," complete with a central heat source, cooking station, water management system, and separate zones for different activities. She maintained regular mealtimes, designated areas for privacy, and established routines that preserved familial roles despite dramatically altered circumstances.

These approaches contrast sharply with what I observed in some households that adopted a more traditionally masculine "emergency headquarters" mentality—spaces organized around equipment rather than activities, focused primarily on managing external threats rather than internal functions, and treating the situation as an aberration to be endured rather than a new normal to be adapted to.

The difference wasn't resources or technical capability, but fundamental perspective: seeing shelter as a living system rather than merely a defensive position. This living systems approach has traditionally been developed through women's roles as homemakers responsible for maintaining family function across changing circumstances.

The practical application of this perspective becomes particularly valuable during extended emergencies, when maintaining basic family operations—meal preparation, personal hygiene, waste management, sleep, social interaction—becomes as important as immediate safety. The ability to establish these functional systems within constrained conditions doesn't develop automatically; it emerges from experience managing household operations through various disruptions.

During a workshop on emergency shelter adaptation, I often use a simple exercise to illustrate this capability: I ask participants to design a living space for a family of four using only the resources found in a typical school classroom during a three-day winter power outage. Those with extensive homemaking experience typically create remarkably functional arrangements that address all basic needs while maintaining family dignity and routine. Those without such background often produce technically adequate but psychologically unsustainable solutions focused exclusively on physical survival.

This distinction highlights a crucial aspect of genuine preparedness that receives minimal attention in conventional prepper literature: the ability to create not just survival conditions but living systems that sustain normal human functioning during abnormal circumstances. This capability has traditionally been developed through women's experiences managing households through various constraints—skills dismissed as mere housekeeping but actually representing sophisticated adaptive expertise.

As you assess your own shelter preparedness, consider whether you've focused primarily on protecting space or creating functional systems within it. Have you developed the capability to establish normalcy within abnormal conditions? Can you maintain essential household operations despite infrastructure disruptions? These capabilities may ultimately prove more valuable than physical fortifications alone.

Beyond the Bunker: Adaptable Housing for Real Emergencies

The underground bunker represents the most iconic prepper fantasy—a self-contained fortress where one can ride out apocalyptic conditions in isolation from external threats. This vision appears constantly in preparedness media, reflecting a predominantly masculine security approach focused on hardened boundaries and total self-sufficiency.

The reality of actual emergencies rarely matches this fantasy. In my decades of both experiencing and studying disaster response, I've observed that the most common shelter challenges don't involve defending against marauders but adapting to changing conditions: managing unusual heat or cold, functioning without expected infrastructure, accommodating different household configurations, or addressing unexpected limitations.

These challenges demand not rigid fortresses but adaptable systems—an approach more commonly found in traditional homemaking practices than tactical security planning. While men have historically focused on defending boundaries, women have typically developed expertise in adapting interior spaces to meet changing needs—a capability that proves invaluable during actual emergencies.

My friend Elena describes this contrast perfectly: "My husband had focused all our preparation on securing the house structure against storm damage. That helped us weather the initial hurricane, but it was my experience managing household systems that got us through the four months without power or running water. The threat wasn't people breaking in—it was maintaining normal life with abnormal resources."

This experience reflects a pattern I've observed repeatedly: the initial security challenges that prepper culture obsesses over typically resolve relatively quickly, while the extended adaptation challenges receive minimal preparatory attention despite consuming the vast majority of actual emergency duration.

The most effective shelter preparation addresses both dimensions but recognizes their different timeframes and requirements. Short-term physical security measures certainly matter, but long-term adaptation capabilities typically determine actual outcomes once immediate threats subside.

Practical preparation for this longer phase involves developing specific adaptability capabilities within your living space:

Thermal flexibility—creating multiple options for heating or cooling spaces as needed

Functional zoning—establishing areas that can serve different purposes

Infrastructure independence—developing systems that maintain essential functions

Spatial efficiency—organizing limited space to support multiple simultaneous activities

Psychological consideration—designing adaptations that maintain dignity

These capabilities represent a fundamentally different approach to shelter preparation than the fortress mentality—focusing on adaptation rather than protection, flexibility rather than hardening, and functionality rather than mere survival.

During an extended power outage some years back, I watched this contrast play out in neighboring households. Those who had invested exclusively in boundary security found themselves technically safe but functionally challenged as basic household operations became increasingly difficult. Meanwhile, households that had developed adaptive systems maintained remarkably normal functioning despite the infrastructure failures.

The difference wasn't resources but perspective and preparation focus. The security-focused households had prepared extensively for threats that never materialized while neglecting the adaptation challenges that actually emerged. The functionally-focused households had prepared for the infrastructure disruptions that actually occurred, creating systems that maintained normal operations despite abnormal conditions.

This pattern reinforces a critical preparedness principle: the most likely emergency scenarios don't involve defending against external human threats but adapting to infrastructure failures and resource constraints. Preparation should prioritize these probable challenges rather than focusing exclusively on the dramatic but less likely scenarios that dominate prepper culture.

As you evaluate your own shelter preparedness, consider whether you've balanced security measures with adaptation capabilities. Have you developed systems that maintain household functionality during extended infrastructure disruptions? Can your space adapt to different thermal conditions, resource limitations, or household configurations? These capabilities represent the overlooked dimension of shelter preparation that often determines actual emergency outcomes.

When Systems Fail: Household Management During Infrastructure Collapse

Most modern households operate as endpoints in complex infrastructure systems, receiving water, electricity, gas, sewage service, and waste removal through municipal connections. When these systems fail during emergencies, households must rapidly transform from passive infrastructure consumers to active system managers—a transition few are adequately prepared for.

This transformation requires developing household-scale versions of systems normally operated at municipal scale, addressing essential functions that most people rarely think about until they're unavailable:

*Water procurement, purification, storage, and distribution
 *Waste collection, treatment, and disposal
 *Energy generation, storage, and application
 *Thermal regulation without conventional heating/cooling
 *Information access without standard communications

Women have traditionally managed these household systems even when infrastructure was functioning normally, creating practical expertise that becomes invaluable during disruptions. This experience develops both technical knowledge and system thinking capabilities that allow for effective adaptation when conventional approaches fail.

During a severe winter storm that left my community without power or water service for nearly two weeks, I observed how this experience translated into practical capability. Households where someone had regular responsibility for internal systems typically adapted more quickly than those where system management had been entirely outsourced to municipal infrastructure.

My neighbor Ruth, who had maintained a rainwater collection system for garden irrigation, immediately repurposed it for household water supply when municipal service failed. Her existing knowledge of basic water management principles allowed her to quickly establish water collection, storage, purification, and distribution systems for her household using available materials.

Similarly, households with experience managing composting systems for garden waste easily adapted to handling human waste when sewage service was disrupted, while those without such background struggled with basic sanitation despite having more sophisticated emergency supplies.

These patterns highlight an important preparedness principle: previous experience managing systems—even at small scale or for different purposes—creates adaptability that theoretical knowledge alone cannot provide. The hands-on system management traditionally practiced through homemaking activities develops capabilities directly applicable to infrastructure disruptions.

Understanding this connection helps explain why individuals with extensive homemaking experience—historically but not exclusively women—often demonstrate superior adaptation capabilities during infrastructure failures despite having less formal technical training than their counterparts. Their practical experience managing household systems creates both knowledge and confidence that facilitate rapid adaptation when conventional approaches fail.

Developing this capability doesn't require becoming a full-time homesteader or abandoning modern conveniences. It simply involves establishing baseline systems knowledge and occasional practice with alternative approaches:

*Understanding where your water comes from and having multiple methods to purify

*Knowing how your waste is processed and maintaining alternatives

*Understanding basic principles of thermal regulation in your specific living space

*Maintaining awareness of energy use in your household and having alternatives

*Practicing system adaptations occasionally to build both confidence and capability

This preparation approach emphasizes developing system understanding rather than merely stockpiling supplies—recognizing that genuine resilience emerges from capability rather than just resource accumulation.

When I teach emergency preparedness workshops, I often ask participants to map their household's invisible systems—tracing the flows of water, energy, waste, and information that they normally take for granted. This exercise typically reveals startling knowledge gaps even among dedicated preppers, who can often describe their bug-out route in meticulous detail but can't explain how their toilet actually works or where their household water originates.

This disconnect reflects a preparedness culture that emphasizes dramatic scenarios over daily functioning—a perspective that inverts actual emergency priorities. In real disasters, maintaining basic household operations despite infrastructure disruptions typically consumes far more time and resources than security concerns, yet receives fraction of preparation attention.

As you assess your own preparedness, consider whether you've developed both the knowledge and practice to manage essential household systems when infrastructure fails. Can you establish water, waste, energy, and thermal management systems using available resources? Have you practiced these adaptations to build capability before emergencies occur? This system-level preparation often determines functional outcomes more decisively than the tactical measures that receive greater attention in prepper culture.

The Psychology of Shelter: Creating Home Amid Chaos

Beyond its physical functions, shelter serves critical psychological purposes that become increasingly important during extended emergencies. The ability to create and maintain a sense of "home" amid disruption significantly impacts both mental health and functional capability—yet this dimension receives minimal attention in conventional preparedness literature.

During extended displacement following a regional flooding event, I observed dramatic differences in psychological outcomes between families who established home-like environments within emergency shelters and those who treated their spaces as merely temporary accommodations. The psychological distinction had profound practical implications, affecting everything from hygiene maintenance to cooperative behavior.

Families who created defined areas for different activities, established regular routines, and maintained familiar objects and practices demonstrated significantly better adaptation to their circumstances. Children in these families showed fewer behavioral problems, adults maintained better emotional regulation, and the households generally required less external support despite facing identical physical conditions.

This pattern highlights a crucial aspect of emergency adaptation that has traditionally fallen within women's domain as homemakers: the creation and maintenance of psychological safety through environmental continuity. This capability involves specific practices that can be developed through intentional preparation:

*Identifying and preserving essential objects that create emotional anchoring

*Establishing and maintaining familiar routines despite disrupted circumstances

*Creating environmental cues that signal safety and normalcy

*Maintaining sensory comfort through attention to light, sound, smell, and touch

*Preserving privacy and personal space despite constrained conditions

These practices don't emerge automatically during emergencies; they require both awareness and preparation. The knowledge of which elements create psychological stability for specific individuals represents a sophisticated form of intelligence traditionally developed through women's roles as family emotional regulators.

My friend Catherine, who worked extensively with disaster-displaced families, notes that this capability often determined long-term recovery trajectories: "The families who could create 'home' wherever they landed generally maintained better function throughout the displacement period and recovered more quickly once it ended. This wasn't about resources but about the psychological capability to establish normalcy within abnormal situations."

This observation aligns with research on disaster resilience, which consistently identifies psychological adaptation as a critical factor in long-term outcomes. Individuals and groups who maintain psychological stability despite physical disruption demonstrate better decision-making, more effective resource management, and higher cooperation levels—all crucial survival factors in extended emergencies.

The ability to create this psychological stability has traditionally been developed through homemaking practices that Western culture often dismisses as trivial or merely decorative. Activities like establishing household routines, creating distinct functional zones within living spaces, maintaining seasonal rituals, and attending to sensory aspects of environments develop psychological management capabilities directly applicable to emergency adaptation.

As you develop your own preparedness strategy, consider whether you've addressed this psychological dimension alongside physical preparations. Have you identified the elements that create emotional stability for your household? Can you replicate these elements under constrained conditions? Have you practiced maintaining normalcy during abnormal circumstances? These capabilities may ultimately prove as important as any physical preparations in determining your emergency outcomes.

Fortress Mentality vs. Actually Living Through a Disaster

The most persistent fantasy in prepper culture involves defending a fortified position against hostile outsiders—a vision that dominates preparedness media despite bearing little resemblance to actual disaster experiences. This disconnect creates dangerous preparedness gaps by focusing resources on unlikely scenarios while neglecting the challenges that consistently emerge during real emergencies.

Having lived through numerous actual disasters and studied countless others, I can confidently report: the dramatic security scenarios that dominate prepper discussions rarely materialize, while the mundane adaptation challenges those same discussions ignore inevitably emerge.

The reality of disaster rarely involves defending your supplies from marauding bands of unprepared people. It typically involves:

*Managing your living space for weeks without functioning utilities
   *Addressing unexpected resource limitations that no stockpile completely anticipated
   *Maintaining physical and mental health despite prolonged discomfort
   *Preserving family functioning and community connections through extended stress
   *Adapting constantly as circumstances change in unpredictable ways

These challenges demand fundamentally different preparation than the fortress mentality provides. Rather than fixed defenses against anticipated threats, they require adaptive capabilities that function across changing circumstances—a distinction that often separates successful disaster navigation from unnecessary suffering.

I witnessed this contrast vividly during an extended power outage that affected our region one particularly harsh winter. A neighbor I'll call Rick had invested extensively in the fortress approach: reinforced doors, window bars, elaborate security systems, and impressive supply stockpiles secured behind multiple locks. When infrastructure failed, he retreated into his defended position exactly as he'd planned.

Meanwhile, my friend Sara had prepared differently, focusing on adaptive systems rather than boundary hardening: alternative heating methods, water management approaches, modular living space arrangements, and community connection networks. When the same infrastructure failed, she adapted her household operations while maintaining connections with neighbors for mutual support.

By week two, Rick was struggling significantly despite his superior resource stockpile. His rigid systems hadn't anticipated the specific challenges that emerged, his isolation prevented resource sharing that would have addressed his gaps, and his fortress mindset created psychological barriers to adaptation. Meanwhile, Sara's household maintained remarkably stable functioning through the same period despite having objectively fewer stored supplies, because her systems could flex to meet emerging conditions.

The difference wasn't resources but approach: Rick had prepared to defend against anticipated threats, while Sara had prepared to adapt to whatever actually occurred. The fortress provided an illusion of security that actually created vulnerability, while adaptive capability created genuine resilience despite less impressive physical preparations.

This pattern repeats across numerous disasters I've either experienced or studied. The fortress mentality consistently produces three dangerous limitations:

First, it creates rigid response systems optimized for specific anticipated scenarios while remaining vulnerable to the inevitable unexpected challenges. No amount of planning can anticipate every possibility, making adaptation capability more valuable than specific defenses.

Second, it typically emphasizes boundary protection over internal system functionality, focusing resources on preventing incursion while neglecting the systems that maintain operations within those boundaries. Securing your perimeter means little if you can't maintain essential functions inside it.

Third, it often generates psychological rigidity that impairs adaptation when circumstances require changing approaches. The fortress mindset tends to create investment in fixed strategies rather than flexible responses—a dangerous limitation when situations evolve unpredictably.

In contrast, the adaptive shelter approach embraces fundamental uncertainty while developing capabilities that function across diverse scenarios. Rather than attempting to anticipate and prepare for specific threats, it focuses on maintaining essential functions through whatever challenges emerge—a strategy consistently more successful in actual disasters.

This adaptive approach has traditionally been exemplified by women's management of households through various disruptions, creating systems that maintain family functioning despite changing constraints. The resulting capabilities—functional flexibility, resource adaptation, system thinking—create practical resilience more relevant to actual emergency conditions than the tactical security skills that receive disproportionate attention in prepper culture.

When I share this perspective in preparedness forums, it sometimes generates resistance from those heavily invested in the fortress fantasy. They present elaborate scenarios justifying their security focus, sharing media examples of disaster-related crime while ignoring the overwhelming evidence that cooperation, not conflict, characterizes most actual disaster responses.

To be absolutely clear: I'm not suggesting security considerations have no place in preparedness. Basic security measures are certainly appropriate within a comprehensive approach. The problem emerges when security concerns dominate preparation to the exclusion of the adaptation capabilities that actual disasters consistently require.

The most effective preparation balances reasonable security measures with substantial investments in adaptive capability, recognizing that most emergency duration will involve living through changing conditions rather than defending against external threats. This balanced approach prepares not just for survival but for actually living through whatever circumstances emerge—maintaining not just biological function but human dignity throughout the experience.

My neighbor Rick eventually discovered this reality when his fortress proved incapable of addressing the extended power outage's actual challenges. By the third week, he had reluctantly abandoned his defended isolation to join community resource-sharing networks that addressed his unanticipated needs. The experience transformed his preparedness approach entirely; his current systems emphasize adaptive capability alongside more modest security measures.

As Rick wryly observed after that transformative experience: "I spent years preparing to defend against desperate unprepared people, only to discover that I was the desperate unprepared person when my plans didn't match reality."

His hard-earned wisdom captures the essential limitation of the fortress mentality: it prepares for dramatic scenarios that rarely materialize while neglecting the adaptive challenges that inevitably emerge. Genuine preparedness requires moving beyond this fantasy to develop capabilities that support not just surviving disasters but effectively living through them— maintaining human dignity and function regardless of what circumstances present themselves.

8

Community Building: The Real Security System

The first rule of my grandmother's kitchen was simple: "Never show up empty-handed." Whether you were bringing fresh eggs, helping hands, or just good gossip, reciprocity was the currency that kept our rural community functioning long before I understood the sophisticated social architecture behind her apple pies and canning parties.

This lesson hit home during when our area got hammered with over four feet of snow followed by temperatures so cold even the snowplows gave up. As roads disappeared and power lines fell, I watched our community split into two distinct response patterns that perfectly illustrate the difference between isolation and connection as survival strategies.

My neighbor Frank—proud owner of a generator the size of a compact car and enough ammunition to start a war— immediately barricaded his driveway and announced via his emergency radio that he and his family were "secure" and would "defend their resources as necessary." Meanwhile, my seventy-year-old neighbor Ruth started organizing a rotation of homes where community members could gather for warmth, shared meals, and pooled resources.

By day three, Frank's generator had failed due to a mechanical issue he couldn't diagnose alone. By day five, his family had joined Ruth's improvised community support network, looking notably sheepish as they carried their rapidly thawing freezer contents to contribute to the communal food supply.

"I thought I could handle anything myself," Frank admitted while helping wash dishes after a shared meal prepared on Ruth's wood stove. "Turns out independence isn't much use when your equipment fails and you've alienated everyone who might have helped."

Ruth, ever diplomatic, patted his arm and said, "That's why we swap apple pies in normal times, dear. So we know who'll share their firewood when it's not so normal."

That moment crystallized something I've observed repeatedly through decades of rural living and multiple emergencies: your community connections are your actual security system. The social capital built through mundane exchanges—babysitting swaps, tool lending, garden surplus sharing, skill teaching—creates resilience that no individual preparation, regardless of how extensive, can replicate.

The Human Safety Net

Let's make note of the big gun in the room: in prepper circles, "security" typically translates to firearms, defensive perimeters, and various strategies for repelling imagined hordes of desperate unprepared people. This approach reflects a fundamentally masculine perspective on safety that emphasizes physical dominance and resource control through force or its implied threat.

The historical evidence from actual disasters tells a dramatically different story about what actually creates security during extended emergencies. Studies show the strength and extent of community relationships—predicts survival outcomes more reliably than material preparations or defensive capabilities.

This reality directly contradicts the "lone wolf" security fantasy popular in prepper culture. The most dangerous situation in a genuine emergency isn't being without a specific resource—it's being without a community that can collectively address unpredictable challenges that inevitably exceed individual capacity.

One particularly memorable example involved a self-proclaimed "security-conscious prepper" who had invested heavily in elaborate property defenses and resource stockpiles while deliberately avoiding community connections. When his water filtration system failed due to a part he hadn't stockpiled, he faced a genuine crisis that the connected households in our area were managing easily through resource sharing. His impressive security measures had effectively imprisoned him with a problem he couldn't solve individually, while keeping him disconnected from the community network that could have easily resolved it.

This pattern repeats across disaster studies worldwide: social connection consistently emerges as the most reliable predictor of resilience, while isolation—regardless of its material advantages—creates critical vulnerabilities when unanticipated challenges exceed individual capacity.

The most effective security strategy isn't accumulating defensive capabilities but building genuine reciprocal relationships within a community of varied skills and resources. These relationships create adaptive capacity that can respond to emergent challenges that no individual preparation, however comprehensive, can anticipate.

This approach to security has traditionally been developed and maintained through women's social roles as relationship cultivators. While men have historically focused on perimeter defense, women have typically invested in the intricate social webs that actually determine community survival during extended crises. The resulting capabilities—network building, favor banking, resource matching, conflict mediation—represent sophisticated survival technologies developed through generations of practical experience.

The Feminine Art of Community Weaving

During a community emergency preparation assessment I conducted some years back, I observed a fascinating gender pattern in social network mapping. When asked to identify their emergency support connections—people they could call on for assistance during a crisis—men typically listed an average of 7-10 individuals, predominantly close family and friends with similar backgrounds and capabilities to their own.

Women in the same community typically identified 15-25 connections spanning diverse skill sets, resource access points, and social positions. More importantly, their networks included critical "bridge" relationships that connected otherwise separate social groups—creating web-like structures that could rapidly mobilize resources across different community segments.

This gender difference in network structure reflects distinct approaches to relationship building with significant implications for emergency resilience. Men's networks tended toward depth with similar individuals, creating strong but narrower support systems. Women's networks emphasized breadth across different social territories, creating more adaptive capabilities during actual emergencies where unpredictable challenges require diverse resources.

These different networking patterns emerge from traditional gender roles that assigned community maintenance responsibilities primarily to women. Across cultures and historical periods, women typically managed the social exchanges—meal sharing, childcare coordination, celebration organizing, care for vulnerable community members—that built and maintained community cohesion. The resulting expertise in network cultivation represents a sophisticated survival adaptation developed through generations of practical experience.

I've witnessed the emergency value of these feminine networking capabilities repeatedly in my community. It was predominantly women who activated the complex social systems that matched displaced households with appropriate temporary housing, coordinated material aid without redundancy or waste, identified and addressed specialized needs, and maintained emotional support throughout the crisis.

The effectiveness of these systems didn't emerge spontaneously during the emergency—it reflected networks deliberately cultivated through previous social exchanges. The women who coordinated aid had spent years building relationships through seemingly mundane activities: organizing community meals, maintaining phone trees, remembering birthdays and personal details, facilitating introductions between disconnected community members, and mediating minor conflicts before they developed into larger divisions.

My friend Elena, who coordinates our community emergency response team, describes this process as "relationship banking"—making regular deposits into social accounts through small assists and exchanges, creating capital that can be withdrawn when larger needs arise. This banking occurs through activities traditionally dismissed as women's social maintenance work: organizing potlucks, remembering children's names and achievements, noting household changes that might indicate needed support, facilitating resource exchanges between community members.

These activities create community resilience more effectively than any physical preparation because they build adaptive capacity rather than merely stockpiling resources. When unexpected challenges emerge—as they inevitably do during actual emergencies—these social networks rapidly mobilize diverse capabilities that no individual or household could maintain independently.

The resulting security isn't based on exclusion and defense but on mutual support and collective capacity—a fundamentally different approach to preparedness than the fortress mentality that dominates masculine prepper culture. Rather than attempting to anticipate and defend against specific threats, this approach builds networks capable of responding to whatever challenges actually emerge.

As you assess your own preparedness, consider whether you've invested in this critical social dimension alongside material preparations. Have you developed reciprocal relationships with diverse community members? Do you participate in the social exchanges that build community cohesion during normal times? Can you activate support networks if your individual capabilities prove insufficient? These social preparations may ultimately determine your outcomes more decisively than many physical preparations.

Strategic Alliance Building

Not all community connections are created equal when it comes to emergency resilience. The most effective preparation involves deliberately cultivating relationships with individuals possessing diverse skills, resources, and social positions—creating a network specifically designed to address varied challenges.

I learned this lesson dramatically during a power outage when my carefully prepared solar system failed due to an inverter issue I couldn't diagnose or repair independently. My stockpiled food and water meant nothing without functioning refrigeration and well pumps. What saved my preparations wasn't another physical backup but a relationship I'd deliberately cultivated with Roberto, an electrician who lived fifteen miles away. One call activated our pre-established mutual aid agreement: he diagnosed and repaired my system, and I later provided his family with preserved garden produce he didn't have time to grow himself.

This exchange represented a strategic alliance I'd intentionally developed before any emergency occurred—recognizing that his technical expertise complemented my food production capabilities in ways that enhanced both our preparedness. Similarly, I've established deliberate exchange relationships with individuals possessing medical knowledge, heavy equipment access, small engine repair skills, and various other capabilities that extend my household's resilience beyond what we could maintain independently.

Creating these strategic alliances involves specific approaches that build genuine reciprocity rather than one-sided dependency:

First, identify your authentic areas of contribution—capabilities you can genuinely provide that others might need. These might include food preservation skills, childcare availability, extra space, specialized tools, transportation resources, or any other capacity you can reliably maintain. The key is genuine capacity to contribute, not just need for assistance.

Second, deliberately connect with individuals possessing complementary capabilities, focusing particularly on skills and resources your household can't efficiently maintain. These connections might develop through community organizations, skill-sharing events, voluntary associations, or direct outreach to individuals with known capabilities.

Third, establish actual exchanges during normal times, creating relationship patterns and expectations that can be activated during emergencies. These exchanges build both trust and practical understanding of each other's capabilities while creating mutual obligation that transcends transactional calculations during actual crises.

I facilitated this process formally for our community through what we call "Skill Swap Saturdays"—monthly events where community members both teach and learn practical skills while building relationships across different social groups. These gatherings have created remarkable community resilience by connecting individuals who might never have developed relationships through their normal social patterns.

During a particularly memorable session, we watched in amusement as Jim, a retired military officer with extensive tactical training, learned canning techniques from Eleanor, an eighty-year-old grandmother who had never fired a gun in her life. Meanwhile, Eleanor's grandson learned basic vehicle maintenance from Jim in an exchange that created both practical capability and social connection between previously separated community segments.

When major flooding struck our region the following spring, these cross-group connections proved invaluable for emergency response. The social bridges established through our skill exchanges allowed rapid resource mobilization across different community networks, creating collective capabilities far beyond what any individual group could have maintained.

This strategic approach to community building reflects traditionally feminine social processes adapted specifically for preparedness purposes. Rather than seeing security as a product of resource hoarding and boundary defense, it recognizes that genuine resilience emerges from exchange networks that extend capability beyond individual limits.

As one participant in our community preparedness program observed after experiencing her first genuine emergency: "I spent years worrying about having enough supplies for my family, but what actually saved us was knowing the right people with the right skills when our preparations proved insufficient. The community we built turned out to be more valuable than anything we stored."

Leadership That Lasts

When normal systems collapse during extended emergencies, leadership becomes a critical factor in community cohesion and function. Yet the dominant models of crisis leadership—typically drawn from military and corporate contexts—often prove poorly suited for the specific challenges of maintaining community during prolonged disruption.

I've observed this leadership gap repeatedly while serving as a designated shelter manager during regional emergencies. Individuals with formal leadership credentials—military officers, corporate executives, institutional administrators—frequently struggle when confronted with the messy, emotionally complex reality of maintaining community function through extended stress without formal authority structures.

Meanwhile, individuals with experience managing families and community organizations—roles traditionally held by women—often demonstrate remarkable effectiveness at maintaining cohesion, resolving conflicts, allocating resources, and preserving morale despite having fewer formal leadership credentials.

The difference lies in fundamentally different leadership approaches developed through different experiential contexts. Traditional masculine leadership models emphasize hierarchy, clear authority lines, rule enforcement, and decisive action—approaches optimized for acute crises requiring coordinated immediate response. Traditional feminine leadership models emphasize relationship maintenance, conflict resolution, need identification, and consensus building—approaches optimized for extended challenges requiring sustained cooperation.

Both approaches have value in different contexts, but extended community emergencies typically demand more of the capabilities developed through family and community management than those developed through hierarchical organization leadership.

During a particularly challenging shelter operation following regional flooding, I watched this distinction play out dramatically. The officially designated shelter manager—a retired military officer with extensive command experience—implemented a leadership approach heavily focused on rule creation, schedule enforcement, and centralized decision-making. While initially creating order, this approach generated increasing resistance as the emergency extended into its second week, with compliance declining and conflicts escalating despite increasingly rigid enforcement attempts.

When circumstances forced a leadership change, the new manager—a woman with extensive experience running community organizations and raising six children—implemented a dramatically different approach. Rather than focusing on rule enforcement, she emphasized:

*Building investment through inclusive decision processes
 *Identifying and addressing unstated needs driving disruptive behaviors
 *Creating appropriate autonomy within necessary boundaries
 *Establishing problem-solving systems rather than just rule structures
 *Matching tasks to individual capabilities and preferences where possible

The transformation was remarkable. Within days, the shelter atmosphere shifted from grudging compliance punctuated by conflicts to genuine cooperation with minimal enforcement requirements. The same population with the same needs under the same constraints demonstrated completely different cohesion based solely on leadership approach.

This experience aligns with research on extended emergency management, which consistently shows that community cohesion during prolonged disruption correlates more strongly with participatory leadership styles than with hierarchical enforcement models. The leadership capabilities developed through traditionally feminine roles—family management, community organization coordination, relationship facilitation—create particularly valuable approaches for maintaining cooperation when formal authority structures are absent.

These capabilities aren't innately gendered despite their historical association with women's social roles. They represent specific skills developed through particular experiences—skills anyone can cultivate through appropriate practice and perspective shifts.

The most effective emergency leaders I've observed combine elements from both traditional approaches, employing directive leadership during acute response phases while transitioning to more collaborative approaches for extended recovery periods. This flexible leadership style—adapting methods to changing circumstances rather than applying a single approach regardless of context—creates resilience through different emergency phases.

As you develop your own preparedness strategy, consider whether you've invested in building these sustainable leadership capabilities alongside more tactical response skills. Can you maintain group cohesion through extended stress without relying on formal authority? Have you developed conflict resolution approaches that preserve relationships despite resource constraints? Can you create decision processes that build investment rather than merely compelling compliance? These leadership capabilities may ultimately prove more valuable than many tactical skills that receive greater attention in conventional preparedness training.

While He's Surveilling the Perimeter, She's Creating Civilization

The scene has played out so many times in our community's emergency shelters that it's become almost comically predictable: as newly arrived men check windows and establish security protocols for the hundredth time, women quietly create the systems that transform emergency shelter into functional community.

During our last extended shelter operation, I watched this gender division unfold with such perfect predictability that I started keeping notes for this book. While a group of earnest men with identical tactical vests established elaborate security rotations for threats that never materialized, the women were busy:

*Creating a childcare rotation that freed parents for essential tasks
  *Establishing meal preparation systems that transform random donations
   *Identifying and addressing specialized needs
   *Developing privacy solutions within the open shelter environment
   *Establishing communication networks that maintain outside connection
    *Organizing shared activities that preserved morale despite uncomfortable conditions

By hour twelve, the men had completed their seventeenth security perimeter check (finding, yet again, no approaching zombies), while the women had established functioning systems for every essential aspect of community life within the shelter. By day three, even the most security-focused men had abandoned their perimeter obsession to join the civilization-building activities that actually determined our collective welfare.

This pattern reflects a fundamental preparedness truth that rarely appears in conventional literature: creating functional community systems ultimately contributes more to survival than defending boundaries against largely imaginary threats. The hard work of establishing shared meals, maintaining sanitation, managing conflicts, supporting vulnerable individuals, and preserving psychological health determines actual outcomes far more reliably than the tactical activities that receive disproportionate attention.

After one particularly grueling shelter operation, a former military officer who had initially focused exclusively on security considerations made a confession during our debrief session: "I spent twenty years training for the wrong apocalypse. I learned to clear rooms and secure perimeters, but it turns out apocalypse looks a lot more like running a really badly equipped summer camp than a tactical operation."

His observation captures something essential about actual emergencies versus prepper fantasies. Real disasters don't primarily demand tactical heroes defending resources against marauders. They require community builders who can establish and maintain the systems that preserve both physical and psychological welfare through extended disruption.

These community-building capabilities have traditionally

been developed through women's social roles as family and group maintainers. The resulting expertise—conflict resolution, resource stretching, morale preservation, vulnerability identification, system creation—represents sophisticated survival technology developed through generations of practical experience managing human groups through various challenges.

The contrast between boundary defense and community building as preparedness strategies becomes particularly stark during extended emergencies. Initial security concerns typically resolve relatively quickly, while community maintenance challenges extend throughout the emergency duration. Yet conventional preparedness culture invests disproportionate resources in security skills that occupy minimal actual emergency time while neglecting community-building capabilities that ultimately determine functional outcomes.

My neighbor Thomas, who spent years accumulating an impressive collection of security equipment while avoiding community involvement, had a transformative experience when regional flooding forced him into a community shelter. After two weeks of watching how actual emergency dynamics unfolded, he sheepishly admitted: "I prepared extensively for a movie version of disaster that never happened, while completely ignoring the reality that did occur. I know exactly how to defend resources I can't use while having no idea how to contribute to the community systems I actually depend on."

His realization reflects a pattern I've observed repeatedly: those most invested in tactical preparedness often discover during actual emergencies that they've developed capabilities with limited practical application while neglecting the community-building skills that actually determine outcomes.

Meanwhile, those who've invested in building community systems—skills traditionally developed through women's social roles—find their capabilities directly applicable to emergency challenges.

This observation isn't meant to dismiss security considerations entirely. Basic precautions certainly have their place within comprehensive preparedness. The problem emerges when boundary defense receives disproportionate investment compared to community building, creating the illusion of security while neglecting the systems that actually determine survival during extended emergencies.

The most effective preparation balances reasonable security measures with substantial investment in community-building capabilities, recognizing that most emergency duration involves living together through challenging circumstances rather than defending against external threats. This balanced approach prepares not just for immediate crisis response but for the extended community maintenance that typically determines actual outcomes.

As my grandmother wisely observed: "Armies might win territories, but only communities preserve what makes those territories worth having in the first place. The real survival skill isn't fighting—it's making life worth continuing despite whatever happens."

Her perspective captures something essential about genuine preparedness that conventional security-focused approaches often miss: survival isn't just about maintaining biological function through crisis but preserving the human connections and systems that make survival meaningful. The capability to build and maintain community through disruption—traditionally developed through women's social

COMMUNITY BUILDING: THE REAL SECURITY SYSTEM

roles—ultimately creates more resilience than any boundary defense strategy.

While tactical skills might occasionally prove useful during brief emergency phases, community-building capabilities remain essential throughout. The ability to create functional human systems amid disruption—to establish civilization within chaos—represents the most consistently valuable preparation for whatever challenges actually emerge.

So by all means, check your perimeter if it makes you feel better. Check it twice if you must. Just make sure someone is creating the community systems you'll actually live within once the perimeter checking gets old—which, based on my shelter management experience, takes approximately six hours. After that, the real work of emergency survival begins: creating human community that sustains both body and soul through whatever challenges emerge.

9

The Practical Wardrobe

The moment I knew my neighbor Trevor had lost touch with practical reality came during a wilderness survival workshop I was teaching. As participants filtered in that crisp October morning, most wore sensible layers appropriate for Maine's notoriously fickle fall weather. And then there was Trevor, resplendent in what appeared to be an entire military surplus store's apparel section, complete with more zippers, clips, and MOLLE webbing than any human could possibly need.

"Desert tan?" I couldn't help asking, noting his head-to-toe khaki ensemble. "In a Maine forest in autumn?"

"It's tactical," he explained with complete seriousness. "The zipper pulls are glow-in-the-dark."

By lunchtime, with temperatures having risen twenty degrees, poor Trevor was sweating profusely while unable to remove layers without undressing completely. Meanwhile, the workshop participants in simple wool layers were easily adapting to the changing conditions by adding or removing pieces as needed.

By mid-afternoon, when an unexpected rain shower swept through our outdoor classroom, Trevor's cotton-blend tactical masterpiece absorbed water like a sponge while the wool-wearing participants stayed relatively comfortable despite the dampness. As we huddled under a tarp waiting for the shower to pass, Trevor looked miserable enough that I took pity on him and loaned him my spare wool sweater.

"I don't understand," he muttered, gratefully pulling on the ancient cardigan I'd knitted years ago. "I spent over $800 on this outfit. The tag said 'extreme conditions.'"

"The first rule of survival clothing," I told him gently, "is that nature doesn't care about your fashion statement. Function beats form every single time."

This lesson—that practical clothing choices dramatically impact survival outcomes—seems increasingly forgotten in an era where "prepper fashion" has become a marketable aesthetic rather than a functional choice. The tactical clothing industry has exploded with options that emphasize military styling over practical functionality, creating garments designed more for looking prepared than actually being prepared.

The reality of emergency clothing needs rarely matches these tactical fantasies. In genuine survival situations, your clothing system becomes a critical component of shelter—your most immediate and personal microenvironment. Yet many preppers invest more thought in distant retreat locations than in the wearable shelter they inhabit continuously.

Beyond Tactical Black: Clothing That Actually Serves Survival

The prepper clothing industry would have you believe that

surviving any emergency requires dressing like a paramilitary operator on a covert mission. This fashion-driven approach has created a sea of muted earth tones, excessive pocket configurations, and "tactical" features that often undermine practical functionality.

After observing how clothing performs during actual emergencies—from blizzards to floods, from extended power outages to evacuation scenarios—I've concluded that genuine survival clothing has little in common with what appears in most prepper catalogs. The most functional emergency wardrobe prioritizes completely different characteristics.

Thermal versatility across varying conditions becomes far more important than color scheme or style. During an extended power outage several winters ago, our community experienced temperature swings from below-freezing nights to surprisingly warm days as buildings with passive solar features overheated without circulation systems. Those with adaptable clothing layers navigated these fluctuations comfortably, while those wearing single-layer "winter tactical" garments suffered in both extremes.

Material performance under varying moisture conditions proves more critical than how many pockets you have. When flooding forced a neighboring community to evacuate, many residents discovered too late that their synthetic "performance" garments became unbearably clammy when humid, while natural fibers like wool maintained reasonable comfort despite atmospheric moisture.

Movement range and physical function supersede tactical styling. During community cleanup after a severe storm, those wearing practical work clothes accomplished significantly more than those sporting restrictive tactical designs better suited to looking rugged in photographs than actually being rugged during labor.

My friend Elena, a search and rescue volunteer with decades of wilderness experience, expresses perfectly the disconnect between marketing and functionality: "If your clothing choices are based primarily on what looks 'tactical,' you're dressing for an Instagram apocalypse, not an actual emergency. The most effective survival clothing rarely looks tactical at all."

This assessment aligns with what I've observed across numerous emergencies. The individuals who maintained the best function in adverse conditions typically wore clothing systems developed through practical outdoor activities—hiking, farming, construction work—rather than garments marketed specifically as "tactical" or "survival" wear.

The most effective emergency wardrobe typically includes:

*Base layers that manage moisture to maintain comfort across varying activity levels, with wool or wool blends significantly outperforming synthetic options for extended wear without washing facilities

*Mid layers that provide insulation while allowing easy adjustment as conditions change, ideally in natural fibers that maintain insulating properties when damp

*Outer layers that protect from wind and precipitation while allowing excess heat and moisture to escape, preventing both external soaking and internal condensation

*Extremity protection suited to likely environmental conditions, with appropriate head, hand, and foot coverings that can adapt to changing circumstances

These practical considerations rarely align with the tactical aesthetic that dominates prepper marketing. Real-world functional clothing often looks disappointingly ordinary—plain wool sweaters, simple cotton-blend work pants, basic rain shells—while providing superior performance in actual emergency conditions.

When my community experienced an extended power outage during a particularly brutal winter, I observed this principle in action. Those who had invested in practical layering systems with appropriate materials maintained comfortable function despite the challenging conditions. Meanwhile, those who had purchased elaborate tactical clothing often discovered that their garments performed poorly during extended wear in real environmental conditions.

The disconnect wasn't surprising given the different development contexts. Most tactical clothing is designed for relatively short operational periods with access to base facilities for cleaning and drying—conditions that rarely match extended emergency scenarios where laundry facilities may be unavailable for weeks or months. The resulting garments emphasize features that photograph well in product marketing while underperforming in sustained adverse conditions.

Your clothing system represents your most immediate shelter and most constant survival tool. It deserves selection based on actual performance rather than aesthetic appeal or marketing claims. As my grandmother wisely noted after living through numerous historical hardships: "In a real emergency, no one cares what you look like—they care whether you can function."

Layering Science: Adaptability in Unpredictable Conditions

The cornerstone of practical emergency clothing isn't a specific garment but a systematic approach that creates adaptability across varying conditions. This layering methodology represents a sophisticated shelter technology developed through generations of practical experience in challenging environments.

During a power outage to our region for nearly two weeks, I witnessed dramatically different outcomes between households that understood layering principles and those relying on single-garment solutions. Families accustomed to layering maintained reasonable comfort despite fluctuating indoor temperatures, while those dependent on either heavy single-layer garments or multiple identical layers experienced either overheating or inadequate insulation as conditions changed.

The science behind effective layering involves understanding how different materials and configurations interact with both the environment and the human body. Each layer serves a specific function within the system. The base layer manages the initial moisture interface between skin and clothing. Contrary to popular tactical marketing claims, synthetic materials typically perform poorly in extended emergency situations where washing facilities are limited. Natural fibers, particularly wool and wool blends, maintain better function and comfort during prolonged wear by absorbing and releasing moisture without developing bacterial growth and associated odors.

During a community emergency shelter operation, this difference became starkly apparent by the third day. Those wearing synthetic base layers had developed significant odor issues and skin irritation, while those in wool or wool-blend undergarments maintained better hygiene with identical washing limitations. The performance gap only widened as the situation extended.

The mid layer provides adjustable insulation that can be modified as conditions or activity levels change. The most functional mid layers offer incremental adjustment options—vests, button-up sweaters, zip-front jackets—that allow fine-tuning without complete garment changes. Materials with high insulation-to-weight ratios that maintain performance when damp, such as wool or modern wool blends, significantly outperform cotton or many synthetics in actual emergency conditions.

My friend Thomas, who worked on disaster response teams across varying climates, describes the importance of mid-layer adaptability: "The constant in emergency situations is change. Your mid layer system needs enough flexibility to handle 30-degree temperature swings and varying activity levels without requiring a complete clothing change or leaving you vulnerable during transitions."

The outer layer serves as a selective barrier between your insulation system and environmental challenges like wind, precipitation, and abrasion. The most functional outer layers provide appropriate protection without trapping internal moisture—a balance many tactical garments fail to achieve due to their emphasis on absolute waterproofing over breathability.

During an extended evacuation following regional flooding, those with breathable water-resistant outer layers maintained better overall function than those wearing fully waterproof tactical rain gear. The supposedly superior tactical garments created internal condensation that eventually soaked insulating layers from the inside, while the more balanced approach maintained better overall dryness despite allowing minor external moisture penetration.

The integration of these layers creates a flexible microclimate that can adapt to both environmental conditions and activity levels—a critical capability during emergencies when both may change unpredictably. Rather than attempting to predict specific conditions and optimize for them, this systems approach creates adaptability across the broad range of circumstances that might actually emerge.

This layering science extends beyond torso protection to include specialized systems for extremities. Hands, feet, and head require particularly thoughtful approaches that balance protection with functionality.

Hands typically need multiple options ranging from high-dexterity light protection to maximum thermal insulation, with transitions between them that don't require complete exposure. The most functional hand systems include layerable options that allow adding or removing protection while maintaining some level of capability throughout.

Feet require perhaps the most careful preparation, as foot health directly impacts overall mobility and function. Effective foot systems include moisture management layers (appropriate socks, often wool), protection appropriate to likely terrain and conditions, and careful attention to fit that prevents both circulation restriction and friction injuries during extended wear.

Head protection needs depend significantly on environmental conditions but generally benefit from adaptable options that can adjust coverage as conditions change. The traditional folk wisdom about heat loss through the head may be somewhat exaggerated, but appropriate head covering still provides significant efficiency in thermal regulation across varying conditions.

The integration of these components into a coherent clothing system creates adaptation capabilities that far exceed what any single "tactical" garment can provide. This systems approach has traditionally been developed through practical experience in challenging environments, where functionality directly impacts survival outcomes.

When you're evaluating potential additions to your emergency wardrobe, consider not just individual garment features but how each piece functions within your overall adaptation system. The most valuable emergency clothing items typically serve multiple functions, transition easily between different configurations, and perform well across varying conditions rather than optimizing for a single scenario.

Wardrobe Longevity: Maintenance and Repair

In genuine long-term emergencies, the ability to maintain your clothing system becomes as important as the initial selection. No garment, regardless of quality or material, can withstand indefinite use without appropriate care and repair. Yet this critical aspect of emergency preparation receives minimal attention in conventional prepper literature, which typically emphasizes acquisition over maintenance.

During a workshop on extended emergency preparation, I asked participants how long they expected their current clothing to remain functional without access to conventional laundering facilities or replacement purchases. The responses revealed a startling preparedness gap—most had never considered clothing deterioration as a significant emergency concern despite its direct impact on shelter capability.

The reality of extended emergencies is that clothing maintenance becomes an essential skill set rather than an optional domestic chore. Your ability to clean, repair, and adapt garments directly affects your functional shelter capability throughout changing conditions.

Cleaning methodologies appropriate to emergency conditions differ significantly from conventional laundering. During a multi-week power outage following a severe winter storm, households with knowledge of non-electric cleaning techniques maintained better hygiene and garment function than those dependent on mechanical washing. Simple technologies like wash basins, agitation tools, and drying systems appropriate to available heat sources proved invaluable for maintaining clothing functionality.

My neighbor Ruth, who grew up in a household without running water, became an unexpected community resource during this period. Her practical knowledge of soap-making, water-efficient washing techniques, and appropriate drying methods helped multiple families maintain clothing hygiene despite infrastructure limitations. This knowledge—typically passed through female family lines but increasingly lost in modern households—represents critical emergency capability rather than merely quaint historical practice.

Beyond basic cleaning, repair capabilities directly impact wardrobe longevity during extended emergencies. Small damages that would be inconsequential with easy replacement access can become critical failure points when shopping isn't an option. Basic mending skills—patching, darning, seam repair, button replacement—transform from occasional convenience to essential maintenance under emergency conditions.

During a community skill-sharing event, I was struck by the gender disparity in clothing repair knowledge. Despite the critical survival implications, garment mending remains overwhelmingly feminized knowledge even within preparedness communities. This gender coding creates a dangerous capability gap in many households where no member possesses these essential skills due to their cultural categorization as "women's work" rather than survival technology.

The most prepared individuals I've encountered maintain not just repair skills but appropriate tools and materials for extended clothing maintenance:

*Mending supplies including various threads, needles, patches, and reinforcement materials suited to their specific wardrobe composition

*Cleaning supplies appropriate for different fabric types under limited water and energy conditions

*Weatherproofing materials for maintaining appropriate water resistance in outer layers

*Replacement components for critical failure points like fasteners, drawstrings, and high-wear areas

These maintenance capabilities extend wardrobe functional lifespan from months to years—a critical difference during extended emergencies when replacement access may be limited or nonexistent. The ability to maintain your clothing system directly impacts your shelter capability throughout changing conditions.

As you assess your own preparedness, consider whether you've developed these maintenance skills alongside your physical supplies. Can you effectively clean and repair your clothing without conventional infrastructure? Have you assembled appropriate tools and materials for extended garment maintenance? Do multiple household members possess these critical skills regardless of gender? These capabilities may ultimately prove as important as the initial garment selection in determining your long-term shelter functionality.

Making Do: Improvisational Garment Creation

The ultimate clothing resilience isn't maintenance or repair but the ability to create functional garments from available materials when conventional options become unavailable. This capability—transforming raw or repurposed materials into practical clothing—represents preparedness depth that transcends dependency on existing supplies.

During a historical preservation project documenting Depression-era survival strategies, I interviewed elderly community members about how their families managed clothing needs during extreme resource constraints. Their accounts revealed sophisticated improvisational capabilities that transformed available materials—feed sacks, worn-out garments, household textiles—into functional clothing that maintained both practical performance and personal dignity.

My great-aunt Eleanor described how her mother created winter coats for seven children using wool blankets, repurposed buttons, and thread unraveled from discarded garments too damaged for direct reuse. These weren't merely emergency coverings but carefully constructed garments designed for specific functional needs while maximizing material efficiency.

This improvisational capability represents a sophistication level rarely acknowledged in modern preparedness discussions. The ability to envision functional garment possibilities within seemingly unrelated materials, then execute those transformations with limited tools, creates resilience beyond what any stored supplies can provide.

The core skills enabling this improvisational capability include:

*Material assessment—understanding how different textiles perform regarding insulation, moisture management, durability, and comfort

*Pattern creation—developing functional garment designs appropriate to available materials and specific needs

*Construction techniques—joining, reinforcing, and finishing textiles using available tools and fastening systems

*Adaptation methods—modifying existing items to serve different functions or fit different users

These capabilities have traditionally developed through practical experience managing household textile needs under resource constraints—knowledge typically passed through female family lines but increasingly lost in our disposable clothing culture.

During a practical skills workshop, I demonstrated how a standard wool blanket could be transformed into a functional cold-weather garment using only scissors and safety pins—no sewing required. The resulting garment provided better environmental protection than many commercial options while requiring minimal tools or specialized knowledge. The participants' surprise at this simple transformation revealed how disconnected many have become from basic material adaptation capabilities.

This knowledge gap represents a significant vulnerability in modern preparedness. Even extensive clothing stockpiles eventually deteriorate or become inappropriate as conditions change, creating dependency unless accompanied by creation capabilities. The ability to transform available materials into functional garments provides adaptation options beyond what any pre-emergency planning can anticipate.

My friend Sarah notes that this improvisational capability often determines long-term outcomes after the initial emergency phase: "Once the immediate crisis passes and stored supplies begin depleting, the people who thrive are those who can create what they need from what's available rather than depending solely on what they stored."

This observation aligns with historical patterns across numerous extended emergencies. The individuals and communities who maintained the best function as conditions evolved were typically those with robust improvisational capabilities rather than merely extensive initial supplies.

Developing these capabilities doesn't require becoming a master tailor before emergencies occur. Basic understanding of material properties, simple construction techniques, and functional garment requirements creates foundation skills that can expand through practical application as needs arise. The most important element is breaking the dependency mindset that views clothing as something that must be purchased rather than potentially created.

As you develop your emergency preparation strategy, consider whether you've included these improvisational capabilities alongside your physical supplies. Can you create or substantially modify garments if replacement needs emerge during extended emergencies? Do you understand the basic principles of functional clothing construction? Have you practiced transforming unconventional materials into useful items? These capabilities may ultimately prove more valuable than extensive initial supplies as conditions evolve beyond what specific preparations anticipated.

Tactical Fashion Disasters vs. Actually Staying Alive

The catalog arrived with perfect ironic timing, landing in my mailbox the same day I was packing for a wilderness survival course I teach annually. The glossy cover featured a stern-faced model in what appeared to be modified military attire, complete with unnecessary straps, superfluous pockets, and a color scheme best described as "apocalypse chic."

Inside, the "Tactical Survival Collection" offered garments that seemed designed more for a dystopian fashion shoot than actual emergency functionality. The descriptions touted features like "combat-ready design" and "tactical advantage" without explaining how these qualities might help during the mundane realities of actual emergencies—like staying dry during extended rain or maintaining mobility while hauling firewood.

As I packed my decidedly *un*tactical clothing for six days of actual wilderness living—well-worn wool layers, simple rain gear, and hiking pants patched so many times they resembled a textile map—I couldn't help creating a mental comparison between tactical fashion fantasies and practical survival realities.

The *Tactical Bodysuit With 37 Pockets* promises "combat readiness for any scenario" but features non-breathable fabric that turns into a personal sauna during any actual exertion. Meanwhile, my 15-year-old wool sweater maintains comfortable temperature regulation across wildly varying conditions from frosty mornings to warm afternoons.

The *Operator-Grade Survival Pants* offer "military-inspired durability" with fashionably angular cargo pockets positioned precisely where they'll dig into your legs when actually sitting on the ground. My simple canvas work pants with strategically reinforced knees allow comfortable movement during real-world tasks like gathering firewood, building shelters, or sitting for extended periods.

The *Elite Tactical Rain Shell* features impressive-sounding "ballistic waterproofing technology" but lacks adequate ventilation, ensuring you'll eventually get soaked from the inside through condensation even if external precipitation doesn't penetrate. My basic breathable rain jacket with adjustable closures and ventilation options maintains better overall dryness through actual precipitation events despite its disappointing lack of tactical styling.

The *Extreme Condition Base Layer* promises "superior moisture management" through synthetic technology but becomes unbearably malodorous after two days without washing—a significant issue during extended emergencies with limited laundering options. My simple wool undergarments maintain reasonable comfort and hygiene for extended periods despite their complete absence of tactical branding.

The *Tactical Advantage Footwear* offers "combat-ready performance" with aggressive styling and minimal break-in period, ensuring impressive blisters during any actual extended wear. My thoroughly broken-in hiking boots with appropriate sock systems maintain foot health during significant mileage despite their regrettable failure to look like something from a military surplus catalog.

This contrast isn't merely stylistic—it reflects fundamentally different approaches to emergency preparation. The tactical fashion approach prioritizes appearing prepared over functional capability, emphasizing features that photograph impressively rather than perform effectively during actual extended use.

My friend Miguel, who served in combat zones before becoming a wilderness guide, puts it perfectly: "The more a clothing item is marketed as 'tactical,' the less likely it is to serve you well in a real extended emergency. The stuff that actually works tends to look boring because it's designed for function rather than appearing badass in your prepper group photos."

His assessment aligns with what I've observed across numerous emergencies and extended wilderness experiences. The individuals who maintain the best function in challenging conditions typically wear clothing systems developed through practical experience rather than marketing-driven design. These systems rarely match prepper fashion expectations but consistently outperform their tactical-branded counterparts in actual challenging conditions.

The most reliable indication of functional emergency clothing isn't its tactical styling or impressive-sounding technology but its proven performance in extended practical use under similar conditions. The wool sweater that's kept sheep warm through countless winter storms will likely serve you better than the synthetic tactical mid-layer developed primarily for its shelf appeal and profit margin.

As you evaluate potential clothing investments for your emergency preparations, consider whether you're being sold tactical fashion or practical function. Are the garment features driven by actual performance needs or by marketing psychology? Does the item have a proven history in relevant conditions, or merely impressive-sounding descriptions? Is it designed for extended use with limited maintenance, or primarily for looking prepared in photographs?

The distinction matters because in actual emergencies, your clothing system directly impacts your survival capabilities. When conditions deteriorate beyond the comfortable boundaries of normal life, functional preparation transcends fashion considerations. Nature remains spectacularly unimpressed by tactical styling while responding quite definitively to practical functionality.

In the moment when your survival actually depends on your preparation choices, you'll care far more about whether your clothing system maintains appropriate body temperature, allows necessary movement, and continues functioning without failure than whether it matched your apocalyptic aesthetic vision.

Choose accordingly.

10

Water Wisdom

The moment I truly understood the gender divide in water management came during a community emergency preparedness fair. At the water station, two approaches emerged so distinctly different that they might as well have been from separate planets.

On one side stood Bruce, proudly displaying his "Ultimate Water Security System"—an impressive array of military-grade water containers, filtration devices that looked like they belonged in a science fiction movie, and enough purification tablets to make the Atlantic Ocean potable. His presentation emphasized "tactical hydration solutions" and "emergency water security protocols" with the grave intensity of someone disarming a nuclear weapon.

On the other side was a seventy-something grandmother demonstrating a simple home water management system she'd been refining for decades. Using ordinary materials and straightforward techniques, she showed how to collect, filter, purify, store, recycle, and conserve water through multiple uses. Her entire setup cost less than one of Bruce's tactical water containers but addressed the complete water cycle rather than just storage.

When a child asked Bruce what happens when his stored water runs out, he launched into an elaborate explanation of his bug-out plan to reach a nearby lake with his portable filtration system. Meanwhile, the grandmother was showing another group how to construct a simple solar still using household materials that could provide clean water indefinitely.

As the fair concluded, I overheard Bruce asking the grandmother about her conservation system that allowed a single gallon of water to serve multiple purposes before eventually reaching her garden. "I've never really thought about using the water more than once," he admitted. "I've just focused on having enough stored."

That exchange perfectly captures the fundamental difference between the "tactical water" approach popular in prepper culture and the sophisticated water wisdom traditionally cultivated through women's roles as household resource managers. One treats water as a static commodity to be acquired and guarded; the other recognizes it as a dynamic resource to be continuously managed through changing conditions.

This distinction matters enormously during actual emergencies, where water management skills typically determine outcomes more decisively than initial storage capacity. Your stored water will eventually deplete, but knowledge of how to find, purify, use, and conserve water creates indefinite sustainability beyond what any stockpile can provide.

The Original Water Managers

Across human cultures throughout history, practical water

management has typically fallen within women's domain as an extension of household resource responsibilities. While men often handled the initial infrastructure (digging wells, building aqueducts), women generally developed the systems for everyday water collection, purification, storage, allocation, and conservation that determined family health and function.

This division of labor wasn't arbitrary but practical. As the primary food preparers, child caregivers, and household maintainers, women directly experienced the consequences of water management decisions in ways that created sophisticated practical knowledge across generations.

My grandmother, who grew up hauling water from a distant spring for her family's daily needs, developed water management techniques that seemed almost magical to my resource-privileged generation. She could intuitively estimate water requirements for different household activities, stretch limited supplies across multiple essential uses, and immediately identify sources of waste that more privileged households overlooked entirely.

"When every drop comes from your own labor," she once told me while demonstrating how to wash dishes with remarkably little water, "you develop a relationship with it. You don't just use water—you think with it."

This thinking-with-water represents a sophisticated cognitive framework developed through intimate practical experience managing limited water resources across variable conditions. Rather than treating water as a single-purpose commodity, traditional women's management systems typically recognized its multi-dimensional potential through sequential uses, appropriate allocation, and careful conservation.

During a drought that affected our region several summers back, I watched this knowledge gap play out dramatically across different households. Families with experience in practical water management maintained relatively normal function despite severe restrictions, while those accustomed to unlimited municipal supply struggled with basic household operations despite having similar restriction levels.

The difference wasn't resources but knowledge—particularly the practical systems developed through generations of women managing household water under constraints. These systems typically included:

*Understanding water quality requirements for different applications, allowing appropriate allocation rather than using potable-quality water for all purposes

*Recognizing sequential use opportunities, where water from one activity becomes the input for another rather than immediate waste

*Developing precise usage techniques that accomplish necessary functions with minimal volume

*Creating contingency systems that adapt to changing water availability across seasons and conditions

*Establishing conservation practices integrated into normal household operation rather than imposed as extraordinary measures

These capabilities represent sophisticated technology developed through practical necessity rather than abstract study. When I interviewed elderly women who had grown up without running water for an oral history project, their water management knowledge contained insights that modern sustainability experts are only now recognizing as innovative—approaches developed through direct experience rather than theoretical research.

My friend Maria, who grew up in rural Mexico helping her mother manage household water collected from a distant source, puts it perfectly: "The first water engineers were women with buckets, not men with degrees. We developed systems that stretched every drop across multiple needs because our families' survival depended on it."

This wisdom hasn't lost relevance in our era of apparent water abundance. As climate change increases water insecurity worldwide, the practical management knowledge traditionally developed through women's household responsibilities becomes increasingly valuable for general resilience—particularly during emergencies when normal supply systems fail.

When our community experienced an extended water service disruption following infrastructure damage, households that had maintained connections to traditional water management knowledge adapted significantly better than those solely dependent on municipal systems. The practical skills that seemed quaintly historical during normal operations suddenly became essential survival technology when infrastructure failed.

As you develop your water preparedness strategy, consider whether you've focused primarily on stockpiling or on management knowledge. Have you developed practical skills for finding, assessing, purifying, using, and conserving water across different scenarios? Can you adapt your water systems to changing conditions rather than depending solely on stored supplies? These capabilities may ultimately prove more valuable than any quantity of stored water once initial supplies deplete.

Sustainable Systems: Beyond the Water Bottle

The most persistent myth in prepper water wisdom is that adequate storage equals adequate preparation. This misconception has created basements full of water containers without the knowledge systems required for sustainable management once those containers empty—which they inevitably will during any extended emergency.

After participating in numerous emergency response situations, I've observed that initial water storage typically transitions to ongoing water management within days or weeks, depending on the scenario. At that transition point, storage capacity becomes largely irrelevant while management capability becomes the limiting factor in continued function.

During a particularly challenging infrastructure failure that affected several communities in our region, I witnessed this transition play out dramatically. Households with extensive water storage but limited management knowledge initially seemed well-prepared but deteriorated rapidly once stored supplies depleted. Meanwhile, households with modest storage but sophisticated management capabilities maintained stable function throughout the extended emergency by establishing sustainable systems appropriate to available resources.

The difference wasn't storage capacity but systematic approach. Sustainable water management typically involves developing multiple capabilities that create resilience through redundancy and adaptation such as collection systems appropriate to your specific environment—whether rainfall, surface water, groundwater, or unconventional sources like atmospheric moisture or plant transpiration. The most resilient approaches maintain options across multiple source types rather than depending on a single collection method.

During a workshop on emergency water systems, I demonstrated how an ordinary household could establish at least five distinct collection methods using materials most people already own. The participants' surprise at these possibilities revealed how narrowly many envision water access beyond municipal systems or commercial bottled sources.

Purification approaches suited to different contamination challenges—from simple filtration for particulates to more advanced treatments for biological, chemical, or radiological threats. The most effective preparation includes both understanding which purification methods address which specific contaminants and maintaining appropriate equipment for challenges likely in your area.

My friend Richard learned this lesson dramatically during a flood that compromised his well. Despite having extensive filtration equipment, he hadn't identified which systems addressed which specific contaminants. His impressive collection of filters proved inadequate for the actual contamination present, forcing him to seek community assistance for appropriate purification knowledge.

Storage systems that maintain water quality while permitting appropriate access and use. Effective water storage involves more than just containers—it requires understanding how storage conditions affect water quality over time, how to prevent contamination during access and use, and how to maintain potability through extended storage periods.

The humble rain barrel illustrates this principle perfectly. I've encountered elaborate commercial rain collection systems that failed due to basic maintenance oversights, while simple homemade systems continued functioning effectively because their owners understood fundamental maintenance requirements rather than depending on technical features they didn't fully comprehend.

Distribution methods that deliver appropriate water quality and quantity to different household functions while minimizing waste or contamination risks. The most effective systems employ gravity where possible, include manual backup options for powered components, and allow selective access based on usage requirements.

During an extended power outage affecting water distribution systems, I watched my neighbor Elaine implement a remarkably effective household water distribution system using ordinary containers, simple siphoning techniques, and strategic placement based on use frequency. Her system—developed through practical experience rather than technical training—maintained efficient function throughout the emergency with minimal physical strain despite her advanced age.

Conservation approaches integrated into normal usage patterns rather than imposed as extraordinary measures during crises. The most sustainable water systems build conservation into basic operation through appropriate fixtures, usage techniques, and sequential applications that maximize utility from each water unit.

My grandmother's kitchen demonstrated this integrated approach perfectly. Every water-using activity incorporated conservation not as a special effort but as normal procedure: washing techniques that minimized volume requirements, capture systems for incidental water that would otherwise waste, and sequential usage planning that allowed a single water unit to serve multiple functions before eventually reaching garden plants.

These system elements typically receive minimal attention in conventional prepper literature, which emphasizes storage volume and purification technology over comprehensive management knowledge. This focus creates dangerous capability gaps once stored supplies deplete and technical systems encounter limitations not addressed in their operating manuals.

The most resilient water preparation emphasizes developing management systems suited to your specific environmental context—recognizing that water challenges during emergencies vary dramatically based on location, season, infrastructure, and scenario. Rather than assuming a universal approach, effective preparation involves understanding your particular water environment and developing appropriate systems for that specific context.

As you assess your own water preparedness, consider whether you've developed sustainable systems beyond initial storage. Can you collect, purify, store, distribute, and conserve water appropriate to your specific environment if normal sources become unavailable? Have you practiced these systems during normal conditions to build capability before emergencies occur? These systems-level preparations often determine long-term outcomes more decisively than initial storage capacity once emergencies extend beyond short-term disruptions.

From Primitive to High-Tech: Purification That Actually Works

One of the most entertaining moments in my emergency preparedness workshops comes when I ask participants to explain exactly how their water filtration devices work. The confident expressions of tactical water commandos typically transform into blank stares as they realize they've purchased equipment they don't actually understand.

"It has a ceramic filter and, um, some carbon stuff?" offered one participant who had just finished describing his $300 "military-grade" filtration system with impressive technical terminology he clearly didn't comprehend.

This knowledge gap represents a dangerous vulnerability. Water purification isn't magic—it's science applied to specific contamination challenges. Without understanding which technologies address which specific contaminants, even the most expensive equipment may prove useless against the particular threats present in your emergency water sources.

Effective water purification preparation begins with understanding the basic contamination categories and which methods address each. Particulates, suspended solids that affect clarity, may carry other contaminants. These can range from visible sediment to microscopic particles, generally addressed through filtration of appropriate size exclusion for the specific particulates present.

During a flood that affected local water sources, I watched several households struggle with rapidly clogging filters because they attempted to use fine-filtration systems directly on heavily silted water. Meanwhile, those who understood filtration as a progressive process implemented simple pre-filtering through cloth or sand to remove larger particulates before employing finer filtration, maintaining system function despite challenging conditions.

Biological contaminants are disease-causing organisms including bacteria, viruses, parasites, and other pathogens. These typically require either killing the organisms through heat (boiling), chemical treatment (chlorine, iodine), ultraviolet exposure, or physical removal through sufficiently fine filtration appropriate to the specific organism sizes.

The distinction between bacteria and virus removal creates particular confusion in emergency filtration. Many commercial filters that effectively remove bacteria remain completely ineffective against viruses due to size differences—a limitation often obscured in marketing materials but critically important during actual emergency application.

Chemical contaminants are dissolved substances ranging from natural minerals to agricultural runoff to industrial pollution. These typically require specific treatment approaches depending on the particular chemicals present, which may include activated carbon adsorption, ion exchange, reverse osmosis, or distillation depending on the specific contaminants.

This category creates some of the most dangerous knowledge gaps in emergency water treatment. During a workshop demonstration analyzing local water sources, participants were shocked to discover that their expensive filtration systems removed some chemical contaminants while leaving others completely untouched—limitations clearly stated in the technical specifications they had never read.

Radiological contaminants—materials that emit ionizing radiation, potentially present in some disaster scenarios. These typically require highly specialized treatment approaches not generally available in consumer purification systems, making source selection and avoidance the primary strategy for most emergency situations.

The most effective purification preparation includes not just equipment for different contamination types but knowledge of when and how to apply different methods based on source assessment. This capability involves both understanding various purification technologies and developing the judgment to select appropriate approaches for specific scenarios.

My friend Elena describes this judgment as more crucial than specific equipment: "I've seen communities with simple but well-understood purification methods maintain safer water than those with advanced technology they didn't fully comprehend. Understanding your tools is more important than how sophisticated they appear."

This wisdom applies across the purification spectrum, from primitive to advanced methods. Some of the most reliable approaches require minimal technology but considerable knowledge. Solar disinfection using UV radiation from direct sunlight can effectively address biological contaminants with nothing more than clear containers and adequate exposure time—but requires understanding specific exposure requirements for different container types and sunlight conditions.

Improvised filtration using available materials like sand, charcoal, cloth, and gravel can remove significant contamination with no commercial equipment—but requires understanding proper layer arrangement, flow rates, and limitations regarding which contaminants this approach effectively addresses.

Basic distillation using simple heating and condensation systems can produce extremely pure water regardless of most source contaminations—but requires understanding energy efficiency techniques, appropriate container materials, and condensation management to produce meaningful volumes.

These knowledge-intensive but equipment-minimal approaches often prove more reliable during extended emergencies than technologically sophisticated systems that users don't fully understand or can't maintain without specialized components.

This reality doesn't mean advanced purification technologies lack value—they can provide excellent treatment with appropriate operation and maintenance. The vulnerability emerges when users depend on equipment they don't comprehend for survival outcomes, creating failure points once operating conditions diverge from manufacturer assumptions or components require maintenance beyond user capability.

The most resilient purification preparation balances technological approaches with knowledge-based methods, creating redundancy through diverse capabilities rather than duplicate equipment. This balanced approach typically includes:

*Understanding multiple purification methods across the technological spectrum

    *Developing assessment skills to identify appropriate methods for specific contamination challenges

    *Maintaining appropriate equipment for likely regional water challenges

    *Practicing knowledge-based methods during normal conditions to build capability before emergencies

    *Establishing appropriate treatment sequences for challenging source waters rather than expecting single-step solutions

This comprehensive approach creates purification capabilities that extend beyond equipment limitations—an essential resilience factor during extended emergencies when replacement parts, consumable media, or power sources may become unavailable.

As you evaluate your own purification preparedness, consider whether you've balanced equipment acquisition with knowledge development. Do you understand how your purification systems actually work? Can you identify appropriate methods for different contamination challenges? Have you developed capabilities across the technological spectrum rather than depending solely on advanced equipment? These knowledge-based preparations often determine long-term outcomes more decisively than initial equipment quality once emergencies extend beyond short-term disruptions.

Conservation Mastery: Using Less While Doing More

The morning after a major storm knocked out power and water service to our community, I watched my neighbor Jerry drag a 55-gallon drum across his yard, cursing continuously as water sloshed over the sides. When I asked what he was doing, he explained he was moving his emergency water supply to his house from the storage shed.

"I figured three gallons per person per day for drinking and basic sanitation," he panted, already soaked from his efforts. "That gives my family about four days before we need to find more."

Meanwhile, my household was implementing a conservation system refined through both historical knowledge and practical experience that extended our similar water volume to nearly two weeks of comfortable function. The difference wasn't storage capacity but usage approach—a distinction that becomes increasingly critical as emergency durations extend beyond initial preparations.

Effective water conservation during emergencies isn't about deprivation but efficiency—using available supplies so effectively that functionality remains high despite limited volume. This capability typically involves specific techniques across different water-using activities. Personal hygiene conservation often creates the most dramatic usage differences between households during water restrictions. Those with experience in limited-water environments typically maintain good hygiene with a fraction of the volume used by those accustomed to unlimited supply.

During a water usage workshop, I demonstrated how to accomplish comprehensive personal cleaning with less than two quarts of water using techniques developed through camping and international travel in water-scarce regions. Participants were genuinely shocked at the difference between this approach and their typical shower usage, which often exceeded 20 gallons for a single shower.

Food preparation and kitchen operations present similar efficiency opportunities through appropriate techniques. Methods like single-container meal preparation, strategic cleaning sequences, and appropriate food choices can dramatically reduce water requirements while maintaining normal nutrition and sanitation.

My grandmother's kitchen wisdom includes dozens of water-efficient cooking techniques that seem almost magical to those accustomed to unlimited supply: using cooking liquid from one food to prepare another, creating meal sequences that utilize a single pot without intermediate washing, and preparing foods in ways that minimize both production and cleanup water needs.

Sanitation management represents perhaps the most crucial conservation domain during extended water restrictions. Appropriate human waste handling, dishwashing procedures, and surface cleaning approaches can maintain necessary sanitation with remarkably little water when properly implemented.

The humble spray bottle ranks among the most valuable conservation tools in this category. During an extended water restriction period, my household maintained excellent kitchen sanitation using spray bottles with appropriate cleaning solutions rather than flowing water—reducing usage by approximately 80% compared to conventional methods while maintaining proper food safety standards.

Laundry typically consumes substantial water in normal operations but can be dramatically reduced through strategic approaches during emergencies. Spot cleaning, extended wear protocols, and efficient batch washing methods can maintain adequate clothing hygiene with minimal water expenditure when properly implemented.

During a multi-week water restriction following regional flooding, my community implemented group laundry systems that dramatically reduced per-household water requirements through efficient batch processing, appropriate pretreatment, and water recycling between compatible laundry stages.

These conservation approaches don't emerge automatically during emergencies—they require both knowledge development and practice during normal conditions to build effective capability. Households that maintain occasional conservation practice during ordinary circumstances typically transition to emergency protocols more effectively than those attempting unfamiliar methods under stress conditions.

The most sophisticated conservation systems integrate multiple usage stages that extract maximum utility from each water unit before ultimate disposal. These sequential systems—sometimes called greywater cascades—direct water from higher-quality needs to lower-quality applications through planned sequences:

*Hand washing water becomes toilet flushing water
  *Vegetable rinsing water becomes plant irrigation water
  *Shower water becomes laundry water
  *Dish soaking water becomes floor cleaning water

These integrated approaches mirror traditional water wisdom developed across cultures through generations of women managing household resources under scarcity conditions. What modern sustainability experts now call "innovative water cycling" represents knowledge that grandmothers worldwide have maintained through practical necessity rather than theoretical interest.

My friend Sophia, who grew up in a Greek village with severe seasonal water limitations, describes this knowledge transfer perfectly: "My grandmother could make three gallons of water accomplish what modern households use thirty to achieve. She taught me to think of water not as something you use once and discard, but as a worker you employ for multiple tasks before releasing it."

This worker metaphor captures the mindset difference between abundance assumptions and conservation mastery. Rather than treating water as a single-purpose commodity, effective conservation approaches recognize its capacity to serve multiple functions sequentially—extracting maximum utility from each unit before final disposal.

As you develop your water preparedness strategy, consider whether you've included these conservation capabilities alongside storage and purification preparations. Have you developed and practiced efficient usage techniques during normal conditions? Can you implement multi-stage water systems that maximize utility from limited volumes? Have you identified household-specific conservation opportunities based on your particular usage patterns? These efficiency capabilities may ultimately extend your functional duration more significantly than increased storage capacity once initial supplies begin depleting.

Water Commando vs. Water Whisperer: Getting Through the Drought

The summer drought had reached critical status by August. Municipal water restrictions limited households to essential uses only, and local officials warned that even those allowances might tighten further if conditions continued. As our community adjusted to the new normal of water scarcity, two distinct approaches emerged that perfectly illustrated contrasting preparedness philosophies.

My neighbor Randy—owner of enough filtration gear to process a small lake—implemented what he called his "water security protocol." This involved elaborately filling and sealing numerous containers from municipal supply before stricter restrictions might occur, constructing a fortress-like arrangement of stored water in his garage, and implementing a rigid usage schedule that had his family members logging every drop consumed like battlefield resources.

Meanwhile, my friend Elaine—an avid gardener with decades of practical resource management experience—took a completely different approach. Rather than focusing exclusively on acquisition and restriction, she implemented an integrated water system that maintained remarkable household function through efficiency, recycling, and strategic usage.

Randy's water commando approach centered on treating water as a dwindling commodity to be guarded and rationed. His family lived in increasing discomfort as restrictions tightened, with personal hygiene particularly suffering under his military-inspired conservation regimen. By week three, family tensions were rising as rapidly as their water stores were depleting, creating a household atmosphere his teenage daughter described as "apocalypse boot camp, but with more yelling about toilet flushing."

Elaine's water whisperer method focused instead on working with available water through its complete potential cycle. Her household maintained nearly normal function despite identical external restrictions by:

*Installing simple greywater diversion from sinks and showers to appropriate garden areas, simultaneously reducing water waste while maintaining critical plantings

*Implementing strategic dishwashing sequences that maximized cleaning capacity from minimal water through proper temperature, soap management, and procedural efficiency

*Creating designated cleaning stations with spray bottles containing appropriate solutions rather than using running

water for most household surfaces

*Establishing personal hygiene approaches that maintained comfort and health while using approximately 20% of normal volumes

The contrast became most apparent when both households hosted family gatherings in the drought's fifth week. Randy's event featured disposable everything to avoid washing, strict bathroom usage limitations that created genuine discomfort for guests, and an atmosphere of scarcity that dominated the supposedly celebratory occasion.

Elaine's gathering included proper dishes comfortably washed through efficient methods, normal bathroom availability managed through simple conservation devices, and an atmosphere that acknowledged the drought without being dominated by it. Her systems approach maintained social normalcy despite identical external constraints.

By the drought's second month, the divergent outcomes became even more pronounced. Randy's commando approach had depleted nearly all his stored supplies while creating significant household stress through increasingly severe usage restrictions. His focus on guarding a dwindling resource had generated conservation through deprivation rather than efficiency, with declining hygiene and rising tensions as the primary results.

Elaine's whisperer method had actually improved over the same period as her household refined their water wisdom through practical experience. New efficiencies emerged through observed opportunities, usage patterns adjusted to seasonal changes, and household members contributed creative improvements based on their particular activities. Rather than guarding a declining stockpile, they were continuously enhancing their relationship with available water through systematic improvement.

The fundamental difference wasn't resources or even initial knowledge, but approach. Randy treated water as a static commodity to be acquired and protected through restrictive control. Elaine recognized it as a dynamic resource to be guided through systems that maximized its utility at each stage—an approach that maintained higher function with lower volume through relationship rather than restriction.

When municipal officials implemented phase three water restrictions that limited households to essential use only, Randy finally sought Elaine's advice after his daughter staged what she called a "hygiene mutiny" in response to his increasingly draconian rationing. His grudging visit to observe her systems revealed the limitations of his commando mentality.

"I've been treating this like a tactical resource problem," he admitted while examining her simple kitchen greywater collection system. "You're treating it like..."

"Like I'm working with the water rather than against scarcity," Elaine finished for him. "Water has properties and patterns. When you understand those, you can accomplish more with less instead of just doing less with less."

Her observation perfectly captures the distinction between the commando and whisperer approaches to resource challenges. One attempts to control scarcity through acquisition and restriction; the other engages available resources through relationship and understanding. Both acknowledge limitations, but one works primarily against constraints while the other works with possibilities.

This distinction applies across all resource domains but

becomes particularly evident with water—our most essential and versatile resource. The commando approach typically creates declining function through increasing restriction, while the whisperer method often maintains or even enhances function through deepening relationship.

As you develop your own water wisdom, consider which approach characterizes your preparation strategy. Are you primarily acquiring and guarding supplies, or developing systems that work with water's natural properties and patterns? Have you focused more on restriction protocols or efficiency methods? Does your approach enhance your relationship with water or simply manage perceived scarcity?

The most resilient preparation incorporates tactical readiness within a broader systems understanding—recognizing that while water storage and purification technology matter, your relationship with water ultimately determines how effectively you navigate scarcity challenges. The water whisperer doesn't reject appropriate technology or reasonable storage, but integrates these elements within a more sophisticated approach based on relationship rather than restriction alone.

In the memorable words Elaine offered to a chastened Randy as he departed with pages of notes about her systems: "Stop commanding your water to last longer, and start whispering with it about how you might work together. It's the oldest conversation in human survival, and women have been having it since we first carried water home."

11

The Mobile Survival Strategy

The hardest decision I've ever made wasn't whether to stay or go—it was acknowledging that staying wasn't an option at all. After thirty years on the same piece of Maine woodland, building a homestead from raw land into a self-sufficient haven, I found myself staring at the approaching forest fire with the crushing realization that everything I'd built might be ash by morning.

The physical preparations—the carefully cultivated gardens, the root cellar packed with preserved harvests, the off-grid power systems I'd invested years perfecting—suddenly meant nothing against the implacable orange glow on the horizon. What mattered now was what we could carry and how quickly we could move.

For most serious preppers, there's a profound emotional investment in place. Whether it's ancestral land passed down through generations or a deliberately chosen retreat location developed with painstaking care, our preparations are typically anchored to specific geography. We think of security in terms of familiar territory—the root cellar we've stocked, the water sources we know intimately, the community connections we've cultivated over decades.

This place-based preparation makes perfect sense. Humans are territorial creatures who function best in environments we understand completely. The prepper's dream of the perfectly prepared homestead speaks to something deep in our psychology—the desire for control, for rootedness, for the security of the known.

Yet the uncomfortable reality is that disasters don't always respect our chosen ground. Sometimes the most prudent decision is to leave everything you've built and move—quickly, efficiently, and with only what you can carry. This necessity creates a fundamental tension in preparedness philosophy: how do you balance the deep investment in place with the potential need for rapid mobility?

My neighbor Ruth, whose family has farmed the same valley for six generations, expressed this tension perfectly as we evacuated together during that fire: "Everything that matters to me is in this place. But nothing in this place matters more than the people leaving it."

You can see the same feelings expressed by some Californians reluctant to evacuate wildfires around Los Angeles. The feeling is universal.

Her words capture the essential wisdom at the heart of balanced preparedness: places matter, but people matter more. The most comprehensive preparation acknowledges that sometimes mobility becomes the only viable survival strategy, regardless of how deeply rooted your primary preparations might be.

This reality demands developing evacuation capabilities

with the same seriousness we apply to our fixed locations—creating mobile survival strategies that maintain essential function when staying put isn't an option. For most preppers, this represents the least developed aspect of their preparation, creating a dangerous vulnerability precisely when resilience matters most.

The Feminine Perspective on Evacuation

Traditional prepper culture typically approaches evacuation through a predominantly masculine lens that emphasizes rapid tactical movement to predetermined alternative locations. This "bug-out" mentality focuses on security during movement, defensive positioning, and individual mobility—often at the expense of the complex human needs that emerge during actual evacuations.

Having both experienced evacuation firsthand and assisted numerous families through forced relocations, I've observed that women typically bring fundamentally different concerns to evacuation planning—considerations that often prove more relevant to actual evacuation challenges than the tactical scenarios that dominate prepper literature.

When our community faced mandatory evacuation during regional flooding, I watched this gender difference emerge clearly in real-time. The men typically focused intensely on routes, vehicles, and security measures, while women more commonly prioritized family cohesion during movement, recognizing that separation during crisis creates both practical problems and psychological trauma that can undermine function. While tactical approaches often divide responsibilities in ways that can separate family members for efficiency, maternal instinct more typically emphasizes maintaining family unity throughout the evacuation process.

My friend Elena, who managed an emergency shelter during that flood, noted that family separation created more acute distress than property loss for most evacuees: "People could accept losing possessions with surprising resilience, but separation from family members, even temporarily, generated anxiety that significantly impaired basic function."

The specific needs of vulnerable family members, including detailed consideration of children, elderly relatives, disabled individuals, and even pets. While tactical evacuation plans might acknowledge these needs as secondary considerations, women more typically center these vulnerabilities in primary planning, recognizing that the most dependent individuals often determine the functional parameters for the entire family unit.

During a community evacuation drill that simulated challenging conditions, I observed that female-led households almost universally incorporated specific provisions for children's psychological comfort—familiar objects, comfort items, and distraction materials—recognizing that maintaining child cooperation directly impacts overall evacuation success.

The logistical complexities of sustained displacement, including considerations for extended living in unfamiliar environments with limited resources. While tactical evacuation often emphasizes the movement itself, women typically think more comprehensively about what happens after arrival—the systems required for daily living in temporary shelter, the resource needs that emerge over time, and the adaptations necessary for different family members.

My neighbor Sarah, who had experienced multiple evacuations with her family, described this perspective difference perfectly: "My husband's evacuation planning stopped at reaching our designated safe location. My evacuation planning started from that point forward—how we would actually live once we got there."

These feminine perspectives on evacuation don't replace tactical considerations—route planning, security awareness, and appropriate timing remain essential elements. But they expand evacuation preparation beyond simplistic bug-out scenarios to address the complex realities of actual displacement experiences.

The most comprehensive evacuation preparation integrates both perspectives, creating plans that address both movement security and sustained function after displacement. This integration recognizes that successful evacuation isn't merely reaching alternative location but maintaining family cohesion and function throughout an inherently traumatic transition.

As you develop your own evacuation strategy, consider whether you've incorporated these broader considerations beyond tactical movement. Does your plan account for the specific needs of all family members throughout the evacuation process? Have you prepared for extended displacement rather than just the movement itself? Does your approach maintain family cohesion during crisis rather than potentially separating members through divided responsibilities? These considerations often determine actual evacuation outcomes more decisively than the tactical elements that receive greater attention in conventional prepper literature.

Beyond the Bug-Out Vehicle: Practical Mobility Preparation

The "bug-out vehicle" occupies nearly mythological status

in prepper culture—typically imagined as some combination of tactical assault vehicle and self-contained survival capsule, bristling with specialized equipment and capable of traversing apocalyptic terrain while repelling opportunistic marauders. This fantasy reflects a deeply masculine approach to evacuation that emphasizes combat readiness over practical mobility.

Having assisted numerous families through actual evacuations across varying circumstances, I can report with confidence that successful evacuation vehicles rarely match this tactical fantasy. The most effective evacuation transportation typically prioritizes reliability, fuel efficiency, appropriate capacity, and operational simplicity over elaborate tactical modifications.

My friend Thomas learned this lesson painfully during a mandatory evacuation. After years of modifying his dedicated "bug-out truck" with expensive specialized equipment, he discovered that its poor fuel efficiency severely limited evacuation range during regional fuel shortages. Meanwhile, families with ordinary but efficient vehicles successfully evacuated much further with less stress, despite their less impressive transportation.

This experience reflects a pattern I've observed repeatedly: the specialized tactical vehicle often creates as many limitations as capabilities during actual evacuations. The most effective preparation typically involves optimizing ordinary transportation rather than creating dedicated bug-out vehicles—a practical approach that addresses evacuation realities rather than tactical fantasies.

This optimization normally includes several key elements often overlooked in conventional bug-out vehicle discussions. Maintenance quality typically determines evacuation reliability more decisively than vehicle type or modifications. A meticulously maintained economy car will generally prove more evacuation-worthy than a neglected tactical vehicle, regardless of theoretical capability differences. The most effective preparation ensures that everyday transportation remains evacuation-ready through regular maintenance rather than relying on specialized vehicles used infrequently.

During a community evacuation exercise, we observed that vehicle performance issues emerged exclusively among rarely-used dedicated evacuation vehicles rather than regularly driven primary transportation. This pattern reinforces a crucial preparation principle: systems used regularly function more reliably than specialized equipment reserved for emergencies.

Capacity configuration significantly impacts evacuation functionality beyond simple cargo volume. Effective evacuation vehicles allow appropriate organization of different resource categories, maintain accessibility to frequently-needed items without unpacking, and accommodate family members comfortably during extended travel. These practical considerations often prove more relevant than theoretical cargo capacity.

My friend Julia, who evacuated with three children and elderly parents during regional wildfires, discovered that her minivan's configurable interior proved vastly more evacuation-suitable than her husband's larger but less adaptable truck. The ability to maintain organized access to essential supplies while accommodating different family members' needs created practical functionality that raw capacity alone couldn't provide.

Operational familiarity during high-stress conditions often

determines evacuation success more significantly than theoretical vehicle capability. Driving an unfamiliar specialized vehicle during emergency conditions typically reduces rather than enhances effective mobility. The most practical preparation ensures that all potential drivers maintain comfort and familiarity with evacuation transportation through regular use.

During an emergency evacuation from approaching wildfires, I witnessed a neighbor struggle dangerously with the specialized driving characteristics of his dedicated bug-out vehicle—a situation he later described as "suddenly trying to learn new equipment while literally fleeing for my life." Meanwhile, families evacuating in their everyday vehicles navigated challenging conditions more effectively despite less theoretical capability.

Fuel consideration becomes particularly crucial during regional emergencies when supply disruptions often occur precisely when evacuation demand peaks. Vehicles with exceptional fuel efficiency or alternative fuel options typically provide greater practical evacuation range than fuel-intensive tactical vehicles, regardless of other capability factors.

The most effective evacuation preparation addresses these practical considerations rather than focusing exclusively on theoretical performance capabilities. This approach typically emphasizes:

*Maintaining everyday vehicles to evacuation standards rather than creating specialized transportation used only during emergencies
*Developing appropriate storage systems within existing transportation rather than assuming specialized vehicles

*Ensuring all family drivers maintain comfort and familiarity with evacuation vehicles through regular use

*Considering fuel efficiency as a primary evacuation capability rather than a secondary concern

*Creating realistic evacuation range expectations based on regional fuel availability during likely emergency scenarios

This practical approach rarely produces vehicles that match the tactical aesthetic popular in prepper media. Instead, it creates genuine evacuation capability based on actual emergency conditions rather than hypothetical scenarios.

As you evaluate your own evacuation transportation, consider whether you've prioritized practical functionality over tactical appearance. Does your approach emphasize reliable mobility appropriate to your specific family needs, or does it reflect influences from tactical fantasy scenarios? The most effective preparation addresses the evacuation challenges most likely in your particular situation rather than generic bug-out assumptions.

Mobile Family Management: The Operational Reality

Beyond transportation considerations, successful evacuation requires effectively managing family function during inherently stressful transition. This operational challenge—maintaining coherent family operation while moving through rapidly changing circumstances—receives remarkably little attention in conventional prepper literature despite determining actual evacuation outcomes more decisively than many more discussed factors.

Having both experienced family evacuation personally and assisted numerous other families through similar circumstances, I've observed that effective mobile family management typically involves several key capabilities that develop through deliberate preparation rather than emerging spontaneously during emergencies. Role clarity during movement reduces coordination overhead and prevents critical oversight during high-stress transitions. The most effective evacuation operations typically establish clear responsibility assignments for different aspects of family function, creating accountability without unnecessary communication requirements.

During a mandatory evacuation preceding a huge storm, I watched my friend Maria implement a family management system she had developed through previous experiences. Each family member, including children with age-appropriate responsibilities, understood their specific roles during different evacuation phases. This clarity enabled smooth function despite extremely stressful circumstances, while families without established role systems frequently experienced debilitating confusion and oversight.

Communication protocols appropriate to evacuation conditions prevent dangerous information gaps during family movement. Effective evacuation management typically includes predetermined communication methods for different scenarios, established information priorities, and contingency approaches when primary communication means become unavailable.

My neighbor Rachel, who evacuated with three generations of family members during regional flooding, had developed specific communication protocols through previous emergency experiences. These systems—including predetermined check-in procedures, information priority hierarchies, and alternative contact methods—maintained critical information flow despite challenging conditions that disrupted normal communication channels.

Decision frameworks that function under stress prevent decision paralysis during rapidly evolving situations. The most effective evacuation management typically includes predetermined parameters for common decision points, clearly established decision authority for different domains, and default protocols when communication becomes impossible.

During an evacuation workshop simulation, I observed dramatic performance differences between families with established decision frameworks and those attempting to create decision processes during stressful situations. The predetermined frameworks enabled rapid adaptation to changing circumstances, while improvised approaches frequently generated decision delays that would have proven dangerous in actual emergencies.

Psychological management strategies that address evacuation-specific stresses prevent function degradation during extended movement. Effective evacuation operations typically include deliberate approaches for maintaining emotional stability across different family members, particularly children and elderly individuals who may experience evacuation as deeply disorienting.

These operational capabilities rarely develop without deliberate preparation before emergencies occur. The most effective approach involves creating specific family evacuation protocols, then practicing key elements during normal conditions to build capability that functions under actual emergency stress.

This preparation need not involve elaborate scenarios or specialized equipment. Simple practices like established "go bag" locations, predetermined responsibility assignments, regular communication procedure reviews, and occasional evacuation simulations can develop fundamental capabilities that function during actual emergencies.

Many families find that camping trips provide excellent opportunities to practice evacuation-relevant skills in low-stress environments—developing capabilities in temporary shelter establishment, limited-resource meal preparation, alternative hygiene approaches, and compact living arrangements that transfer directly to evacuation scenarios.

My own family used annual camping excursions explicitly as evacuation practice, gradually refining our systems through practical experience rather than theoretical planning alone. When actual emergency evacuation became necessary, these practiced capabilities functioned smoothly despite the inherently stressful circumstances—a stark contrast to families attempting to develop operational systems during the emergency itself.

As you develop your own evacuation preparation, consider whether you've addressed these operational aspects alongside more obvious physical considerations. Have you established clear roles and responsibilities for different evacuation phases? Do you have communication protocols appropriate to likely emergency scenarios? Have you developed decision frameworks that function under stress conditions? Have you practiced these systems during normal conditions to build capability before emergencies occur? These operational preparations often determine evacuation success more decisively than many more visible aspects that receive greater attention in conventional prepper discussions.

Packing Priorities: What Actually Matters

Perhaps no aspect of evacuation preparation generates more controversy than packing strategy—determining what to bring and what to leave when rapid departure becomes necessary. Conventional prepper approaches typically emphasize either tactical equipment focused on security concerns or long-term sustainability tools designed for extended off-grid living. Both approaches often miss the practical realities of actual evacuation needs.

Having assisted numerous families through emergency evacuations across varying circumstances, I've observed consistent patterns in what actually proves useful versus what typically becomes deadweight. These patterns rarely match conventional bug-out packing lists, which often reflect fantasy scenarios rather than documented evacuation experiences.

The most useful evacuation supplies typically share several characteristics regardless of specific emergency types including immediate practical utility within the first 24-72 hours and addressing actual needs that emerge during initial evacuation phases rather than hypothetical long-term scenarios. Items that don't serve clear functions during this critical period typically become burdens rather than assets during actual evacuations.

During a hurricane evacuation assistance operation, I watched hundreds of families discover this reality firsthand. Those who had packed based on immediate practical needs maintained better function throughout the evacuation, while those who had prioritized long-term theoretical utility often found themselves burdened with equipment that served no purpose during the actual emergency phase while lacking items that would have addressed immediate challenges.

Appropriate proportion between weight/volume and functional value, recognizing that every item carried represents both transportation capacity used and mobility limitation imposed. The most valuable evacuation items provide high functional utility relative to their physical burden rather than simply addressing hypothetical needs regardless of carry cost.

My friend Thomas, who evacuated through challenging conditions during regional wildfires, described this realization perfectly: "I had to make real-time decisions about what stayed and what went as conditions worsened. What I discovered was that theoretical utility meant nothing compared to the immediate question: Is carrying this worth the mobility it costs us right now?"

Multi-purpose functionality that addresses different needs through reconfigurable application rather than single-purpose specialization. The most effective evacuation supplies typically serve multiple functions through different usage approaches, creating adaptability without requiring separate items for each potential need.

During an evacuation workshop focused on practical packing strategies, I demonstrated how relatively few multi-purpose items could address dozens of potential needs through creative application—a stark contrast to the specialized equipment approach that dominates many prepper packing lists. The resulting load reduction created mobility advantages that would prove crucial during actual evacuation conditions.

Familiarity and practiced usage that enables effective application under stress conditions rather than requiring new skill development during emergencies. Items that family members use regularly typically provide more practical value than specialized equipment requiring unfamiliar operation, regardless of theoretical capability differences.

These characteristics rarely align with conventional bug-out packing approaches, which typically emphasize theoretical scenarios over documented evacuation experiences. The resulting disconnect creates dangerous preparation gaps that often become apparent only during actual emergencies—precisely when correction opportunities no longer exist.

The most effective evacuation packing strategy typically prioritizes several categories that address documented needs rather than theoretical scenarios:

Identity and financial documentation that enables access to external support systems, financial resources, and legal status verification—functions that become critically important during most actual evacuation scenarios yet receive minimal attention in many prepper approaches.

Secure appropriate medication and medical supplies to maintain essential health function during evacuation periods, including prescription medications, basic first aid supplies, and specific items needed for individual family health conditions.

Practical comfort items are also crucial. These items maintain psychological stability for vulnerable family members, particularly children and elderly individuals who may experience severe distress from displacement. Often dismissed as luxuries in tactical packing approaches, these comforting things frequently determine functional outcomes more significantly than much more expensive specialized equipment.

Communication tools appropriate to likely emergency scenarios, enabling both family coordination during movement and connection to external information sources guide effective evacuation decision-making.

Basic sustenance supplies sufficient for the realistic evacuation period likely in your specific regional context, need to focus on ready-to-consume options that minimize preparation requirements during transitional circumstances.

Adaptable clothing appropriate to likely environmental conditions, should emphasize layering strategies that accommodate temperature variation rather than specialized tactical garments that often prove less functional during actual evacuation scenarios.

Multi-purpose tools that address the most common practical needs encountered during documented evacuations are better than specialized equipment designed for theoretical scenarios.

This practical approach rarely produces the impressive equipment collections that dominate prepper media but typically creates more functional evacuation capability based on actual emergency patterns rather than hypothetical scenarios.

As you develop your own evacuation packing strategy, consider whether your approach reflects documented evacuation experiences or theoretical assumptions. Have you prioritized items with immediate practical utility during realistic evacuation timeframes? Does your approach balance functional value against mobility limitations? Have you emphasized familiar multi-purpose items over specialized equipment? These practical considerations often determine evacuation outcomes more decisively than the tactical elements that receive greater attention in conventional prepper discussions.

The 70-Pound Bug-Out Bag vs. What You'll Actually Carry

The scene has played out in evacuation scenarios so consistently that emergency managers have developed a name for it: "The Ditch Line." About two miles from evacuation starting points, abandoned backpacks and equipment begin appearing along evacuation routes—jettisoned by individuals discovering the difference between theoretical packing lists and practical carrying capability under actual emergency conditions.

The typical prepper bug-out bag, weighing anywhere from 50 to 70 pounds and brimming with specialized equipment for extended wilderness survival, represents one of the most persistent and dangerous myths in preparedness culture. This approach fails not because the equipment lacks value in absolute terms, but because it fundamentally misunderstands the practical realities of actual evacuation scenarios.

During a wilderness search and rescue operation for a family that had attempted to evacuate through forest land during regional flooding, we discovered their abandoned bug-out bags less than three miles into their journey. The father later explained: "They seemed perfectly manageable during practice hikes around the neighborhood. But with the actual emergency stress, difficult conditions, and needing to help the children... they became impossible within the first hour."

This experience reflects a reality that military personnel understand intimately but prepper culture often ignores: carrying capacity diminishes dramatically under stress conditions, unfamiliar terrain, and extended movement requirements. The bug-out bag that seemed reasonable during brief test carries becomes unbearable during actual evacuation conditions—particularly when family responsibilities require physical and mental resources beyond personal movement.

The resulting abandonment means that carefully selected

equipment becomes completely useless, creating a dangerous capability gap precisely when resilience matters most. This outcome doesn't reflect personal weakness or inadequate determination, but simple physical reality—the human body has finite carrying capacity that stress conditions further reduce.

More concerning, heavy packs significantly impair mobility itself—reducing speed, increasing injury risk, and limiting route options during evacuation. The theoretical capability provided by extensive equipment becomes irrelevant when that same equipment prevents reaching safety in the first place.

The alternative isn't abandoning preparation but embracing realistic parameters based on documented evacuation experiences rather than prepper fantasy scenarios. The most effective approach typically involves:

*Limiting pack weight to approximately 20% of body weight for physically fit adults, with further reductions for individuals with limited carrying capacity. This parameter aligns with extensive research on sustainable carrying loads under stress conditions rather than theoretical maximums.

*Prioritizing items with immediate practical utility during realistic evacuation timeframes over long-term hypothetical value. Most actual evacuations resolve within days or weeks through reaching alternative shelter, making many extended survival items unnecessary weight.

*Selecting multi-purpose equipment that addresses multiple needs through different applications rather than specialized tools for specific scenarios. This approach creates functional capability without the weight penalties of redundant equipment.

*Emphasizing knowledge and skill development that creates capability without corresponding physical weight. The most valuable evacuation assets often exist between your ears rather than on your back, creating resilience that requires no carrying capacity.

Developing realistic evacuation scenarios based on your specific regional context rather than generic wilderness survival assumptions. Many evacuations involve reaching alternative shelter through relatively developed areas rather than extended wilderness self-sufficiency.

This practical approach produces evacuation capabilities that function under actual emergency conditions rather than theoretical scenarios. The resulting equipment complement rarely matches impressive prepper display photos but typically proves far more useful during genuine evacuations.

My friend Jason, a military veteran with extensive evacuation experience in both professional and civilian contexts, captures this reality perfectly: "The most valuable bug-out bag is the one you'll actually have with you when needed—not the one abandoned when reality hits. I'd rather have 20 pounds of perfectly selected gear than 70 pounds of theoretically valuable equipment I had to ditch when things got real."

This wisdom aligns with documented patterns across numerous evacuation scenarios. The individuals who maintain the best function throughout emergency movement are rarely those with the most impressive initial equipment but those with the most realistic carrying expectations and most carefully prioritized selections.

As you evaluate your own evacuation packing strategy, consider whether your approach reflects realistic parameters or prepper fantasy scenarios. Have you tested your carrying capacity under challenging conditions similar to actual evacuations? Does your selection prioritize immediate practical utility over theoretical long-term value? Have you considered the mobility penalties associated with heavy carrying loads? These practical considerations often determine whether your carefully selected equipment remains with you when needed or becomes part of someone else's "ditch line" discovery after the emergency passes.

The most effective preparation acknowledges human limitations rather than imagining superhuman capability under stress conditions. By embracing realistic parameters based on documented evacuation experiences, you create genuine resilience that functions when actually needed rather than theoretical capability that fails under real-world conditions.

12

Tools of the Trade

The day I realized I'd become what I once gently mocked was both humbling and hilarious. It happened last spring when my brother-in-law visited and discovered what I now reluctantly call my "tool sanctuary" in the converted garden shed behind my house.

"Good Lord, Riki," he said, staring wide-eyed at the meticulously organized walls of hand tools, power equipment, and yes—I admit it—specialized gadgets arranged by function, frequency of use, and seasonal application. "You've got more gear than the hardware store."

I followed his gaze around the room, suddenly seeing it through his eyes: the three different types of axes (each with a specific purpose, I assure you), the collection of hand planes that would make a colonial woodworker weep with envy, the embarrassingly comprehensive selection of gardening implements, and—most damning of all—the special drawer dedicated solely to tools I'd purchased for single, specific projects and hadn't touched since.

"I can explain," I started, but then burst out laughing at

myself instead. "Actually, no. I've become exactly what I used to tease the men in my life about. I have officially contracted Gear Acquisition Syndrome."

He grinned and picked up a peculiar-looking device from my workbench. "And what the hell does this do?"

"That," I said with the passionate enthusiasm of a true convert, "is a specialized bark spud for green woodworking that I used exactly once three years ago to make a single stool that currently serves as my kindling holder."

We both dissolved into laughter, and I had to face the uncomfortable truth: somewhere along my journey of practical preparedness, I'd crossed over into the territory I once viewed with amused skepticism. I had become a gear head!

This transformation didn't happen overnight. For most of my life, I maintained a somewhat minimalist approach to tools, focusing on versatile basics while quietly shaking my head at the men who seemed to acquire specialized equipment with religious fervor. I prided myself on solving problems with whatever was at hand rather than purchasing single-purpose solutions.

Then came the ice storm, which left our community without power for nearly three weeks. As I struggled to maintain basic household functions with my modest tool collection, I watched my neighbor—he of the legendary tool crib that I'd previously considered excessive—become the community's salvation. His specialized equipment and extensive spare parts inventory kept generators running, helped repair storm damage, and maintained essential services when municipal systems failed.

That experience began my reluctant conversion. With each subsequent challenge—from fallen trees to failed well pumps, from garden expansions to unexpected home repairs—

I gradually expanded my tool collection. Each new acquisition came with a solemn promise to myself: "This one is truly essential. I won't become one of those people who needs a specialized tool for every conceivable task."

Yet here I stood, surrounded by evidence to the contrary, finally admitting what the men in my life have known all along: the right tool for the job isn't just a luxury—it's sometimes the difference between success and failure, especially when normal support systems are unavailable.

This revelation hasn't completely transformed my perspective on preparedness priorities. I still believe that skills trump supplies and that relationships create more resilience than possessions. But I've developed a more nuanced appreciation for the role of appropriate tools in creating genuine capability—and a much more sympathetic understanding of the gear-acquisition impulse I once dismissed as primarily masculine weakness.

So consider this chapter my humble apology to tool enthusiasts everywhere, along with what I've learned about balancing the genuine utility of appropriate equipment with the ever-present temptation of gear for gear's sake. We'll explore how to build a truly functional tool collection that enhances resilience without becoming its own liability—a lesson I'm still learning every time I eye that new Japanese garden knife catalog that somehow keeps finding its way to my mailbox.

Redefining Essential Tools Beyond Weapons

Let's address the mysterious box in the prepper room: when many people think "essential tools" in preparedness contexts, their minds immediately go to weapons. The fantasy of defending homesteads against marauding bands of unprepared people has created a preparation imbalance where many households possess multiple tactical firearms but lack basic tools for repairing a leaky roof or maintaining a water pump.

I've watched this imbalance play out during actual emergencies, where the ability to repair, adapt, and maintain proved far more valuable than defensive capabilities. During a particularly severe ice storm that left our region without power for weeks, household functionality correlated much more strongly with repair capability than security preparations. Families with comprehensive tool kits maintained comfort and safety through equipment adaptation and infrastructure repairs, while those with impressive security systems but minimal maintenance tools often struggled with basic functions.

This observation isn't meant to dismiss security considerations entirely. Appropriate protective measures certainly have their place within comprehensive preparedness. The imbalance emerges when security tools receive disproportionate investment compared to the maintenance and repair equipment that addresses daily needs during extended emergencies.

My own journey toward tool appreciation began with maintenance necessities rather than tactical considerations. After watching a neighbor's generator fail during that ice storm due to simple maintenance issues they couldn't address without specific tools, I began building my collection around practical capabilities: keeping essential systems functioning, adapting available resources to changing needs, and repairing rather than replacing when acquisition isn't an option.

This approach led me to develop what I call "capability categories"—tool groupings based on the essential functions they support rather than traditional classifications:

Energy system tools maintain whatever provides power to your essential needs, from generators to solar systems to wood heat. These typically include specific maintenance implements for your particular energy sources, diagnostic tools appropriate to your systems, and repair equipment suited to your technical capabilities.

During the extended power outage following Hurricane Sandy, my friend's modest DIY, shed mounted solar system continued functioning throughout the emergency because she had both the tools and knowledge to maintain it, while much more expensive roof systems failed due to minor issues their owners couldn't address without specific equipment and expertise.

Water management tools support collection, purification, storage, distribution, and disposal systems—the complete water cycle that maintains basic hygiene and hydration. These range from simple plumbing implements to purification maintenance equipment to watershed management tools appropriate to your specific water sources.

When regional flooding contaminated local wells, households with appropriate water management tools typically maintained safe supply through filtration system adaptations and storage system protections. Those without such capabilities often faced water insecurity despite having had clean supply sources before the emergency.

Food system tools support the complete cycle from production through preservation and preparation. These include appropriate gardening implements, processing equipment, preservation tools, and preparation options suited to available energy sources under emergency conditions.

During a storm that caused extended power loss during

harvest season, families with hand-powered food processing tools preserved their garden production despite the electricity disruption. Those dependent on electric preservation equipment often lost significant food resources that had taken months to produce.

Structural maintenance tools keep your physical shelter functioning through damage or degradation. These include basic construction implements, weatherization equipment, improvisational repair tools, and adaptation capabilities for changing shelter needs as conditions evolve.

When severe winds damaged numerous homes in our community, those with appropriate repair tools implemented immediate protective measures that prevented minor damage from becoming major destruction. Those without such capabilities often experienced significant property deterioration while waiting for professional assistance that was overwhelmed by regional demand.

Medical support tools extend beyond the standard first aid kit to include equipment that supports extended care capabilities when professional medical services are unavailable. These typically include diagnostic implements appropriate to your training level, treatment tools for conditions you're qualified to address, and maintenance equipment for existing medical supplies.

After a winter storm isolated our community for nearly a week, a neighbor with diabetes managed her condition effectively because her household maintained appropriate monitoring and treatment tools. Without such capabilities, her health would have deteriorated significantly before professional medical access was restored.

This capability-based approach typically creates very different tool priorities than either traditional gender-based divisions or conventional prepper checklists. Rather than accumulating tools based on catalog categories or tactical considerations, it builds functional capability across essential domains that actual emergencies consistently impact.

As I developed my own tool collection through this lens, I discovered something surprising: many of the most valuable emergency tools weren't tactical, flashy, or even particularly expensive. They were often modest implements designed for specific functional capabilities that become disproportionately important when normal systems fail.

My hand-operated well pump—installed as a backup to my electric system—has proven more valuable during actual power outages than many far more expensive preparations. I hug my hand-operated well pump every day. You should too!

My basic plumbing repair kit has addressed more genuine emergency needs than equipment with far more impressive marketing. My collection of manual food processing tools has maintained household function during multiple extended power outages where electrical alternatives became useless.

This experience has completely transformed my understanding of "essential tools" from weapons-focused security preparation to comprehensive functional capability across daily need domains. The resulting approach emphasizes maintenance, repair, and adaptation tools that support continuous operation of basic systems rather than dramatic response to acute threats.

As you evaluate your own tool preparation, consider whether you've developed balanced capability across these essential domains or focused disproportionately on single categories. Can you maintain all your critical systems when replacement isn't an option? Do you have appropriate tools for adapting available resources to changing needs? Can you implement repairs across essential domains when professional services are unavailable? These capabilities often determine your actual resilience more decisively than many more dramatic preparations that receive greater attention in conventional prepper discussions.

Multi-purpose Equipment Selection for Space and Resource Efficiency

I learned my most valuable lesson about multi-purpose tools during an extended power outage when my carefully organized tool collection remained largely inaccessible in my unlit workshop. The handful of multi-purpose implements I'd thoughtfully placed in our emergency kit proved far more useful than my extensive specialized collection simply because they were actually available when needed.

This experience highlighted a fundamental preparedness principle: the perfect specialized tool becomes worthless when inaccessible, while a decent multi-purpose tool in hand provides immediate capability. This reality demands thoughtful balance between specialized efficiency and versatile adaptability—particularly when space, weight, and resource limitations become significant factors.

I've now completely reorganized my approach to tool preparation based on what I call "concentric capability circles"—tool arrangements that balance specialization and versatility based on likely accessibility during different emergency scenarios. The **innermost circle** consists of truly multi-functional tools maintained in immediately accessible locations. These versatile implements provide moderate capability across multiple functions rather than optimized performance in single applications. Examples include quality multi-tools, combination tools like hammer-hatchets, and adaptable implements with interchangeable components.

During a flash flood evacuation, my neighbor discovered that her carefully packed specialized tools remained in her flooded basement while her modest multi-tool provided the only immediately available capability. This experience demonstrated that moderate function immediately available consistently outperforms optimized function that remains inaccessible during actual emergencies.

The **middle circle** includes moderately specialized tools that address core functions across essential capability domains. These implements balance functional optimization with reasonable versatility within their primary application areas. Examples include basic hand tools with multiple applications within their domains, mid-range power tools with various attachments, and adaptable equipment that serves complementary functions.

When a severe ice storm isolated our community, households with thoughtfully selected middle-circle tools typically maintained better function than those with either minimal multi-tools or extensively specialized collections. This balanced approach provided sufficient capability for most common needs without requiring excessive space or resource allocation.

The **outer circle** contains highly specialized tools for specific applications within your particular context and capabilities. These implements optimize performance within narrow functional domains at the cost of versatility across broader applications. Examples include specialized repair equipment for specific systems, optimized tools for particular production processes, and technical implements for domain-specific applications important in your context.

During extended recovery after a regional hurricane, households with appropriate specialized tools for their specific systems maintained better long-term function than those limited to basic capabilities alone. This specialized capacity becomes particularly valuable during extended emergencies when temporary solutions prove insufficient for ongoing needs.

This concentric approach creates balanced capability that functions across different emergency durations and access limitations. Rather than either minimal multi-tools that prove insufficient for extended needs or extensively specialized collections that become partially or completely inaccessible during actual emergencies, it builds adaptable capacity appropriate to different scenarios.

Implementing this approach involves making intentional decisions about which tools belong in which circles based on several key factors:

*Function critical*ity determines which capabilities require dedicated specialized tools versus which can be adequately addressed through more versatile implements. Capabilities that directly impact survival needs typically warrant greater specialization than convenience functions.

Usage frequency influences appropriate specialization level, with frequently used functions generally justifying more optimized tools than rarely needed capabilities. Functions employed regularly develop user proficiency that maximizes specialized tool benefits, while rarely used functions often benefit more from intuitive multi-purpose designs.

Space/weight constraints significantly impact specialization decisions, particularly for mobile preparations or limited storage situations. As constraints increase, multi-functionality becomes increasingly valuable despite modest capability compromises.

User skill levels affect appropriate tool selection across versatility/specialization spectrums. Higher skill levels typically extract greater benefit from specialized tools, while limited experience often achieves better results with more forgiving multi-purpose implements.

Resource limitations influence optimal balance points between quantity and quality, with budget constraints sometimes favoring fewer high-quality versatile tools over larger quantities of specialized implements.

These considerations create significantly different optimal selections for different households and contexts. The appropriate tool collection for an urban apartment with minimal storage differs dramatically from suitable preparations for a rural homestead with dedicated workshop space. The optimal selection for a highly skilled user varies substantially from appropriate choices for those with limited technical experience.

My own journey through this balance point has been humbling and educational. After initially favoring minimal versatile tools based on space considerations, I gradually accumulated extensive specialized implements as capability expanded—only to discover during actual emergencies that accessibility often limited specialized tool utility precisely when their capabilities would have proven most valuable.

This experience led to my current *hybrid* approach: maintaining highly versatile implements in multiple accessible locations while organizing specialized tools in clearly categorized systems that can be quickly accessed or transported as specific needs emerge. This arrangement balances immediate basic capability with accessible specialized function when circumstances permit.

As you evaluate your own tool preparation, consider whether you've developed appropriate balance between versatility and specialization based on your specific constraints and capabilities. Have you ensured immediate access to basic functionality across essential domains? Can you access more specialized capability when circumstances permit? Does your approach match your actual usage patterns and skill levels? These balanced considerations often determine your practical capability more decisively than theoretical tool performance during actual emergency conditions.

Tool Maintenance for Extended Use Without Replacement

The most expensive, specialized tool becomes worthless when it fails without repair options—a reality I learned painfully during an extended power outage when my chainsaw developed fuel line problems I couldn't address with my available maintenance supplies. Despite having invested in a premium saw with impressive specifications, I found myself borrowing my neighbor's ancient but meticulously maintained model because mine had become an expensive paperweight.

This experience highlighted a crucial preparedness principle that receives remarkably little attention in conventional discussions: maintenance capability often determines tool longevity more decisively than initial quality. During extended emergencies when replacement becomes difficult or impossible, your ability to maintain functional operation through appropriate care and repair creates resilience beyond what any initial purchase quality can provide.

This reality becomes particularly important for tools that experience substantial stress during emergency use—often precisely when their function becomes most critical and replacement least available. Power tools subjected to extended operation, cutting implements used beyond normal duration, mechanical devices operated outside optimal conditions—all experience accelerated wear that demands appropriate maintenance capability to sustain function.

After my chainsaw embarrassment, I completely reoriented my tool preparation approach to emphasize maintenance capability alongside initial quality. This approach involves several interconnected elements that create genuine longevity rather than merely theoretical durability:

Preventative maintenance supplies appropriate to your specific tools represent the first line of defense against failure during critical use. These include appropriate lubricants, cleaning materials, adjustment implements, and basic wear components specific to your particular equipment.

During a community recovery effort following a severe storm, I watched two identical generator models experience dramatically different outcomes based solely on maintenance preparation. The household with appropriate supplies implemented preventative maintenance during extended operation, maintaining function throughout the emergency. The household without such supplies experienced progressive deterioration culminating in complete failure precisely when alternative power remained unavailable.

Repair components for common failure points extend function when preventative maintenance proves insufficient. These typically include replacement parts for components that experience highest wear, repair materials for common breakage points, and alternative parts that can substitute when exact replacements become unavailable.

My friend Thomas, who maintains extensive garden equipment, discovered this necessity during an extended supply chain disruption that made commercial parts unavailable. Because he had thoughtfully stockpiled components for the most common failure points in his critical equipment, he maintained garden production capability while others experienced equipment downtime waiting for parts that remained backordered for months.

Appropriate tools for maintaining tools create meta-capability that extends function across your entire equipment inventory. These implements allow appropriate adjustment, repair, and adaptation of your broader tool collection, preventing the frustrating situation of owning the perfect tool for a job but lacking the maintenance implement needed to make it functional.

During a wilderness expedition where equipment repair became necessary miles from alternative resources, I witnessed the value of this capability directly. A participant with appropriate tool maintenance implements addressed a critical equipment failure that would have otherwise ended the expedition, demonstrating that sometimes the most important tool is the one that keeps other tools functioning.

Knowledge resources for maintenance procedures transform physical supplies into practical capability. These resources—whether printed manuals, saved digital instructions, or personal reference notes—provide critical guidance when memory proves insufficient for complex maintenance processes.

When our community experienced extended power loss following a severe ice storm, households with appropriate repair documentation maintained equipment function more effectively than those attempting to remember complex procedures under stress conditions. This preparation element costs relatively little but dramatically enhances maintenance capability when normal information access becomes unavailable.

Skill development through regular practice transforms theoretical maintenance capability into practical function. Regular implementation of maintenance procedures during normal conditions builds both proficiency and confidence that function under emergency stress, when unfamiliar processes often prove difficult to implement effectively.

I observed this capability gap clearly during a community emergency when equipment owners with regular maintenance practice implemented critical repairs efficiently under pressure, while those attempting unfamiliar procedures often created additional problems through improper technique despite having appropriate supplies and documentation.

These maintenance elements combine to create tool longevity far beyond what initial quality alone can provide—a critical resilience factor during extended emergencies when replacement becomes difficult or impossible. The resulting capability transforms brittle dependence on specific implements into robust functionality that adapts to inevitable wear, damage, and failure through appropriate intervention.

My own journey toward maintenance enlightenment hasn't been without embarrassing setbacks. Despite my preventative planning, I still occasionally discover gaps in my preparation when specific issues arise. During one memorable wind storm, I found myself improvising a chainsaw chain repair using decidedly non-standard methods because I'd failed to stock the specific maintenance component needed despite having numerous less critical supplies.

This experience reinforced another maintenance reality: perfect preparation remains impossible, making adaptability and improvisational repair knowledge valuable supplements to specific maintenance supplies. The ability to create functional alternatives when ideal components remain unavailable adds resilience layer beyond even comprehensive maintenance preparation.

As you evaluate your own tool maintenance preparation, consider whether you've developed appropriate capability across your critical equipment domains. Do you maintain suitable preventative supplies for your essential tools? Have you identified and prepared for common failure points in your specific equipment? Can you implement necessary maintenance procedures under emergency conditions without external guidance? These capabilities often determine your extended tool function more decisively than initial purchase quality during actual emergency conditions when replacement remains unavailable.

Skill Development: Becoming the Human Multi-tool

The summer I broke my dominant wrist during haying season taught me something profound about the relationship between tools and skills. Despite having every specialized implement needed for continuing critical farm operations, I suddenly couldn't use most of them effectively. What saved our harvest wasn't alternative equipment but my neighbor's teenage daughter Sarah, who lacked my collection but possessed remarkable adaptability born from years of hands-on experience.

The most valuable multi-purpose tool isn't found in any kit—it's the adaptable human using the kit. Your skill development creates capability that transcends specific implements, allowing effective function across varying conditions with whatever tools become available.

This perspective transforms preparation priorities from accumulating specialized equipment to developing adaptable capability that functions regardless of specific tool availability. The resulting approach emphasizes skill development across essential domains as foundational preparation rather than supplemental enhancement.

My experience recovering from that injury completely reoriented my preparation balance between equipment acquisition and skill development. I still value appropriate tools—perhaps more than ever—but I now recognize them as capability extensions rather than capability sources. This approach develops what I call "skill redundancy layers" that maintain function despite equipment limitations:

Fundamental skills that require minimal specialized tools create baseline capability independent of specific equipment. These include core manual processes, basic manipulation techniques, and fundamental operations that human capability can accomplish with minimal external enhancement.

During a regional evacuation following widespread flooding, I observed that individuals with strong fundamental skills typically adapted more effectively to equipment limitations than those dependent on specific implements for basic functions. This adaptability emerged not from superior preparation but from greater skill development that created function without specialized equipment.

Adaptability across similar tool categories allows effective operation of available implements regardless of specific familiarity. This capability emerges from understanding fundamental principles behind tool function rather than just specific operation procedures for particular models or brands.

My friend Michael, a contractor with extensive experience across different work sites, demonstrated this capability impressively during a community recovery project when he effectively utilized unfamiliar tools based on functional understanding rather than specific experience. His adaptability maintained productive operation despite using equipment significantly different from his personal collection.

Improvisational capability that creates functional alternatives when ideal tools remain unavailable. This skill level transforms available materials into appropriate implements based on understanding underlying functional principles rather than depending on purpose-built equipment.

During an extended power outage that coincided with critical food preservation needs, I watched my neighbor Elena create remarkably effective processing implements from available materials when her electrical equipment became inoperable. Her improvisational capability maintained essential function despite equipment limitations that would have created complete capacity loss for those without similar skills.

Cross-domain knowledge that identifies unexpected tool applications beyond their intended purposes. This perspective recognizes functional potential rather than designated applications, creating capability that transcends conventional tool limitations through creative adaptation.

When a severe storm created urgent community needs without adequate specialized equipment, individuals with cross-domain creativity identified numerous unconventional applications for available tools that addressed critical functions despite lacking purpose-designed implements. This adaptive capability emerged from understanding functional principles rather than remaining constrained by conventional applications.

These skill layers develop through intentional practice rather than emerging spontaneously during emergencies. The most effective preparation approach integrates skill development within regular activities, creating capability through consistent application rather than occasional emergency drills.

My own journey toward becoming a more adaptable "human multi-tool" involves deliberate practice across diverse applications—using different equipment types for similar functions, attempting tasks with intentionally limited tools, and occasionally imposing artificial constraints that build adaptability rather than optimizing immediate efficiency.

This approach often appears inefficient from conventional

productivity perspectives. Using a hand saw instead of a power saw, processing food with manual implements rather than electric alternatives, or intentionally employing unfamiliar tools rather than comfortable favorites might reduce immediate productivity. However, these practices build adaptive capacity that creates genuine resilience when preferred options become unavailable during actual emergencies.

The resulting capability transforms your relationship with tools from dependence to partnership—recognizing implements as valuable extensions of human capability rather than capability sources themselves. This perspective shift creates preparedness depth beyond what any equipment collection alone can provide, maintaining function across varying conditions regardless of specific tool availability.

As you evaluate your own preparedness balance between tools and skills, consider whether you've developed adaptable capability independent of specific equipment. Can you accomplish essential functions with minimal specialized implements? Do you understand fundamental principles that allow adaptation across different tool types? Can you create functional alternatives when ideal equipment remains unavailable? These capabilities often determine your practical resilience more decisively than any specific tool collection during actual emergency conditions when preferred equipment may become inaccessible or inoperable.

Humorous Guide: "Gear Acquisition Syndrome vs. Actually Being Prepared"

In the spirit of honest self-assessment and good-natured accountability, I present this field guide to identifying whether you're building genuine preparedness or simply satisfying the universal human urge to acquire shiny new things. As someone who has fallen victim to Gear Acquisition Syndrome while earnestly believing I was enhancing my preparedness, I offer these observations from the recovering gear-aholic perspective.

You Might Have Gear Acquisition Syndrome if...

*Your tool organization system has been expanded three times, yet you still need "just one more" specialized storage solution to properly arrange your growing collection. Meanwhile, your skill practice area remains approximately the size of a postage stamp because your gear has annexed all available space.

*You can provide the precise technical specifications, manufacturing origin, and comparative advantages of every tool in your collection, yet when asked to demonstrate its practical application, you respond with, "Well, I haven't actually used it yet, but the reviews were amazing."

*You possess specialized implements for scenarios so specific they could only occur during a precise alignment of planets that happens once every 2,300 years, yet you're still using a butter knife as a screwdriver for regular household repairs because your "good tools" are being saved for "when they're really needed."

*You've devoted more time to researching the perfect bug-out bag than actually practicing evacuation scenarios, resulting in a masterpiece of organizational engineering that weighs roughly the same as a small refrigerator and has never moved further than from your closet to your living room.

*You own multiple tactical flashlights powerful enough to signal alien civilizations in neighboring galaxies, yet during your last power outage, you couldn't find a single one because they were all neatly packed in waterproof cases stored somewhere in the very dark basement you needed illumination to navigate.

*Your preparedness bookshelf contains seventeen different volumes on advanced survival techniques, all with pristine, uncracked spines, while your actual skill practice consists entirely of watching wilderness survival videos while snacking on decidedly non-emergency food supplies.

*You've invested in specialized food storage containers with oxygen absorbers, Mylar bags, and military-grade waterproofing, yet you rotate your stock approximately once per decade, usually after discovering that five-year shelf life doesn't actually mean "will remain edible until the end of time."

*Your tool collection includes implements whose purposes are so obscure you've had to create elaborate scenarios to justify their acquisition: "Well, if the power grid fails while I'm simultaneously experiencing a flat tire in the woods during an unexpected blizzard while being pursued by wolverines, this specialized widget will definitely prove essential."

You Might Actually Be Prepared if...

*Your tools show appropriate wear patterns from regular use, maintenance, and skill practice. The most valuable tools in genuine preparedness are rarely the shiniest—they're the ones that have developed patina from actual application.

*You can maintain essential functions with multiple different tool options, having practiced accomplishing necessary tasks with varying implement types rather than depending on specific equipment availability.

*Your preparation priorities align with documented needs from actual emergencies rather than theoretical scenarios from preparedness fiction, emphasizing capabilities repeatedly proven valuable during genuine disasters.

*You've experienced and addressed actual tool failures during normal use, developing both specific repair capabilities and general adaptation strategies based on practical limitations rather than theoretical performance.

*Your skill development consistently receives greater investment than your equipment acquisition, recognizing that capability ultimately resides in the user rather than the implement.

*Your preparedness discussions focus more on what you've actually done than what you're planning to acquire, emphasizing development of proven capability rather than theoretical potential.

*You regularly incorporate tools and skills into daily life rather than reserving them exclusively for emergency scenarios, building practical familiarity through consistent application rather than occasional specialized practice.

Your preparation approach acknowledges and addresses your actual limitations rather than assuming idealized performance during emergency conditions, developing realistic capabilities based on demonstrated rather than imagined capacity.

The journey from gear acquisition to actual preparedness often passes through the valley of humbling experience, where theoretical capability meets practical limitation. My own expedition through this terrain has been filled with embarrassing discoveries about the gap between what I thought my tools made possible and what my actual skills could accomplish under pressure.

Yet this journey has also revealed something wonderful: genuine preparedness emerges not from perfect equipment but from the integration of appropriate tools with developed skills, creating capability that transcends specific implements. The resulting resilience doesn't depend on having the perfect tool for every conceivable scenario but on developing the adaptability to work effectively with whatever becomes available when actual needs arise.

So by all means, acquire the tools appropriate to your context and capabilities—just remember that the most important preparedness tool is the one currently being developed between your ears. Your knowledge, adaptability, and practiced skills will ultimately determine your functional resilience more decisively than any equipment collection, no matter how impressive.

And if you occasionally succumb to the universally human temptation of acquiring "just one more" specialized implement that promises to solve problems you don't actually have... well, welcome to the club. We meet on Thursdays in various garages, workshops, and garden sheds around the country, surrounded by tools we absolutely needed at the time of purchase and will definitely use someday. Probably. Maybe.

13

The Information Economy

The moment I truly understood the value of information happened during the great ice storm of '98, which knocked out power to most of Maine for weeks. As the community gathered in our town hall—the only building with a working generator—I watched a fascinating scene unfold that perfectly captured the difference between information hoarders and information sharers.

In one corner stood Malcolm, clutching his prized ham radio like it contained nuclear launch codes. He'd been telling everyone for years about his "communications preparedness," but when asked to help establish contact with neighboring communities, he hesitated. "I need to conserve my battery for emergency transmissions," he explained, despite the generator humming outside. What he meant, of course, was that his radio was a status symbol, not a community tool.

Meanwhile, my seventy-year-old neighbor Ruth sat at a folding table with a simple spiral notebook, creating what she called a "community knowledge inventory." As people arrived at the shelter, she asked them two questions: What do you know how to do? What do you need help with?

By evening, Ruth had created something far more valuable than any radio network—a complete map of our community's practical knowledge and needs. She connected George, who knew generator repair, with three families whose heat depended on fixing their equipment. She linked Susan, a retired nurse, with an elderly couple who needed medication management. She identified which households had expertise in food preservation, water purification, emergency childcare, and dozens of other critical skills.

That lesson has stayed with me through every subsequent emergency. In genuine crisis situations, information becomes its own form of currency—often more valuable than physical supplies. The ability to preserve, share, and apply critical knowledge directly impacts survival outcomes, yet this aspect of preparedness receives remarkably little attention compared to stockpiling tangible resources.

The humbling truth is that no individual or household can maintain comprehensive knowledge across all domains relevant to extended emergencies. Even the most diligently prepared among us have knowledge gaps that could become life-threatening under specific circumstances. The solution isn't attempting to become walking encyclopedias of survival information, but developing effective systems for knowledge preservation, sharing, and application.

My own emergency information management began with meticulously organized three-ring binders containing printed instructions for everything from water purification to emergency childbirth. I imagined myself calmly flipping to the appropriate section as each crisis arose, following step-by-step guides with the serene competence of a NASA mission controller.

Reality, as usual, had other plans. During an actual evacuation, I discovered my carefully crafted information system was both too bulky to transport easily and too rigidly organized to adapt to the chaotic circumstances we actually encountered. I had created a knowledge monument rather than a usable tool.

This experience began my journey toward more effective information management that balances comprehensive content with practical accessibility—a system that acknowledges both the critical value of preserved knowledge and the messy reality of actual emergencies. That journey has taught me that information preparedness isn't about having all the answers, but creating systems that help you find the right answers when they're needed most.

And yes, I still occasionally tease Malcolm about his sacred radio, though these days he's slightly more willing to share. Progress comes in small steps.

Knowledge Preservation Beyond the Digital Cloud

One of the most dangerous illusions of our digital age is the belief that information is immortal because it exists "in the cloud." (Which cloud, *cumulus*?)

This misconception creates a false sense of security about knowledge preservation that vanishes quickly during actual infrastructure disruptions. When the power fails, the internet disappears, and electronic devices eventually discharge, all that supposedly permanent information becomes instantly inaccessible—precisely when it might be most critical.

I learned this lesson painfully during an extended power outage when I discovered that my carefully collected digital library of preparedness information had become completely inaccessible. My laptop battery lasted roughly five hours, my phone about twelve, and then all those meticulously organized files might as well have been on Mars for all the good they did me.

Meanwhile, my neighbor Walter—whom I'd previously considered charmingly old-fashioned for his preference for printed materials—calmly consulted his reference library by lantern light, using information I could no longer access despite having identical content theoretically "at my fingertips." His physical books and manuals required no electricity, no firmware updates, and no connectivity to deliver their critical knowledge.

This experience completely transformed my approach to information preservation. While I still maintain digital resources for convenience during normal conditions, I've developed physical knowledge preservation systems specifically designed for accessibility during infrastructure disruptions:

Critical reference guides in durable printed formats cover essential information across domains most relevant to likely emergency scenarios. These include medical references appropriate to my training level, repair manuals for key equipment, preservation instructions for seasonally available foods, and safety protocols for managing household emergencies.

During a two-week power outage following a severe winter storm, I witnessed the value of this approach firsthand. Households with appropriate physical reference materials maintained better function across various domains than those dependent on digital information that became inaccessible as devices discharged.

Personal skill documentation captures household-specific information that generic references don't address. These records include customized procedures for our particular equipment, notes on adaptations we've found effective for our specific context, and documentation of lessons learned through previous emergency experiences.

My friend Elena, who manages a small homestead with numerous interconnected systems, discovered the value of this documentation when she became seriously ill during a regional ice storm. Her family members, suddenly responsible for maintaining unfamiliar systems, could follow her personalized operation guides despite having limited prior experience—maintaining function that would have deteriorated without this documented knowledge.

Community wisdom collections preserve local knowledge particularly relevant to regional conditions and challenges. These compilations include information about local resources, regionally appropriate techniques, and community-specific considerations that generic preparedness literature typically doesn't address.

When flooding affected our region several years ago, communities with established local knowledge documentation navigated the emergency more effectively than those relying solely on general emergency guidance. The specific information about local water systems, regional evacuation patterns, and community resource locations provided critical advantages that generic preparation couldn't deliver.

Of course, Walter—my printed-material mentor—couldn't resist pointing out the irony when he visited and saw my newly established physical reference library. "Welcome to the eighteenth century," he said with a grin. "We've been expecting you."

His good-natured teasing highlighted an important preparedness principle: sometimes the most resilient approaches aren't the newest or most technically sophisticated, but those proven effective through extended historical use. Physical knowledge preservation systems have served human civilization through countless disruptions long before digital alternatives existed—a track record worth considering when evaluating information resilience.

This perspective doesn't mean rejecting digital tools entirely, but recognizing their limitations during infrastructure disruptions. The most robust approach combines formats for different circumstances: digital for convenience during normal conditions, physical for reliability during disruptions, and—most importantly—internalized knowledge for immediate application without reference dependency.

As my grandmother wisely noted when reviewing my elaborate documentation systems: "The best place to store emergency information is in your head. Everything else is just backup." Her observation highlights another crucial aspect of knowledge preservation: information you've actually internalized through practice doesn't require preservation systems at all.

When developing your own knowledge preservation approach, consider which information truly requires documentation versus which capabilities you should develop through practice until they become automatic. The most effective preparation balances comprehensive documentation with practical skill development, recognizing that some knowledge serves you best when referenced while other information needs to be immediately accessible through established capability.

And maybe invest in a good bookshelf. Those reference materials aren't getting any lighter, and as I've discovered, "the cloud" gets surprisingly heavy when printed on actual paper.

Communication Systems That Survive Infrastructure Collapse

The day our neighborhood emergency communication plan faced its first real test began with a transformer explosion that took out power to our entire county. By evening, as households switched to backup systems, another surprise emerged: cell towers quickly overwhelmed as thousands of residents simultaneously attempted to check on loved ones. Within hours, even landline phones failed as their backup batteries depleted.

Amid this communication blackout, I watched with mild amusement as Malcolm—yes, the same one from our town hall gathering—finally had his moment of glory. His previously mocked ham radio setup suddenly transformed from eccentric hobby to vital community link. As he established contact with the next town to coordinate emergency services, I had to admit that perhaps his years of radio enthusiasm hadn't been entirely misplaced.

"The irony isn't lost on me," he said with a barely suppressed grin when I complimented his system. "I've been preparing for this moment for twenty years while everyone called me paranoid."

"You were paranoid," I countered. "You were also right."

His laugh acknowledged both truths. Emergency communication preparation often walks the line between prudent readiness and obsessive over-preparation. Finding appropriate balance requires understanding which communication capabilities genuinely matter during different disruption scenarios—a distinction that often gets lost in technical discussions focused more on equipment specifications than practical application.

After participating in numerous actual communication disruptions, I've observed that effective emergency communication systems typically share several key characteristics regardless of their technical sophistication:

Power independence allows continued function when grid electricity becomes unavailable. The most resilient communication tools maintain operation through self-contained power sources, low energy requirements, or external power options compatible with emergency generation capabilities.

During an extended regional power outage, I watched communication systems differentiate primarily based on energy resilience rather than technical capability. Impressively sophisticated equipment became useless as batteries depleted without recharging options, while simpler systems with sustainable power solutions maintained function throughout the emergency.

Multi-directional information flow supports both transmission and reception—a critical distinction often overlooked in preparedness discussions that emphasize broadcasting capability over information gathering. The most valuable emergency communication often involves receiving critical updates rather than just sending messages.

When severe flooding isolated several communities in our region, households with weather radio receivers obtained critical evacuation information despite cellular network failures. This reception capability proved more immediately valuable than transmission options, highlighting the importance of balancing information input and output in communication preparation.

Appropriate transmission range matches your actual communication needs rather than maximizing theoretical distance. While transcontinental capability might seem impressive, most genuine emergency communication happens within much shorter ranges—typically involving family members, immediate neighbors, and local emergency services.

My neighbor Sarah, who prepared with her family's specific needs in mind, developed a simple communication system focused on maintaining contact between household members during community emergencies. Her solution—primarily short-range radios with established meeting protocols—addressed her actual priorities more effectively than more sophisticated options optimized for impressive but unnecessary range.

Operational simplicity ensures function under stress conditions when complex procedures become difficult to implement correctly. The most reliable emergency communication systems prioritize straightforward operation that works when users experience stress, limited visibility, or physical constraints that compromise fine motor skills.

During a nighttime evacuation exercise, I observed that

communication equipment requiring complex setup or operation frequently failed to establish effective contact despite working perfectly under ideal conditions. Meanwhile, simpler systems maintained reliable communication despite challenging circumstances—demonstrating that theoretical capability proves worthless when stress or environmental factors prevent proper operation.

These characteristics often lead to very different communication preparation than what appears in conventional prepper discussions, which typically emphasize impressive technical specifications over practical resilience factors. The resulting approach balances multiple complementary systems rather than depending on single high-capability options:

Short-range communication typically provides the most immediately useful capability during common emergencies. Simple two-way radios, predetermined meeting points with written messages, and visual signaling systems often maintain critical family and neighborhood communication when infrastructure fails.

Medium-range options connect to nearby communities and local emergency services when additional coordination becomes necessary. These systems might include citizen-band radio, GMRS/FRS radio with enhanced setups, or community relay networks that extend effective range through multiple transmission points.

Long-range capabilities serve specialized needs when regional information becomes critical. Though less frequently needed in common emergencies, options like amateur (ham) radio, shortwave receivers, or satellite communication systems provide valuable capability in specific scenarios where wider information gathering and transmission matter.

The most resilient approach integrates these ranges rather than viewing them as competing alternatives. My own communication preparation includes options across this spectrum, with selection and training emphasis proportional to likely usage in probable scenarios. This balanced preparation acknowledges both the critical importance of communication during emergencies and the practical reality that different situations require different capabilities.

Malcolm, to his credit, eventually developed a similar balanced perspective—though I suspect he still secretly hopes for the scenario where only his elaborate ham radio setup can save the community. (*Right, Malcolm?*) During our most recent emergency preparedness meeting, he actually demonstrated a surprisingly practical short-range system alongside his impressive distance setup.

When I commented on this evolved approach, he shrugged with unexpected self-awareness. "Turns out the most important message is the one that actually gets delivered, not the one that could theoretically travel furthest."

His observation captures essential wisdom for emergency communication preparation: practical effectiveness outweighs theoretical capability every time. The ability to reliably exchange critical information with those most immediately relevant to your specific situation creates more genuine resilience than impressive technical specifications that might never prove practically necessary.

As you develop your own communication preparation, consider whether your approach addresses your actual emergency priorities or reflects fascination with technical capabilities. Have you established reliable contact methods for family members during local disruptions? Can you receive critical emergency information when normal channels fail? Do your systems maintain function without grid electricity? These practical capabilities typically determine your actual communication resilience more decisively than maximum range or technical sophistication.

And perhaps consider befriending your local Malcolm. As I've learned, sometimes the communication enthusiasts we gently tease during normal times become the community resources we gratefully rely upon when normal systems fail. Just maybe don't tell him I said that—his radio setup is impressive enough without additional encouragement.

Documentation: The Unsexy Superhero of Preparedness

Let's face it: in the world of emergency preparedness, documentation ranks somewhere between dental floss and tax preparation in terms of excitement. Nobody posts Instagram photos of their meticulously organized reference binders or creates YouTube videos about their revolutionary file labeling system. Documentation lacks the tactical appeal of gear collections or the pastoral charm of homesteading skills.

Yet during actual emergencies, this unsexy preparedness element frequently determines outcomes more decisively than many more glamorous preparations. I've watched households with comprehensive documentation navigate emergencies with remarkable effectiveness while those with impressive gear but poor information management struggled with basic functions.

My own appreciation for documentation developed after an embarrassing incident during a power outage when I couldn't remember the specific steps for safely connecting our backup generator—a procedure I had performed multiple times but hadn't documented because I was "completely familiar with the process." As I stood in the dark garage with my flashlight, trying to recall whether the fuel shutoff valve should be opened before or after the electrical connection, I made a humbling discovery: memory becomes remarkably unreliable precisely when reliable information matters most.

Since that instructive failure, I've developed what my family teasingly calls my "documentation obsession." It's a comprehensive approach to recording critical information before it's urgently needed. This system addresses several distinct documentation needs that emerge during different emergency phases:

Operational procedures for equipment and systems that function differently during emergencies than during normal conditions. These documented processes include activation sequences for backup systems, shutdown procedures for preserving equipment during disruptions, and appropriate operation guidelines for emergency-specific functions.

During a sudden evacuation due to approaching wildfires, my friend Thomas discovered the value of this documentation when stress and time pressure made even familiar procedures difficult to recall accurately. His pre-written equipment shutdown sequence prevented potential damage that could have resulted from hasty improvisation under pressure.

Location information identifying exactly where critical resources, tools, or components are stored. These references become particularly valuable when emergency functions require accessing items used infrequently or when individuals who didn't place the resources need to locate them quickly.

When my neighbor became seriously ill during a winter storm that prevented medical evacuation, her family members—suddenly responsible for maintaining household function—relied heavily on her documented storage system to locate critical supplies they hadn't personally organized. This information prevented potentially dangerous delays in accessing necessary resources.

Contact protocols containing not just basic information but complete communication procedures for different emergency scenarios. These documents include primary and alternative contact methods, predetermined check-in schedules, prioritized communication sequences, and decision triggers for different response options when initial contact attempts fail.

During a regional flooding event that separated family members across different locations, households with documented communication protocols typically reestablished contact more quickly than those improvising connection attempts under stress conditions. The predetermined procedures eliminated confusion about which contact methods to try in which sequence, creating efficiency when communication options became limited.

Knowledge transfer references capturing critical information in formats accessible to individuals without specialized background. These documents translate technical knowledge into practically applicable instructions that enable function without requiring comprehensive understanding of underlying principles.

When a medical emergency coincided with infrastructure disruption, a neighbor with minimal healthcare background successfully implemented appropriate first aid using documentation specifically designed for non-professional application. The carefully crafted instructions—including clear triggers for different intervention levels—enabled effective response despite limited prior training.

The most valuable emergency documentation shares several key characteristics that distinguish it from less effective information management approaches:

Clarity under stress conditions ensures usability when users experience the cognitive limitations that typically accompany emergencies. Effective documentation uses simple language, clear sequential steps, explicit decision criteria, and visual reinforcement that functions despite stress-impaired information processing.

Accessibility without infrastructure maintains usability when normal information retrieval systems become unavailable. Physical documentation stored at usage locations, waterproof reference cards carried by users, and visually distinct guides attached to equipment all provide critical information when digital systems, central storage locations, or normal environmental conditions become inaccessible.

Appropriate detail calibration provides sufficient information without overwhelming users during high-stress application. Effective emergency documentation typically includes more procedural detail than might seem necessary during normal conditions, while simultaneously eliminating interesting but non-essential background information that could create confusion during urgent implementation.

Update mechanisms that maintain accuracy despite system changes. The most reliable documentation includes both regular review protocols and immediate update triggers when modifications occur, preventing dangerous misalignment between documented procedures and actual system requirements.

These documentation principles initially struck me as excessively meticulous—the kind of overly careful approach that gets knowing eye-rolls from more "practical" preparedness enthusiasts. My conversion to documentation evangelism emerged not from theoretical consideration but from repeated experiences where good documentation created successful outcomes while poor information management contributed to failures.

During a particularly memorable emergency response effort, I watched two households with nearly identical equipment and supplies experience dramatically different outcomes based almost entirely on documentation quality. The family with clear, accessible procedures maintained effective function throughout the emergency, while the household without such documentation struggled increasingly as stress and fatigue degraded recall of procedures that remained perfectly operational but inadequately documented.

This experience highlighted something essential about emergency documentation: it doesn't just preserve information—

it extends cognitive function during precisely the conditions where normal mental processes become most compromised. When stress, fear, sleep deprivation, and environmental challenges combine to impair thinking, good documentation serves as an external cognitive support system that maintains capability despite these limitations.

Of course, documentation enthusiasm does occasionally warrant the gentle teasing it receives. During a community preparedness workshop, my friend Michael—another documentation convert—and I found ourselves engaged in an embarrassingly earnest debate about the optimal labeling system for emergency reference binders. As we passionately discussed color-coding versus alphanumeric organization, a workshop participant leaned over and whispered, "Is this what happens when preppers get old? They transition from tactical gear to filing systems?"

We both laughed at ourselves, acknowledging that documentation enthusiasm probably wouldn't feature prominently in any apocalyptic movie scripts. Yet we've both experienced enough real emergencies to know that sometimes the most important survival tool isn't a tactical knife but a well-organized three-ring binder containing exactly the information needed at exactly the moment it becomes critical.

So perhaps consider adding documentation development to your preparedness priorities—not because it's exciting or impressive, but because it repeatedly proves valuable during actual emergencies when memory fails, stress impairs processing, and clear procedures make the difference between functional success and dangerous failure. The resulting preparation won't win admiration on prepper forums, but it might just save your bacon when normal cognitive function becomes another casualty of emergency conditions.

Just maybe don't get into heated debates about labeling systems in public. Some stereotypes about documentation enthusiasts are, unfortunately, occasionally warranted.

Teaching and Skill Transmission: The Ultimate Emergency Resource

The most dramatic moment of the community workshop I was leading on emergency preparation wasn't a manufactured scenario but an actual medical emergency. As I demonstrated proper storage methods for emergency water supplies, an elderly participant suddenly clutched his chest and collapsed—a genuine heart attack unfolding in our community center.

What happened next perfectly illustrated a principle I'd been teaching all day: in genuine emergencies, transmittable knowledge becomes the most valuable resource. Instead of rushing forward myself, I quickly identified three participants with medical backgrounds and guided them through establishing a coordinated response while simultaneously instructing others in supporting roles appropriate to their capabilities.

As the situation stabilized and professional medical help arrived, one participant commented: "You just demonstrated exactly what you've been teaching—the difference between having knowledge and transmitting knowledge in an emergency."

She was right. Throughout that emergency and countless others I've experienced, the ability to effectively transfer critical information under stress conditions repeatedly proves more valuable than individual expertise alone. One person who knows emergency procedures can help only those immediately present; one person who can effectively teach those procedures can create capability that extends far beyond their personal reach.

This reality directly contradicts the prepper fantasy of the survivalist expert who single-handedly saves the day through superior knowledge. In actual emergencies affecting more than a few individuals, the limitation isn't usually knowledge existence but knowledge distribution—getting critical information to those who need it when conventional education systems become unavailable.

My friend Robert, who coordinates emergency response training, describes this challenge perfectly: "In most disasters, it's not that nobody knows what to do—it's that the knowledge doesn't reach the people facing immediate decisions. Effective emergency education isn't about creating experts but about developing knowledge transmission systems that function when normal teaching methods fail."

This perspective transforms preparation priorities from accumulating personal expertise to developing effective knowledge transmission capabilities—skills that enable sharing critical information under the challenging conditions emergencies typically create:

Stress-appropriate teaching methods maintain effectiveness despite the cognitive limitations emergencies typically impose. These approaches emphasize simple sequential instructions, hands-on demonstration, immediate application opportunities, and multi-sensory reinforcement that functions despite attention limitations and processing constraints.

During a community response to regional flooding, I observed that emergency skills transmitted through these methods typically resulted in successful application, while information shared through conventional explanation often failed to create functional capability. The difference wasn't content but delivery method—specifically adapting teaching approaches to the cognitive conditions emergencies create.

Just-in-time knowledge formatting organizes critical information for immediate application rather than comprehensive understanding. These approaches provide exactly the information needed for the immediate task without requiring background knowledge, theoretical context, or extensive preparation that emergency conditions rarely permit.

When a severe storm created widespread damage throughout our community, households with access to just-in-time guides for emergency repairs typically implemented effective temporary solutions, while those attempting to learn comprehensive repair methods often achieved nothing practical before professional help became available. The focused approach created immediate capability where conventional learning methods proved too time-intensive for emergency conditions.

Capability-appropriate instruction matches teaching content and methods to learner capacity rather than instructor expertise. These approaches identify what information particular individuals can effectively implement given their existing capabilities, then provide exactly that content without overwhelming them with knowledge beyond their immediate application ability.

During an extended power outage affecting vulnerable community members, I watched caregivers effectively implement simplified emergency protocols specifically designed for their capabilities while struggling with more technically comprehensive instructions despite the latter containing "better" information from expert perspectives. The matched approach created practical function where theoretically superior knowledge failed to generate useful capability.

Distributed expertise networks connect individuals with different knowledge areas rather than attempting to create universal capabilities across all participants. These systems identify who knows what, establish communication methods between knowledge holders, and develop shared understanding of when to consult different expertise sources based on specific emergency needs.

When our community experienced a complex emergency involving multiple simultaneous challenges, our established expertise network allowed appropriate knowledge to reach decision points despite no individual possessing comprehensive capability across all required domains. This distributed approach created collective capability far beyond what any individual expert could have provided.

These transmission-focused approaches often differ dramatically from conventional prepper priorities, which typically emphasize developing comprehensive personal expertise across numerous domains. The resulting shift creates preparation that acknowledges both the critical importance of emergency knowledge and the practical reality that such knowledge creates resilience only when effectively shared beyond individual experts.

My own journey toward this understanding began with attempting to learn everything about everything—a preparedness approach that quickly proved both impossible and unnecessary. The turning point came during a community emergency where I discovered that my greatest contribution wasn't personally implementing my knowledge but effectively teaching critical procedures to others who could extend implementation far beyond my individual capacity.

This experience completely reoriented my preparation priorities from accumulating personal expertise to developing effective teaching capabilities for emergency contexts. While continuing to develop important skills, I simultaneously practice transmitting that knowledge under simulated emergency conditions—discovering through sometimes humbling experiences which teaching approaches function under stress and which prove theoretically sound but practically useless.

The resulting preparation creates resilience that extends beyond personal capability to enhance community function during actual emergencies. Rather than depending solely on what I personally know and can implement, this approach develops networks of transmittable knowledge that create distributed capability—a resource that consistently proves more valuable during genuine emergencies than isolated expertise regardless of how impressive that individual knowledge might be.

After all, as that heart attack incident demonstrated so dramatically, even the most knowledgeable individual can become the person needing help rather than providing it. When that role reversal occurs—as it eventually does for everyone—the most valuable preparation isn't what you personally know but what you've effectively taught others who can implement critical knowledge when you can't.

This perspective doesn't diminish the importance of developing personal expertise but places it within a broader understanding of emergency knowledge as a transmittable resource rather than a personal possession. The most valuable emergency capability isn't knowing everything yourself but creating systems that get the right knowledge to the right people at the right times—particularly when conventional education methods become unavailable precisely when critical information matters most.

Radio Silence vs. Actually Coordinating Survival

Every community seems to have at least one—the information prepper who has diligently prepared for emergencies by hoarding critical knowledge with the same enthusiasm others reserve for stockpiling beans and bullets. They've accumulated impressive expertise across multiple domains but share it with the reluctance of a dragon guarding gold, apparently operating under the bizarre assumption that knowing something others don't provides security during scenarios where cooperative function determines collective survival.

I encountered our local information dragon during a community emergency when several families needed to quickly implement water purification methods after contamination affected their supply. Despite having extensive knowledge on this exact topic—evidenced by his impressive reference library visible through his living room window—he declined to host a quick teaching session that could have helped neighbors avoid waterborne illness.

"I've spent years learning this," he explained when I asked directly for his assistance. "People should have done their own preparation instead of expecting others to solve their problems."

The irony, of course, was that his information hoarding

actually damaged his own security by creating preventable health issues in households directly surrounding his own. The waterborne illness that subsequently affected several families created community challenges that eventually impacted even his carefully isolated household—a perfect demonstration that information isolation provides illusory security in scenarios where community function directly affects individual outcomes.

This pattern repeats across numerous emergencies I've either experienced or studied: information sharing creates community capability that enhances everyone's resilience, while information hoarding generates preventable failures that eventually compromise even the most carefully prepared households. This reality directly contradicts the "knowledge as power" mentality that keeps critical information carefully guarded precisely when its broadest application would most benefit everyone—including the knowledge holders themselves.

The most effective emergency information approach recognizes that certain knowledge categories create maximum value through widespread distribution rather than restricted access. These types typically include:

Basic safety protocols that prevent injuries, illness, or resource contamination through appropriate handling methods. These fundamental procedures—water purification, food safety, sanitation management, fire prevention—create their greatest value when widely implemented throughout affected communities rather than practiced by isolated experts alone.

During a water contamination emergency affecting our region, communities with broadly distributed purification knowledge experienced significantly lower illness rates than those where such information remained concentrated among preparedness enthusiasts who hadn't effectively shared their expertise. The resulting capability difference affected not just prepared individuals but entire community function during the extended emergency.

Resource management techniques that optimize limited supplies through appropriate usage, preservation, and allocation methods. These approaches—food storage rotation, water conservation, energy efficiency, supply sharing systems—create community resilience through widespread implementation rather than isolated practice.

When our area experienced extended supply disruption following regional infrastructure damage, neighborhoods with widely shared resource management knowledge maintained better function throughout the emergency than those where such expertise remained concentrated among a few prepared households. The distributed capability extended available resources for everyone through efficient usage rather than creating islands of abundance amid preventable scarcity.

Mutual support systems that coordinate complementary capabilities across different households based on their particular resources and needs. These coordination approaches—skill sharing networks, equipment lending systems, resource exchange mechanisms—create community capability greater than what any individual household could maintain regardless of preparation level.

During an extended power outage affecting vulnerable community members, neighborhoods with established support coordination systems maintained better overall function than those where households operated in isolation despite similar aggregate resource levels across both areas. The coordinated approach created more efficient resource utilization through appropriate matching of capabilities with needs.

These knowledge categories demonstrate a fundamental principle of genuine emergency resilience: some information provides its greatest value through broad distribution rather than restricted access. The resulting community capability enhancement typically benefits even the most thoroughly prepared households by creating more stable collective function throughout extended emergencies—a security factor that isolated preparation alone cannot provide regardless of its thoroughness.

My own journey toward this understanding included some embarrassingly dragon-like phases where I carefully guarded certain preparedness knowledge out of misguided concerns about resource competition during potential emergencies. The transformation toward information sharing came through actual emergency experiences where I repeatedly observed that community capability directly affected individual outcomes regardless of personal preparation levels.

This perspective doesn't suggest indiscriminately broadcasting all information regardless of context or consequence. Certain knowledge categories—specific resource locations, security vulnerabilities, specialized technical details—may warrant more careful distribution based on trustworthiness, need-to-know considerations, or potential misuse risks. The key distinction involves identifying which information creates its maximum value through broad distribution versus which might justifiably warrant more controlled sharing.

When I attempted to explain this perspective to our local information dragon after the water contamination incident, his response perfectly captured the fear-based thinking that often drives information hoarding: "If I teach everyone everything I know, what value do I have in an emergency?"

This question reveals a fundamental misunderstanding of how community emergencies actually function. In genuine disasters affecting more than isolated individuals, value comes not from monopolizing critical knowledge but from contributing to functional community systems that enhance everyone's resilience—including your own. The most respected and integrated community members during actual emergencies are typically those who share capability-enhancing knowledge rather than hoarding it behind walls of imagined self-sufficiency.

As you develop your own emergency information approach, consider whether you've fallen into dragon-like tendencies regarding certain knowledge categories that would actually create their greatest value—including for your own household—through broader distribution. Have you developed effective methods for sharing critical information with those who would benefit most from its application? Do you participate in knowledge exchange systems that enhance community capability beyond what your individual household could maintain? Have you recognized which information categories create their maximum value through widespread implementation rather than restricted access?

And perhaps consider whether your preparation approach reflects the reality of actual community emergencies rather than individualistic fantasy scenarios where isolated expertise supposedly creates security amid collective dysfunction. The most effective preparation acknowledges the inconvenient truth that most disasters affecting more than a handful of people create interdependencies that directly link individual outcomes to community function—making information sharing a practical security enhancement rather than a theoretical vulnerability.

Just don't expect immediate conversion if you share this perspective with your local information dragon. Those gold hoards of carefully guarded knowledge don't get abandoned easily, even when their isolation demonstrably creates vulnerabilities rather than security. Sometimes the most we can hope for is incremental progress—perhaps beginning with water purification methods that might actually benefit the knowledge hoarder by preventing illness in the neighbors who would otherwise be coughing through the shared wall.

Progress comes in small steps, after all—preferably documented clearly in waterproof ink with appropriate revision dates noted for accurate reference during future emergencies. But that's just the documentation enthusiast in me speaking. Some preparedness stereotypes are, unfortunately, occasionally warranted.

Financial Preparedness: Beyond the Bitcoin Bunker

The moment I truly understood the gender divide in financial preparedness happened at a community workshop on economic resilience. As the facilitator introduced the topic of preparing for potential financial disruption, he asked participants to share their primary economic concerns.

One after another, the men in the room outlined elaborate

scenarios involving currency collapse, hyperinflation, and banking system failures, complete with detailed plans for precious metals acquisition, cryptocurrency investments, and strategic fund positioning across multiple financial instruments. Several had complex spreadsheets tracking historic monetary collapses and international exchange rates.

When my neighbor Ruth—a seventy-year-old widow who had survived, even *thrived* through multiple recessions with remarkable stability—finally spoke, the room grew quiet.

"I've lived through the oil crisis of the 70s, double-digit inflation in the 80s, the tech bubble, and the 2008 crash," she said calmly. "Never once did my ability to survive depend on gold coins or investment strategies. It depended on three things: keeping my fixed expenses low, maintaining practical skills that people always need, and having strong community connections where resources could flow both ways."

She paused, looking around the room with gentle amusement. "The best financial preparation isn't what you can hoard during good times, but what you can contribute during bad ones."

The uncomfortable shifting among the spreadsheet enthusiasts told me her simple wisdom had struck a nerve. While they had been plotting theoretical strategies against global monetary collapse, Ruth had been quietly implementing practical economic resilience through daily decisions that created genuine stability regardless of larger financial conditions.

This contrast highlights a fundamental difference in approaches to financial preparedness. The predominantly masculine approach often focuses on protecting abstract value through various financial instruments and alternative currencies. The traditionally feminine approach typically emphasizes reducing vulnerability through practical skill development, expense management, and reciprocal community economics.

Both approaches offer valuable elements for comprehensive preparation. The tragedy is that prepper culture overwhelmingly emphasizes the former while undervaluing the latter—creating financial vulnerability even among those who believe themselves thoroughly prepared for economic disruption.

My own journey in financial preparedness began firmly in the former camp. I diligently researched historic economic collapses, diversified into recommended "crisis-proof" investments, and accumulated the supposedly essential precious metals that would see me through any monetary catastrophe. I was prepared for currency collapse, banking system failure, and global economic reset—all while carrying substantial monthly expenses, lacking several practical skills that would prove valuable during actual financial strain, and maintaining relatively weak economic connections within my community.

The transformation in my thinking began when unexpected medical expenses coincided with a regional economic downturn, creating personal financial pressure despite no collapse of the larger monetary system. My carefully selected crisis investments remained intact but largely irrelevant to my immediate needs, while my high fixed expenses, underdeveloped practical skills, and limited community economic connections created genuine vulnerability despite my theoretical "preparation."

This experience sparked a complete reassessment of financial resilience that balanced protecting abstract value with creating practical economic capability—an approach that acknowledges both the potential for systemic disruption and the more common personal financial challenges that typically emerge during normal economic fluctuations.

As we explore this balanced approach to financial preparedness, I invite you to consider whether your own strategy might benefit from similar integration. Are you prepared only for dramatic systemic collapse, or have you developed the practical economic resilience that serves you through both financial apocalypse and ordinary financial disruption? The most comprehensive preparation addresses both possibilities while recognizing that the latter occurs far more frequently than the former.

Women's Approach to Financial Resilience During Economic Collapse

When my grandmother died at 94, having lived independently until her final weeks, I discovered something remarkable while helping settle her modest estate. Despite never earning more than a secretary's salary and living through the Depression, multiple wars, and numerous economic upheavals, she had maintained continuous financial stability through every disruption. She left no substantial assets by modern standards, yet had never experienced genuine financial distress despite the tumultuous economic events spanning her long life.

As I sorted through her meticulous records, the secret to her resilience emerged not from clever investment strategies or crisis financial instruments, but from practical approaches traditionally associated with women's economic management:

Expense minimization formed her first line of financial defense. Rather than focusing primarily on increasing income or returns, she maintained remarkably low fixed expenses relative to her resources. Her mortgage was paid off years early through consistent additional principal payments. She maintained minimal ongoing obligations that could become burdensome during income disruption. She distinguished clearly between necessary expenditures and optional ones, creating substantial buffer between her needs and her resources.

When regional manufacturing decline created widespread financial hardship in her community, I watched families with substantially higher incomes experience genuine distress while my grandmother maintained comfortable stability despite her modest resources. The difference wasn't earnings but the relationship between expenses and income—a ratio she managed with meticulous attention through daily decisions rather than dramatic financial strategies.

Practical skill development created her second resilience layer. Rather than depending solely on monetary resources to meet needs, she maintained extensive practical capabilities that reduced her dependence on purchased solutions. Her impressive home maintenance skills, advanced food production and preservation capabilities, and remarkable textile talents (she could create, repair, or repurpose nearly anything involving fabric) dramatically reduced her vulnerability to both service disruptions and price increases in essential domains.

During a prolonged regional economic downturn when many households struggled with basic expenses, my grandmother's practical capabilities allowed her to maintain comfortable function despite reduced monetary resources. While others faced difficult choices between essential needs due to financial constraints, her skills created non-monetary solutions to many requirements that would otherwise have strained her limited budget.

Reciprocal economic relationships formed her third stability layer. Rather than focusing exclusively on individual financial position, she maintained extensive exchange networks that facilitated resource flows beyond formal economic systems. Her community trading, skill sharing, and cooperative resource usage created economic capability exceeding what her individual position might have supported through market mechanisms alone.

When her community experienced economic disruption following industrial restructuring, these informal economic networks maintained significant function despite formal system contraction. Households within these exchange relationships weathered the downturn with notably less distress than those operating solely through conventional economic participation, regardless of their pre-disruption financial position.

These approaches reflect financial wisdom developed through women's historical experiences managing household economics through various constraints. While men typically focused on income generation through formal economic participation, women often developed sophisticated strategies for maintaining household function despite limited, uncertain, or disrupted resource flows—creating practical resilience applicable to both personal financial challenges and larger economic disruptions.

The resulting capabilities differ significantly from conventional prepper financial preparation, which typically emphasizes protecting abstract value through alternative investment vehicles rather than reducing fundamental vulnerability through practical economic approaches. Both perspectives offer valuable elements, but the feminine approach typically provides more immediate utility during actual disruptions while requiring less specialized knowledge and fewer resource commitments to implement effectively.

My friend Elena, who maintained remarkable stability through both the 2008 financial crisis and subsequent personal economic challenges, describes this perspective perfectly: "The most valuable financial preparation isn't figuring out how to maintain wealth during system failure, but how to maintain function with or without wealth regardless of what happens to larger systems."

Her observation highlights a crucial distinction between approaches. Traditional prepper financial strategies typically focus on preserving purchasing power through economic disruption—maintaining ability to acquire resources through market mechanisms despite system difficulties. The historically feminine approach more typically focuses on reducing dependence on market acquisition altogether—developing capabilities that maintain function regardless of market conditions or purchasing power fluctuations.

This distinction creates very different preparation emphasis. Rather than complex financial instruments, alternative currencies, or strategic asset positioning, the feminine approach typically prioritizes:

Fixed expense reduction that creates genuine financial buffer through daily choices rather than specialized crisis preparation. These practical decisions—whether to take on debt, how housing costs relate to income, which ongoing obligations to accept—create immediate resilience through ordinary financial management rather than requiring dedicated crisis preparation.

Self-provision capability in essential domains that reduces vulnerability to both market disruptions and price fluctuations. These practical skills—food production and preservation, home and property maintenance, basic medical care, household item creation and repair—create non-monetary solutions to needs that would otherwise require market participation regardless of economic conditions.

Community economic integration that establishes resource flows beyond conventional market mechanisms. These relationships—skill and service exchanges, tool and equipment sharing, cooperative resource usage, local economic interdependence—create capability beyond individual resource limitations by facilitating exchanges not entirely dependent on formal economic systems.

These approaches won't make for exciting apocalyptic financial planning seminars. They involve choices more mundane than precious metals investment strategies and certainly less thrilling than cryptocurrency speculation as economic collapse hedges. Yet they typically create more practical resilience against both dramatic disruptions and ordinary financial challenges than many more sophisticated preparation approaches.

As you evaluate your own financial preparedness, consider whether you've balanced abstract value protection with practical vulnerability reduction. Have you developed capabilities that maintain function regardless of larger economic conditions? Does your preparation address both dramatic system disruption and personal financial challenges? Have you integrated traditionally feminine financial resilience strategies alongside conventional protection approaches? This balanced preparation often determines actual outcomes more decisively than specialized financial instruments alone when genuine economic difficulties emerge.

Practical Assets That Maintain Value When Currency Fails

The most illuminating conversation I've had about crisis-resilient assets occurred not with a financial advisor or economic theorist, but with my friend Sarah's grandmother, who had lived through multiple wars, political upheavals, and economic collapses across different countries before immigrating to America in her fifties.

When I asked what financial preparations she recommended based on her experiences, she laughed gently. "The things that maintained real value weren't what you could lock in a safe," she explained. "They were what you carried between your ears, what you could do with your hands, and who would help you when you needed it most."

Her perspective—echoed by many who have experienced genuine economic collapse rather than merely theorized about it—highlights something crucial about truly resilient assets: the most valuable ones during severe disruption typically aren't financial instruments or even physical commodities, but practical capabilities and relationships that function regardless of currency stability.

This reality directly contradicts conventional prepper wisdom about crisis-proof assets, which typically emphasizes precious metals, land, or specific durable commodities expected to maintain exchange value when traditional currencies fail. While these tangible assets certainly offer advantages over purely abstract financial instruments during severe disruption, they share a fundamental limitation: their practical utility depends on functioning exchange systems where others recognize and accept their value.

My own thinking about resilient assets transformed dramatically after serving on a disaster response team following a regional economic crisis compounded by natural disaster. I watched households with substantial "crisis-proof" asset positions still struggle to meet basic needs because local exchange systems had temporarily collapsed, while those with practical capabilities and strong community connections maintained better function despite less impressive financial preparations.

This experience highlighted several asset categories that demonstrated remarkable resilience precisely because they maintained utility independent of external valuation or exchange systems:

Production capabilities that generate essential resources without requiring purchase maintain function regardless of currency stability or market access. These assets—gardens, orchards, energy generation systems, water collection and purification setups—create value through direct provision rather than exchange, functioning when both conventional and alternative currencies lose practical utility.

During an extended regional crisis where normal supply chains collapsed and local exchange became severely constrained, households with food production capabilities maintained significantly better nutrition than those depending on purchased supplies—regardless of what financial assets or even precious metals the latter possessed. The practical ability to generate essential resources proved more valuable than any theoretical exchange medium when actual markets ceased functioning normally.

Practical skill assets that transform available materials into needed resources maintain value regardless of economic conditions. These capabilities—food preservation, construction and repair, textile creation and maintenance, energy system management—create value through transformation rather than acquisition, functioning when purchasing power becomes irrelevant due to supply constraints or exchange system failures.

When severe flooding combined with economic disruption to create both financial instability and supply shortages, individuals with practical creation and repair capabilities maintained better function than those with significant financial resources but limited transformation skills. The ability to create and adapt using available materials proved more valuable than theoretical purchasing power when desired goods simply weren't available for purchase at any price.

Tool assets that extend human capability maintain practical utility regardless of their nominal value in any currency system. These implements—quality hand tools, appropriate food production and preservation equipment, durable textile processing tools, sustainable energy technology—create value through capability enhancement rather than exchange potential, functioning when monetary systems of all types lose practical relevance.

Following a devastating hurricane that created both physical destruction and economic disruption, communities where essential tools had been maintained and distributed through intentional redundancy recovered function more quickly than those with centralized resources regardless of their collective financial position. The practical capabilities these tools enabled proved more valuable than any monetary resources when basic function required direct creation rather than market acquisition.

Knowledge assets preserved in accessible formats maintain critical value during both information system disruptions and economic instability. These resources—practical reference materials, local adaptation information, skill documentation in physical formats—create value through capability enhancement regardless of currency conditions or digital system function.

During an extended infrastructure disruption that affected both economic function and information access, households with comprehensive physical reference materials maintained better practical capability than those dependent on digital knowledge resources—regardless of their financial preparations. The ability to access critical information without functioning infrastructure proved more valuable than any financial position when knowledge needs couldn't be addressed through functioning information systems.

Relationship assets within local communities maintain function when formal economic systems falter. These connections—skill exchange networks, mutual aid relationships, cooperative resource management systems—create value through reciprocity rather than market mechanisms, functioning when conventional economy contracts or temporarily collapses.

In the aftermath of a regional economic crisis where conventional employment and commerce became severely constrained, communities with established reciprocal exchange networks maintained better overall function than those primarily dependent on formal economic participation despite similar aggregate resource levels. The ability to facilitate non-monetary resource flows proved more valuable than conventional financial positions when traditional economic mechanisms temporarily failed.

These asset categories rarely feature prominently in conventional financial preparedness discussions, which typically emphasize maintaining purchasing power rather than reducing dependence on purchasing altogether. Yet historical evidence from actual economic collapses consistently shows that direct capability often maintains function more effectively than even the most theoretically sound exchange media when systems experience genuine disruption.

This perspective doesn't suggest completely abandoning conventional financial preparation or reasonable alternative currency positions. These approaches certainly offer value within their appropriate contexts and particularly during moderate disruptions where exchange systems maintain some function. The limitation emerges when preparation emphasizes these elements exclusively without developing the practical capabilities that function when exchange itself—regardless of the currency medium—becomes temporarily impossible.

As you evaluate your own asset position for resilience

against severe disruption, consider whether you've balanced exchange media with direct capability. Have you developed production assets that generate essential resources without requiring purchase? Do you possess practical skills that transform available materials into needed items? Have you established relationship assets that facilitate reciprocal exchange beyond monetary systems? These capability-based assets often determine actual resilience more decisively than any financial instrument or alternative currency when systems experience genuine collapse rather than mere fluctuation.

Sustainable Economic Activity During Prolonged Disruption

The most persistent fantasy in prepper economic thinking involves the "self-sufficient homestead" where a single family unit supposedly maintains complete independence through various disruptions. This mythical narrative dominates preparedness literature despite substantial historical evidence that successful adaptation to prolonged economic disruption typically involves not isolation but strategic interdependence through local economic systems that maintain function when larger structures fail.

I encountered this reality directly while documenting community responses to an extended regional economic crisis following industrial collapse. The households that maintained the highest function weren't those attempting complete self-sufficiency, but those participating in local economic networks that facilitated specialized production, resource exchange, and capability sharing despite larger system dysfunction.

This observation aligns with historical patterns across diverse disruptions worldwide. From the Depression-era United

States to economic collapse in Argentina, from Soviet Union dissolution to various regional crises globally, the most effective adaptation typically emerges through local economic structures rather than isolated household units—regardless of how thoroughly the latter prepared for independent function.

The resulting approach to sustainable crisis economics differs dramatically from conventional prepper wisdom, emphasizing integration within resilient local systems rather than isolation from vulnerable larger ones. This perspective recognizes a fundamental reality: economic specialization creates efficiency that even the most dedicated generalists cannot match, making appropriate interdependence more resilient than attempted self-sufficiency for most households in most circumstances.

My friend Thomas, who made it through his region's economic collapse following industry relocation, describes this approach perfectly: "The question isn't whether you'll participate in economic exchange during disruption, but which exchanges you'll participate in and with whom. Complete self-sufficiency is usually both impossible and undesirable when compared to strategic participation in appropriate local systems."

His perspective highlights several key elements of sustainable crisis economics that receive insufficient attention in conventional preparation discussions:

Strategic production specialization based on specific capabilities and resources creates more efficient output than attempting comprehensive self-provision across all domains. This focused approach—concentrating production efforts where your particular skills, tools, land, and interests create maximum efficiency—generates greater value than divided attention across numerous less productive activities.

During a prolonged regional economic downturn, I observed households that focused their production in areas where they held comparative advantage maintained better overall function through strategic exchange than those attempting comprehensive self-provision across all domains. The efficiency gains through appropriate specialization created surplus beyond self-provision requirements, enabling exchange that enhanced overall position more effectively than isolated production alone could have achieved.

Deliberate redundancy coordination within local networks prevents critical capability gaps while avoiding wasteful duplication across participating households. This cooperative approach—identifying essential functions and ensuring multiple production sources within the network rather than within each household—creates system resilience without requiring universal capacity development across all participants.

When our community experienced extended economic disruption following industry departure, neighborhoods that had established intentional redundancy coordination maintained more comprehensive capability than either isolated households or uncoordinated groups, regardless of individual preparation levels. The distributed approach ensured critical functions remained available throughout the network while allowing individual households to maintain reasonable specialization rather than attempting universal capacity development.

Appropriately scaled exchange mechanisms facilitate resource flows when conventional economic structures contract or temporarily fail. These systems—from formal arrangements like local currencies and structured barter networks to informal approaches including gift economies and mutual aid agreements—create transaction capability based on direct relationship rather than abstract financial instruments, functioning when larger economic structures cannot maintain effective operation.

Following regional economic collapse that severely constrained conventional commerce, communities with established alternative exchange systems maintained significantly higher function than those solely dependent on traditional economic mechanisms despite similar aggregate resource levels. The available transaction channels facilitated resource flows that maintained overall capability despite disruption to larger structures that would otherwise have prevented effective exchange.

Value-appropriate pricing mechanisms allow sustainable exchange despite disrupted currency systems and fluctuating valuation benchmarks. These approaches—typically emphasizing direct relation between production costs and exchange rates rather than speculative or status considerations—maintain function when conventional pricing systems become destabilized through currency fluctuation or supply constraint.

During a period of severe currency instability that made conventional pricing mechanisms increasingly unreliable, local producers who established direct cost-relationship exchange rates maintained more consistent economic activity than those attempting to continuously recalibrate to fluctuating currency values. The simplified approach created transaction stability that supported ongoing exchange despite the challenging conditions that disrupted conventional commerce.

Reciprocal skill utilization networks enable capability sharing beyond direct resource exchange. These systems—from formal arrangements like time banks and service exchange programs to informal approaches including cooperative work patterns and skill-sharing events—create value flows beyond tangible resources, maintaining function when material exchange alone would prove insufficient for comprehensive needs.

When economic contraction severely constrained conventional employment and service markets in our region, communities with established skill exchange systems maintained higher overall function than those dependent solely on traditional labor markets despite similar demographic compositions. The alternative capability deployment channels facilitated value flows that addressed needs conventional economics could no longer efficiently serve given the disrupted conditions.

These elements combine to create local economic resilience that functions despite larger system disruption—providing sustainable activity patterns that maintain capability through prolonged contraction rather than merely surviving until theoretical recovery. The resulting approach emphasizes strategic participation rather than isolation, recognizing that appropriate interdependence typically creates more resilience than attempted self-sufficiency for most households in most circumstances.

My own journey through this understanding has substantially transformed both my financial preparation and my community participation. Rather than focusing exclusively on isolated household resilience, I've invested significantly in developing appropriate local systems that enhance collective capability during potential disruptions. This approach recognizes that my individual outcomes during genuine economic challenges will likely depend more on the function of these local networks than on any personal financial position I might establish, regardless of how theoretically sound my isolated preparation might be.

As you develop your own approach to sustainable crisis economics, consider whether you've balanced individual preparation with appropriate system participation. Have you identified your most efficient production specialties rather than attempting comprehensive self-provision? Are you participating in redundancy coordination that ensures critical capabilities without requiring universal capacity development? Have you helped establish appropriate exchange mechanisms that can function when conventional economic structures cannot? These systemic factors often determine actual outcomes more decisively than individual financial position alone when larger economic structures experience genuine disruption rather than mere fluctuation.

Planning for Recovery: Preserving Crucial Financial Information

While preparing for economic disruption certainly matters, preparing for eventual recovery often proves equally important yet receives far less attention in conventional prepper discussions. This oversight creates dangerous vulnerability even among those who navigate the initial crisis successfully, as they remain unprepared for the complex challenges that typically emerge during economic reestablishment.

I witnessed this recovery gap directly while assisting a community rebuilding after both natural disaster and economic disruption. Households that had maintained comprehensive financial documentation navigated the complex recovery systems with relative efficiency, while those without such records often experienced substantial delays despite having successfully managed the actual crisis period. The distinction wasn't crisis preparation but recovery readiness—specifically, information preservation that facilitated reengagement with formal systems once they began functioning again.

This experience highlighted a crucial preparedness element often overlooked in dramatic collapse scenarios: maintaining information continuity between pre-crisis and post-crisis periods. The ability to establish clear financial identity, ownership, obligations, and entitlements when systems reactivate often determines long-term outcomes more significantly than many more dramatic preparation elements that receive greater attention.

My friend Elena describes this reality perfectly: "The households that recovered most completely weren't necessarily those who weathered the crisis most comfortably, but those who could efficiently navigate the bureaucratic systems that inevitably emerge during rebuilding. That navigation depends almost entirely on documentation most people never think to preserve until it's already lost."

Her observation identifies several documentation categories that deserve specific preservation attention despite their unglamorous nature:

Identity verification materials establish your legal personhood and system relationship when formal structures reactivate. These documents—birth certificates, social security cards, passports, driver's licenses, marriage certificates, professional credentials—create your official existence within reconstituting systems, functioning as the foundation for nearly all subsequent recovery engagement.

During a prolonged regional crisis where many households lost documentation through evacuation, property damage, or simple neglect, those who had preserved identity verification materials navigated recovery programs substantially more efficiently than those attempting to reestablish official identity through compromised systems. The available verification created administrative capability that dramatically expedited assistance access compared to households facing similar circumstances without such documentation.

Property ownership records establish your legal claim to assets when ownership systems resume function. These documents—property deeds, vehicle titles, significant purchase receipts, inheritance records, intellectual property registrations—create your official relationship to specific resources within reconstituting legal structures, functioning as evidence for claims that might otherwise remain unrecognized during recovery.

Following a devastating hurricane that destroyed many local government buildings where property records were stored, households with preserved ownership documentation reestablished their claims significantly more quickly than those dependent on compromised public records systems. The available evidence created legal clarity that expedited everything from insurance processing to reconstruction permitting compared to similarly situated households without such documentation.

Financial obligation records establish clarity about debts, payments, and responsibilities when creditor systems resume operation. These documents—mortgage statements, loan agreements, payment records, tax filings, contractual obligations—create accurate accountability within reconstituting financial structures, preventing both unnecessary penalties and potential exploitation during system reestablishment.

When our region experienced severe economic disruption that temporarily suspended numerous financial services, households that maintained comprehensive obligation records navigated the eventual resumption with notably fewer complications than those without documented histories. The available evidence prevented both missed responsibilities and inappropriate claims as systems reactivated with inevitable administrative confusion following the extended disruption.

Entitlement verification material* establish your eligibility for benefits, services, and assistance when provision systems resume function. These documents—insurance policies, program enrollments, service contracts, membership agreements—create your official qualification within reconstituting support structures, enabling appropriate access that might otherwise face substantial verification delays during recovery.

During community rebuilding following both economic crisis and natural disaster, households with preserved entitlement documentation accessed support services dramatically faster than those attempting to establish eligibility without such records. The available verification created administrative efficiency that expedited assistance compared to households facing similar circumstances without documented claim evidence.

Digital information preservation systems maintain electronic records through conditions that might compromise standard storage methods. These approaches—physically isolated backups, protection from electromagnetic risks, redundant storage across multiple locations—create information resilience beyond what conventional digital systems typically provide, maintaining critical data despite potential infrastructure disruptions that would otherwise compromise electronic records.

When severe flooding damaged numerous households in our community, those with appropriately preserved digital financial information navigated both immediate response and longer-term recovery more efficiently than those who lost electronic records to either direct damage or infrastructure failure. The available information created capability that supported better decisions throughout both crisis and rebuilding phases despite the challenging circumstances that compromised standard record systems.

These documentation elements combine to create information continuity between disruption and recovery—preserving critical data that enables efficient system reengagement when formal structures resume function. The resulting capability supports not just immediate crisis navigation but longer-term rebuilding, which typically involves complex administrative processes that function dramatically more efficiently with appropriate documentation than without it.

My own approach to this preparation aspect involves what I call "resurrection files"—comprehensive documentation packages preserved in formats and locations specifically designed to survive whatever disruptions might compromise primary records. These collections include both physical and appropriately protected digital copies of all critical documents, structured for efficient access and protected against various potential compromise scenarios from physical destruction to electronic disruption.

This documentation focus admittedly lacks the dramatic appeal of many more conventional preparation elements. Organizing and preserving financial records simply doesn't generate the same enthusiasm as stockpiling precious metals or establishing cryptocurrency positions as economic collapse hedges. Yet historical evidence consistently shows that recovery often presents more complex and consequential challenges than the actual crisis period—challenges that appropriate documentation addresses more effectively than many more exciting preparation approaches.

As you develop your own financial resilience strategy, consider whether you've adequately addressed the recovery phase alongside the crisis period. Have you preserved comprehensive identity documentation in formats likely to survive potential disruptions? Are your property records protected against possible compromise scenarios? Have you maintained obligation evidence that would establish clear responsibility during system reactivation? These unglamorous but crucial preparations often determine long-term outcomes more decisively than many more dramatic elements that receive greater attention in conventional prepper discussions.

Crypto-Apocalypse Planning vs. Actually Handling Economic Crisis

The scene at the preparedness conference perfectly captured the disconnect between theoretical economic collapse preparation and practical financial resilience. In the main exhibition hall, eager attendees crowded around polished presentations promising "crisis-proof wealth protection" through elaborate cryptocurrency strategies, precious metals positioning, and offshore account structures—complete with complex graphs showing historical currency collapses and projections of imminent financial apocalypse.

Meanwhile, in a sparsely attended side room with folding chairs and no multimedia presentation, a panel of people who had actually lived through various economic collapses—from Argentina's crisis to Zimbabwe's hyperinflation—shared practical lessons bearing little resemblance to the exciting strategies being promoted next door.

"I had gold coins hidden in my house when our currency collapsed," one panelist explained. "They remained completely unused while my vegetable garden and sewing skills kept my family fed and clothed. The theoretical value of those coins meant nothing when no one was in position to exchange anything for them."

Another nodded agreement. "Everyone focuses on protecting abstract value, but in real collapse, abstract value temporarily ceases to exist. What matters is direct capacity to meet needs without depending on any exchange system at all. The question becomes not 'how do I maintain purchasing power?' but 'what can I do without needing to purchase?'"

A third panelist smiled ruefully. "The people who navigated our economic crisis most successfully weren't those with the cleverest financial instruments or alternative currency positions, but those who had minimized their vulnerability through practical skills, low fixed expenses, and strong community connections. Financial preparation mattered far less than vulnerability reduction."

The contrast between rooms couldn't have been starker—exciting theories about protecting wealth through financial sophistication versus sobering experiences about maintaining function through practical preparation. This distinction isn't merely academic; it creates dramatically different preparation priorities with significantly different practical outcomes when genuine economic challenges emerge.

To illustrate this difference concretely, let's examine how different preparation approaches might function during three distinct economic challenge scenarios:

Scenario 1: *Personal Financial Crisis (Job Loss, Medical Expense, Divorce)*

The most common economic emergency isn't systemic collapse but personal financial disruption—challenges affecting individual households amid normally functioning larger systems. These situations test resilience through individual circumstance rather than collective crisis.

The Crypto-Apocalypse Preparation Approach:
  - Alternative currency positions remain largely irrelevant to immediate needs
  - Precious metals investments typically require liquidation at disadvantageous terms

- Complex financial instruments often lack immediate accessibility when needs arise
  - Offshore structures provide minimal benefit for ordinary financial difficulties

The Practical Resilience Approach:
  - Low fixed expenses create extended financial runway
  - Emergency funds in accessible, liquid forms provide immediate response capability
  - Minimal debt obligations reduce vulnerability to income interruption
  - Practical skills provide non-monetary solutions
  - Community connections offer support options beyond financial resources alone

Historical evidence consistently shows the latter approach provides more effective navigation through personal financial challenges despite its less exciting theoretical framework. The practical capabilities—expense management, accessible reserves, reduced obligations, direct provision skills, and community support—address actual needs more effectively than sophisticated financial positions designed for entirely different scenarios.

Scenario 2: *Systemic Financial Instability (Severe Inflation, Banking Restrictions, Market Disruption)*
Less common but still recurring are periods of significant system stress without complete collapse—challenges affecting broad populations through institutional strain rather than total failure. These situations test resilience through system navigation rather than system replacement.

The Crypto-Apocalypse Preparation Approach:
 - Alternative currency positions often experience their own volatility
 - Precious metals may maintain relative value but frequently face liquidity challenges
 - Complex financial instruments typically become less reliable
 - Offshore structures may provide theoretical protection but not really

The Practical Resilience Approach:
 - Diversified resource storage reduces exposure to single system vulnerabilities
 - Multiple financial access methods across different institutions provide options
 - Practical skills create direct solutions when normal acquisition becomes constrained
 - Local economic participation establishes exchange options
 - Reduced consumption minimizes exposure to inflation impacts/supply constraints

Historical examples from various financial instability periods consistently show balanced practical approaches navigating system stress more effectively than either complete conventional participation or elaborate alternative positioning alone. The practical capabilities—resource diversification, access redundancy, direct provision skills, local economic participation, and reduced consumption requirements—create functional options regardless of which specific system components experience strain.

Scenario 3: *Complete Economic Collapse (Currency Failure, Market Cessation, Institutional Breakdown)*

The rarest but most discussed scenario involves genuine system failure—challenges affecting entire populations through comprehensive institutional collapse rather than mere dysfunction. These situations test resilience through system independence rather than system utilization.

The Crypto-Apocalypse Preparation Approach:
- Alternative currencies typically face implementation challenges
- Precious metals maintain theoretical value but often experience limitations d
- Complex financial instruments generally cease functioning
- Offshore structures become largely irrelevant when basic exchange systems fail

The Practical Resilience Approach:
- Direct production generate essential resources without requiring functioning markets
- Practical skills create needed items regardless of exchange system availability
- Tool assets enable continued function independent of external supply chains
- Knowledge resources provide critical information despite information disruptions
- Community economic integration establishes local exchange

Historical examples from genuine economic collapses consistently show practical approaches maintaining better function than even the most theoretically sound financial positioning. The direct capabilities—production capacity, transformation skills, enabling tools, essential knowledge, and community integration—maintain critical function when exchange itself temporarily ceases, regardless of what exchange medium one might theoretically possess.

These scenario comparisons reveal something crucial about effective financial preparation: resilience emerges not from sophisticated preservation of abstract value but from practical reduction of fundamental vulnerability. The households that maintain the best function through various economic challenges—from personal difficulties to systemic collapse—typically achieve this through balanced approaches emphasizing practical capability development alongside reasonable financial positioning.

This perspective doesn't suggest abandoning all conventional financial preparation or reasonable hedging strategies. These approaches certainly offer value within appropriate contexts, particularly during moderate disruptions where exchange systems maintain some function. The limitation emerges when preparation emphasizes these elements exclusively without developing the practical capabilities that maintain function when exchange itself becomes compromised or temporarily impossible.

As you evaluate your own financial resilience strategy, consider whether you've balanced abstract value protection with practical vulnerability reduction. Have you developed capabilities that maintain function regardless of exchange system status? Does your preparation address personal financial challenges alongside potential systemic disruptions? Have you invested in practical skills and community connections that create resilience beyond what financial instruments alone can provide? This balanced preparation often determines actual outcomes more decisively than any specific financial position when genuine economic challenges emerge—whether personal difficulties or broader systemic disruptions.

And perhaps consider attending those sparsely populated side rooms at preparedness conferences, where people with actual experience share practical wisdom that rarely makes the main stage but consistently proves more valuable when theory meets reality. The resulting preparation might generate fewer exciting apocalyptic discussions but will likely serve you far better through the economic challenges most likely to actually emerge during your lifetime—from personal financial setbacks to the broader systemic strains that periodically affect even the most stable economies.

After all, as one of those experienced panelists noted with a wisdom born from genuine hardship: "The best financial preparation isn't figuring out how to remain wealthy during collapse, but how to maintain dignity and function regardless of what happens to wealth altogether."

14

What About the Children?

The morning after our community's first major blizzard of the season had finally passed, I found myself trudging through knee-deep snow to check on my neighbor Ruth and her two young grandchildren. The storm had knocked out power throughout the region, and temperatures had plunged well below zero overnight. As I approached their farmhouse, I spotted seven-year-old Emma in the yard, methodically building snow sculptures with a look of intense concentration.

"Morning, Emma," I called out. "Everything okay after the storm?"

She looked up, her face serious beneath her wool hat. "We're having an adventure," she said matter-of-factly. "Gran says the power's sleeping, so we're camping inside." She pointed to her snow creation. "I'm making a map of our house, but with snow. See? This is where we sleep now—all together by the woodstove."

Inside, I found Ruth calmly preparing breakfast on the woodstove while four-year-old Ben carefully arranged their battery-powered lanterns. The house was cold except for the living room, where Ruth had created a cozy nest of blankets around the heat source. What struck me wasn't just their physical preparation, but the atmosphere—there was no panic, no sense of emergency, just purposeful activity tinged with the gentle excitement of doing things differently.

"They think it's an adventure," Ruth whispered later as the children played a board game by lantern light. "We've practiced for this—not as a scary emergency, but as another way of living when needed." Her eyes grew momentarily distant. "Children can handle almost anything if they feel secure in their people and have a framework for understanding what's happening."

Ruth's approach captures the essence of the most profound preparedness question many of us face: how do we prepare the children in our lives for an uncertain future without burdening them with adult fears? How do we equip them with the skills and resilience they'll need without stealing the security that childhood requires? And perhaps most importantly, how do we raise children who can thrive in whatever world awaits them—not just survive in it?

These questions touch something deeper than stockpiles or skills. They reach into our hopes, fears, and fundamental values—forcing us to confront what truly matters in how we prepare the next generation.

Seeds of Resilience: Preparation Without Fear

The most dangerous misconception about preparing children for uncertainty is that we face a binary choice: either shelter them completely from difficult realities or expose them fully to adult concerns about the future. This false dichotomy creates either unprepared children or unnecessarily burdened ones—neither outcome serving their development or future resilience.

My friend Elena explains this balance beautifully: "Children need both security and capability to develop healthy relationships with uncertainty. Security comes from trusted adults who maintain appropriate protective boundaries; capability comes from graduated challenges that build confidence through mastery. Without security, capability becomes overwhelming. Without capability, security becomes brittle."

This balanced approach differs significantly from what I've observed in some prepper families, where children are either completely shielded from preparation activities or inappropriately immersed in adult fears about societal collapse. The most effective preparation for children occupies the thoughtful middle ground—building skills and awareness within developmentally appropriate frameworks that emphasize confidence rather than fear.

During a summer program I ran for rural children, we taught wilderness skills through what we called "adventure learning"—framing basic survival capabilities as exciting challenges rather than emergency preparation. The children learned fire-building, water purification, basic first aid, and food foraging without ever discussing disaster scenarios or collapse concerns. Instead, we emphasized connection to nature, problem-solving, and self-reliance in positive contexts.

One mother later told me that during an unexpected overnight power outage, her eight-year-old daughter had confidently helped prepare a cold meal and set up alternative lighting using skills from our program. "She wasn't scared at all," the mother marveled. "She just said 'Oh, I know what to do' and stepped right up."

This experience reflects a crucial principle in children's preparedness: skills taught in positive, confidence-building contexts transfer effectively to actual challenges without requiring fear-based motivation. Children don't need to worry about societal breakdown to benefit from knowing how to build a fire, grow food, or handle basic medical needs. These capabilities can develop through ordinary learning framed around competence and connection rather than catastrophe.

The most effective approaches typically incorporate several key elements that build resilience without creating anxiety. Age-appropriate skill development should be embedded in regular family activities rather than separated as special "emergency training." Children who routinely help preserve garden harvests, maintain emergency supplies as normal household tasks, and learn basic self-reliance skills within everyday family functioning develop capability without corresponding anxiety.

My neighbor Sarah involves her children in seasonal food preservation as a normal family activity. They've learned to can, dehydrate, and freeze garden produce without any framing around disaster preparation—yet these skills would prove invaluable during actual supply disruptions. The children take pride in their growing mastery without carrying adult anxieties about why these capabilities might someday matter.

Graduated independence appropriate to developmental stages that builds decision-making confidence through successful challenge navigation. Children who regularly practice making consequential choices within appropriate boundaries develop critical adaptive capabilities that transfer directly to emergency situations.

During a community resilience program, I watched children across different age groups tackle progressively more complex challenges—from simple fire-building for younger children to overnight wilderness experiences for teenagers. The graduated nature of these experiences built confidence through appropriate stretching rather than overwhelming challenge, creating resilience through success rather than stress.

Problem-solving frameworks that emphasize resourcefulness, adaptability, and creative thinking rather than rigid procedural responses. Children who regularly engage with open-ended challenges develop cognitive flexibility that proves invaluable during actual emergencies, when circumstances rarely match pre-planned scenarios.

My friend Michael, who teaches outdoor education, structures his children's programs around what he calls "resource-limited challenges"—activities that present authentic problems with deliberately constrained materials. The children develop remarkable ingenuity through these experiences without any framing around emergency preparation, building adaptive capability that functions across diverse situations.

Emotional regulation skills that create foundational resilience applicable across all life challenges. Children who develop the ability to recognize, name, and appropriately respond to their emotional states maintain better function during all stressful situations, including emergencies.

During a workshop on childhood resilience, I observed a simple practice where children learned to identify their emotional states using color associations, then apply corresponding regulation techniques appropriate to each state. This approachable method gave children concrete tools for managing their internal experiences without complex psychological concepts—skills directly applicable during emergency situations.

These approaches build genuine preparedness without corresponding anxiety—creating capabilities that serve children well regardless of what futures they ultimately face. The resulting resilience emerges not from fearful anticipation but from confidence in their own developing capabilities and trust in supportive adult frameworks.

As my friend Elena notes: "The most prepared children aren't those who worry about potential disasters, but those who believe in their ability to handle challenges because they've successfully navigated appropriate ones before. Confidence, not concern, creates true readiness."

Learning Through Anything: Educational Continuity in Disruption

Among the most profound impacts of major disruptions on children is the potential loss of educational continuity—not just formal academic progression, but the broader developmental benefits that structured learning provides. During extended emergencies, maintaining educational frameworks serves functions far beyond academic advancement, providing crucial psychological stability through routine, purpose, and cognitive engagement.

During a lengthy power outage that closed local schools for nearly three weeks, I observed striking differences between families who established alternative educational structures and those who treated the disruption as an extended vacation. Children in households with continued learning routines maintained better emotional regulation, engaged in more constructive activities, and demonstrated greater overall resilience throughout the challenging period.

My friend Rebecca, a homeschooling mother of three, found her family better prepared for this disruption than many conventionally schooled households. "We've always seen learning as something that happens with or without formal institutions," she explained. "When the schools closed, we adjusted our approaches to the new constraints but maintained the fundamental understanding that learning continues regardless of circumstances."

This perspective—that education transcends institutional structures—creates remarkable resilience in children's developmental trajectories during disruptions. The most effective approaches typically incorporate several key elements that maintain educational continuity despite challenging circumstances. Flexible learning frameworks must adapt to available resources rather than requiring specific materials or environments. Families who maintain simple, adaptable educational structures can continue meaningful learning despite significant constraints on normal materials and settings.

During a workshop on educational resilience, I demonstrated how basic literacy, numeracy, and critical thinking development could continue using only materials commonly found in most households. Parents were often surprised at how effective these simple approaches could be in maintaining educational progression without specialized resources—a crucial capability during extended emergencies when normal educational materials may be unavailable.

Integrated learning opportunities that recognize educational value in necessary activities during disruption. The most resilient educational approaches identify and enhance the natural learning embedded in practical emergency responses rather than treating education as separate from survival needs.

My neighbor points out that emergency situations provide extraordinary opportunities for applied learning across multiple domains: measuring and rationing supplies develops mathematical thinking; keeping journals of experiences builds literacy; observing environmental changes enhances scientific understanding; solving practical problems develops critical reasoning.

Cross-age teaching structures that allow older children to support younger ones' learning, creating both educational continuity and meaningful purpose during disruption. These approaches recognize that knowledge transmission doesn't require adult specialists but can occur through appropriately structured peer relationships.

During a community-wide flooding event that displaced numerous families for several weeks, I watched a remarkable educational ecosystem emerge in the emergency shelter. Teenagers organized reading circles for younger children, middle-schoolers created math games using available materials, and even elementary-aged children took responsibility for teaching specific skills they had mastered to others.

Non-electronic educational resources maintained as part of standard emergency preparation. The most educationally resilient families include basic learning materials—books, paper, writing instruments, manipulatives, reference materials—in their emergency supplies, recognizing these as essential rather than optional resources.

During a preparedness workshop focused on families, I was struck by how few had included educational materials in their emergency planning. When asked about priorities in limited packing scenarios, many parents listed numerous comfort items for children but had not considered basic educational resources—a perspective that often shifts dramatically during actual extended emergencies when cognitive engagement becomes crucial for psychological wellbeing.

These approaches create educational resilience that maintains children's developmental progression despite significant disruption to normal structures. The resulting continuity serves not just academic advancement but broader psychological needs for meaning, purpose, and growth that remain essential during challenging circumstances.

This perspective recognizes education not as a luxury to be abandoned during emergencies but as an essential component of human resilience, particularly for developing minds. By maintaining adaptable learning frameworks during disruptions, we provide children with crucial psychological anchors that support overall wellbeing beyond the specific knowledge being developed.

As you consider your family's preparedness strategy, evaluate whether you've addressed educational continuity with the same seriousness as physical needs. Have you developed adaptable learning approaches that function without institutional support? Do you maintain appropriate non-electronic educational resources as part of your emergency supplies? Have you identified how necessary emergency activities could incorporate meaningful learning opportunities? These educational preparations often determine long-term impacts on children's development more significantly than many physical preparations that receive greater attention in conventional preparedness planning.

Hearts and Minds: Psychological Support Through Crisis

Perhaps the most consequential aspect of children's emergency experience—yet often the least addressed in preparedness literature—involves the psychological impact of disruption on developing minds. How children interpret and integrate crisis experiences shapes not just their immediate coping but their long-term relationship with adversity, uncertainty, and their own capability amid challenge.

My friend Sophia emphasizes this critical dimension: "Children can emerge from significant disruption either psychologically strengthened or wounded, depending largely on how their experiences are framed, supported, and processed with caring adults. The same objective circumstances can produce entirely different psychological outcomes based on the emotional scaffolding provided."

This understanding—that children's subjective experience of crisis matters as much as objective circumstances—highlights the importance of deliberate psychological support strategies during emergencies. The most effective approaches typically incorporate several key elements that protect psychological wellbeing while building emotional resilience:

Age-appropriate explanations of circumstances that provide honest information without overwhelming detail. Children need sufficient understanding to make sense of their experiences without being burdened with complexities beyond their developmental capacity to process.

During a community evacuation from approaching wildfires, I observed how different communication approaches affected children's psychological responses. Families who provided simple, truthful explanations appropriate to their children's developmental stages generally maintained better emotional regulation than those who either provided no explanation (creating anxiety through mysterious circumstances) or shared overwhelming details (creating anxiety through excessive information).

Emotional validation that acknowledges and normalizes feelings about disruption without magnifying them. Children need permission to experience their authentic emotional responses while receiving assurance that such feelings are normal, manageable, and not themselves dangerous.

My neighbor Ruth describes her approach as "making room for feelings without letting them take over." She created regular "feeling check-ins" during disruptions where family members could express their emotional experiences without judgment, followed by simple coping activities appropriate to different emotional states—physical movement for anxiety, creative expression for confusion, connection for fear.

Maintained routines that provide psychological anchoring despite changed circumstances. Even simple predictable patterns can create crucial psychological stability during otherwise chaotic experiences, giving children orientation points that support emotional regulation.

During an extended power outage that significantly disrupted normal household functioning, I watched several families create improvised but consistent routines that maintained remarkable psychological stability for their children despite challenging physical conditions. Even basic predictable rhythms—regular meal times, consistent evening activities, predictable sleep arrangements—provided structural support for emotional wellbeing amid significant disruption.

Agency opportunities appropriate to developmental capabilities that allow children to contribute meaningfully to family response. Children who participate in emergency response through manageable, consequential tasks maintain better psychological function than those treated as helpless dependents requiring complete protection.

My friend Elena involves her children in age-appropriate emergency responsibilities—her teenager manages communication systems, her middle-schooler organizes supplies, her youngest takes charge of monitoring battery-powered lighting. These roles provide not just practical assistance but crucial psychological benefits through purposeful contribution to family welfare during challenging circumstances.

Processing frameworks that help children integrate emergency experiences into healthy narratives rather than traumatic ones. How children understand and story their experiences significantly impacts long-term psychological outcomes, making meaning-making support a crucial component of emotional care during disruptions.

During a community recovery program following a destructive flood, I participated in a children's activity that helped them create illustrated books about their experiences. The facilitators provided thoughtful guidance that helped the children construct narratives emphasizing not just what had been lost but what had been discovered—about themselves, their families, and their communities—through the challenging experience. This meaning-making process visibly transformed how many children related to their emergency experiences.

These approaches create psychological resilience that helps children navigate disruption without developing traumatic responses that could affect their long-term relationship with uncertainty. The resulting emotional capabilities serve them not just during specific emergencies but throughout lives that will inevitably include various challenges and difficulties.

As my friend Sophia notes: "The goal isn't raising children who never feel afraid, sad, or confused during emergencies—these are normal, healthy responses to difficult circumstances. The goal is raising children who know these feelings are manageable, temporary, and not the entirety of their experience even during significant challenges. This confidence in their emotional capability alongside their practical skills creates true resilience."

This balanced approach recognizes that psychological preparation matters as much as physical readiness—particularly for developing minds still forming their fundamental relationships with challenge, uncertainty, and their own capabilities amid difficulty. By attending thoughtfully to the emotional dimensions of children's emergency experiences, we protect not just their immediate wellbeing but their long-term psychological development through whatever challenges they may face.

The Protection Paradox: Safety Without Helplessness

Perhaps the most nuanced challenge in preparing children for uncertainty involves navigating what I call the "protection paradox"—the tension between keeping children safe and developing their independent capabilities. Overemphasize protection, and we raise children unprepared for self-sufficiency; overemphasize independence, and we may expose children to inappropriate risks or responsibilities beyond their developmental readiness.

This balancing act becomes even more complex in emergency contexts, where normal risk parameters shift and children's capabilities may suddenly become crucial components of family resilience rather than developmental exercises for the future. How we navigate this tension shapes not just children's emergency readiness but their fundamental relationship with their own capabilities and limitations.

This approach—developing capability within appropriate protective frameworks rather than maximizing either protection or independence alone—creates children who understand both their growing competencies and their legitimate limitations. The most effective strategies typically incorporate several key elements that balance safety with capacity development. Graduated responsibility progression that systematically expands children's capability zones through appropriate challenges should be matched to developmental readiness. Rather than sudden emergency skill requirements or continuous overprotection, this approach creates progressive competence through manageable stretching experiences.

During a community resilience program, I watched children of different ages engage with increasingly complex emergency skills—from basic fire safety for younger children to comprehensive emergency response protocols for teenagers. The graduated nature of these experiences built capability without premature responsibility, creating confidence through appropriate challenge rather than either anxiety through overextension or limitation through excessive protection.

Clear distinction between adult responsibilities and appropriate child roles during emergencies. Children need both protection from inappropriate burdens and opportunities for meaningful contribution, requiring thoughtful frameworks that distinguish between adult accountability and valuable child participation.

WHAT ABOUT THE CHILDREN?

My neighbor Sarah established clear emergency responsibility boundaries with her children through what she called "capability conversations"—ongoing discussions about which aspects of emergency response belonged to adults and which represented appropriate child domains. These distinctions protected her children from inappropriate responsibility while still honoring their developing capabilities through meaningful roles.

Skill development separate from scenario application, allowing capability building without premature emergency framing. Children can develop numerous valuable competencies through ordinary activities without requiring disturbing context about why these skills might someday prove crucial.

During a children's summer program focused on practical skills, I observed how children enthusiastically learned fire-building, outdoor cooking, basic first aid, and water purification without any framing around disaster scenarios. The skills developed just as effectively through adventure frameworks as they would have through emergency preparation contexts, but without corresponding anxiety about why such capabilities might become necessary.

Safety skills that emphasize discernment rather than rigid rules, developing judgment alongside specific practices. The most resilient children learn not just what to do in predetermined scenarios but how to assess and respond to novel situations through principled understanding rather than procedural memorization.

My friend Elena teaches what she calls "thinking safety" rather than just rule-following. Her children learn not only specific practices but the underlying principles that inform them, allowing flexible application across varying circumstances. This approach creates adaptive capability rather than brittle procedural responses that may fail when actual conditions don't match predicted scenarios.

Appropriate emotion management regarding safety concerns, modeling healthy vigilance without anxiety transmission. How adults frame and discuss potential dangers significantly impacts how children relate emotionally to risk, uncertainty, and their own safety practices.

During a workshop on communicating with children about emergency preparation, I emphasized the crucial distinction between appropriate seriousness and anxiety-producing urgency. Adults who present safety considerations with calm importance rather than fearful intensity generally raise children with healthier relationships to potential risks—neither dismissive of genuine concerns nor preoccupied with hypothetical dangers.

These balanced approaches create children who understand both their genuine capabilities and their legitimate need for protection in different contexts—a nuanced self-awareness that serves them well during actual emergencies. Rather than either helpless dependence or premature self-reliance, they develop appropriate agency within realistic recognition of their developmental stage.

As my friend Thomas notes: "The most prepared children aren't those who have been completely protected from all potential harm, nor those prematurely burdened with adult responsibilities. They're children who have developed genuine capabilities within appropriate protective frameworks, who understand both what they can handle and when they need assistance. This balanced self-awareness creates true resilience in challenging circumstances."

This perspective recognizes that genuine safety emerges not from maximum protection but from developing appropriate capability within necessary boundaries. By thoughtfully navigating the protection paradox, we raise children who can participate meaningfully in family emergency response without inappropriate responsibility—contributing to collective resilience while continuing their essential developmental processes.

Raising Little Commandos vs. Raising Resilient Humans

I first met Tyler and his eight-year-old son at a community emergency preparedness fair where organizers were demonstrating child-appropriate preparation activities. Tyler approached a display with visible skepticism, his son trailing behind wearing a miniature tactical vest complete with multiple pouches and what appeared to be a child-sized survival knife.

"We don't do arts and crafts," Tyler announced dismissively, gesturing toward the table where children were creating personal emergency contact cards decorated with colored markers. "We train. Jason here can already field-strip my backup firearm and has memorized three different escape routes from our property."

An organizer nodded pleasantly. "That's certainly one approach," she said, before asking Jason directly, "What do you do when you feel scared about emergencies?"

The boy's face went blank, his eyes darting toward his father before answering with rehearsed precision, "Fear is a weakness. We eliminate the threat and execute the mission."

Later that evening, the organizer shared her concerns about the interaction. "That child has been trained in procedures but not prepared as a person," she observed. "He's being raised as a miniature commando, not a resilient human being with both capabilities and appropriate emotions."

This encounter captures a crucial distinction in approaches to raising children with emergency preparedness. One path emphasizes tactical skills, procedural responses, and emotional suppression—raising children as miniature operators oriented toward threats and missions. The other develops practical capabilities within broader human development, including emotional intelligence, adaptable thinking, and appropriate agency—raising children as resilient persons equipped to navigate uncertainty while maintaining their essential humanity.

The tactical child-raising approach typically emphasizes:

*Procedure memorization over principle understanding, training children to follow specific protocols rather than comprehend the reasoning that might allow adaptation to unexpected circumstances

*Adult-mimicking equipment and terminology that create the appearance of preparation without developmentally appropriate foundations

*Emotion suppression framed as "mental toughness," teaching children to deny rather than appropriately manage natural feelings about challenging circumstances

*Scenario-specific responses rather than adaptive thinking capabilities that function across diverse situations

*Security priorities that overshadow broader developmental needs, focusing primarily on physical survival while neglecting psychological, social, and emotional dimensions

The resilient human-raising approach typically develops:

Foundational principles that inform flexible responses across varying circumstances, emphasizing understanding over mere procedural compliance

Age-appropriate skills that build genuine capability within developmental readiness rather than miniaturized adult preparations

Emotional intelligence that acknowledges and appropriately manages authentic feelings rather than suppressing them

Adaptive thinking capabilities that create functional responses to novel situations rather than just rehearsed scenarios

Integrated development that addresses emergency preparation within broader human needs, recognizing that children require more than survival skills to truly thrive amid uncertainty

The differences between these approaches become starkly apparent during actual emergencies, when children raised as "little commandos" often struggle with unexpected circumstances, emotional responses, or situations requiring adaptive rather than procedural thinking. Meanwhile, children raised with integrated resilience typically navigate challenges more effectively, maintaining both practical capability and psychological wellbeing through disruption.

My friend Sophia observes that the tactical approach often reflects adult anxiety more than thoughtful child development: "Parents who focus exclusively on training tactical responses in children are frequently managing their own fears about uncertainty through the illusion of control. Real preparation means raising children who can think adaptively, manage emotions appropriately, and maintain their essential humanity even during challenging circumstances."

This balanced approach recognizes that genuine resilience emerges not from procedural training alone but from integrated development of both practical capabilities and human qualities that maintain well-being through difficulty. The resulting preparation serves children not just during specific emergency scenarios but throughout lives inevitably filled with various challenges and uncertainties.

As you consider how to prepare the children in your life for an uncertain future, reflect on whether your approach leans toward creating little commandos or resilient humans. Are you focusing primarily on tactical skills and procedural responses, or developing integrated capabilities within broader human development? Are you teaching children to suppress emotions or manage them appropriately? Are you training for specific scenarios or developing adaptive thinking that functions across diverse challenges?

The most prepared children aren't junior survivalists equipped with miniature tactical gear and rehearsed protocols, but developing humans with appropriate skills, emotional intelligence, and adaptive capabilities that serve them regardless of what specific futures they may face. By raising resilient people rather than little commandos, we prepare children not just to survive whatever challenges emerge but to maintain their essential humanity while navigating them—perhaps the most important preparation we can provide for an uncertain future.

15

Beyond Survival by Creating the World We Want

The storm that changed everything for our community arrived with little warning in late October—an unseasonable blizzard that collided with a warm front to create what meteorologists blandly termed a "precipitation event" and what we experienced as apocalyptic ice followed by three feet of wet, heavy snow. Kind of *The Perfect Storm 2*. (Shouldn't they do that sequel?)

The resulting devastation took down not just our power grid but virtually every system we'd taken for granted: communications, transportation, water delivery, and the intricate just-in-time supply chains that kept our grocery shelves stocked.

For the first seventy-two hours, our community operated in pure survival mode. Those with generators shared power for critical medical equipment. Those with woodstoves opened their homes as warming centers. Those with preserved food and water established feeding stations. We were, by both necessity and long practice, focused entirely on making it through each day intact.

By day ten, with regional infrastructure still in shambles and outside help unable to reach our isolated area, something remarkable began to happen. The conversation at our community gathering spots gradually shifted from "How do we survive this?" to "How do we want to live through this?" It was a subtle but profound transformation—the moment when crisis response evolved into intentional rebuilding.

I remember sitting in Ruth's kitchen—her woodstove cranking out blessed heat while two dozen neighbors crowded around with steaming mugs of coffee and tea—when the conversation took this decisive turn. Tom, our town's retired engineer, had just finished updating everyone on the latest damage assessment when Ruth asked a question that changed everything.

"Before we automatically rebuild everything exactly as it was," she said, stirring a massive pot of venison stew, "shouldn't we talk about what wasn't working so well before all this happened?"

The room fell silent for a moment before erupting into what became a three-hour conversation about everything from our town's inadequate senior housing to the food insecurity that had plagued many families even before the storm. People who had never spoken at town meetings suddenly found their voices, offering insights and suggestions that would have been dismissed as impractical just weeks earlier.

By midnight, impromptu committees had formed around different aspects of rebuilding, each tasked with developing plans that addressed both immediate needs and longer-term community resilience. As I walked home that night, picking my way carefully along snow-packed streets illuminated only by stars, I realized we had crossed a threshold. We were no longer disaster victims waiting for restoration of normality. We had become architects of a new normal, one we were deliberately choosing rather than passively receiving.

That night marked the beginning of what I now recognize as the most important phase of emergency response—the transition from survival to intentional rebuilding. It's a phase rarely discussed in preparedness literature, which tends to focus overwhelmingly on the dramatic early stages of disaster while giving little attention to the extended, complex process of reconstruction that inevitably follows any significant disruption.

Yet it's precisely this reconstruction phase that determines whether a disaster becomes merely a traumatic memory or a transformative opportunity. The choices communities make during rebuilding—often under the radar of dramatic news coverage—shape their fundamental resilience for decades to come. And these choices have historically been heavily influenced by women working deliberately to create not just recovery but improvement—building back not just what was, but what should be.

My own journey through this process has transformed not just my community but my understanding of what true preparedness actually means. The tactical skills and material preparations that helped us survive those first chaotic days proved far less important than the social fabric we'd been quietly weaving for years before any storm clouds appeared. It was that fabric—the relationships, trust networks, and shared values—that ultimately determined not just whether we would survive, but how we would rebuild.

This final chapter shares what I've learned about this crucial but neglected aspect of preparedness—the part that begins when immediate survival needs are met, and the deeper work of creating community resilience truly begins. It's the chapter I wish I'd read before facing our own disaster, and the wisdom I hope you'll carry forward long after the excitement of stockpiling supplies and learning tactical skills has faded.

Because ultimately, preparedness isn't about surviving the end of the world—it's about building the capacity to create the world we actually want to live in, regardless of what storms may come.

Moving from Crisis Response to Community Rebuilding

The day we realized our "temporary" emergency shelter would need to become semi-permanent housing for nearly thirty families whose homes had been destroyed, I watched a fascinating transformation unfold. The same space that had functioned adequately as an emergency refuge suddenly seemed hopelessly inadequate for ongoing community life.

"People need more than cots and meal times," Ruth observed as we surveyed the crowded gymnasium. "They need privacy, dignity, purpose, and some sense of normalcy. We need to stop thinking about this as emergency management and start thinking about it as community creation."

Her distinction perfectly captured the fundamental shift required when moving from crisis response to sustained rebuilding—a transition that demands entirely different approaches, skills, and priorities. The capabilities that serve communities well during initial disaster response often prove insufficient or even counterproductive during extended recovery, creating a dangerous gap precisely when long-term outcomes hang in the balance.

I've now witnessed this transition through multiple community emergencies, and the pattern remains remarkably consistent. The initial response phase typically emphasizes:

- Centralized decision-making for rapid deployment
   - Resource distribution based on immediate survival needs
   - Short-term solutions to acute problems
   - Technical expertise for system restoration
   - Command structures that prioritize efficiency

These approaches serve critical purposes during immediate emergency response, helping communities address urgent threats to life and safety. But they become increasingly problematic as recovery extends beyond initial stabilization, eventually creating friction rather than function if maintained too long without evolution.

Effective rebuilding phases typically shift toward approaches that emphasize:

- Participatory decision processes that build community investment
   - Resource allocation addressing both short and long-term resilience
   - Sustainable solutions to underlying vulnerabilities
   - Social expertise for relationship rehabilitation
   - Collaborative structures that prioritize inclusivity

This transition rarely happens automatically. In the absence of deliberate effort to shift approaches, many communities remain stuck in emergency response patterns long after their utility has expired—creating dependency, frustration, and missed opportunities for genuine improvement.

My friend Elena describes this critical juncture perfectly: "The moment when outside emergency managers start packing up is precisely when the most important work begins. That's when communities either fall back into recreating their pre-disaster vulnerabilities or seize the opportunity to address the underlying issues that made the disaster so devastating in the first place."

Her observation highlights something crucial about effective rebuilding: it requires communities to recognize and navigate this transition point consciously rather than drifting through it without deliberate direction. The communities that emerge stronger from disasters typically do so because they actively shift their approach when immediate survival is no longer the primary concern.

In our own community's experience, this transition began with small but significant changes in how we organized our collective efforts. The emergency response team that had effectively managed initial survival needs gradually evolved into a recovery coordination network with very different structure and function:

- *Daily emergency briefings became weekly community planning sessions*
  - *Centralized resource distribution evolved into cooperative exchange systems*
  - *Technical repair teams expanded to include social reconstruction groups*
  - *Short-term emergency shelter transformed into intentional interim housing*
  - *Command hierarchies shifted toward facilitative leadership*

approaches

These changes didn't happen overnight or without friction. Those who had effectively led initial response efforts sometimes struggled to adapt their approaches for the different requirements of extended rebuilding. Community members accustomed to emergency directives occasionally resisted the slower, more inclusive processes rebuilding required. The transition demanded patience, flexibility, and persistent commitment to evolution rather than simply maintaining what had worked during crisis.

The key insight emerging from our experience echoes what research on disaster recovery consistently demonstrates: effective rebuilding requires a deliberate transition in both mindset and methodology. Communities that consciously navigate this shift typically create more sustainable recovery than those that either remain stuck in emergency response patterns or prematurely abandon coordination efforts altogether.

For my own part, I found this transition surprisingly challenging despite understanding its importance intellectually. The urgency and clarity of emergency response had provided a certain adrenaline-fueled simplicity that rebuilding processes lacked. The complex, nuanced, sometimes frustratingly slow work of collaborative reconstruction initially felt less immediately rewarding than the dramatic life-saving efforts of early disaster response.

Yet I gradually recognized that this less glamorous phase ultimately determined whether our community would merely survive the disaster or genuinely thrive beyond it. The patient, persistent work of rebuilding—identifying underlying vulnerabilities, developing sustainable solutions, building inclusive systems—created resilience that no amount of emergency response capability alone could provide.

As you consider your own preparedness journey, I encourage you to extend your thinking beyond the dramatic early phases of disaster that dominate preparedness literature. How might your community navigate the transition from emergency response to intentional rebuilding? What structures might facilitate this evolution when immediate survival is no longer the primary concern? Who might lead different aspects of reconstruction based on capability rather than traditional authority?

These questions receive far less attention than tactical response skills or material preparation, yet they ultimately determine whether communities merely weather disasters or transform through them. The answers won't make for exciting prepper conference presentations or dramatic survival stories, but they may well prove more important to your community's long-term resilience than many more dramatic preparations that receive greater attention.

After all, as one of our elders wisely noted during our own rebuilding process: "Anyone can help people survive a disaster. The real challenge is helping them create something worth surviving for."

Women's Historical Role in Post-Disaster Reconstruction

When I began researching community recovery patterns following various disasters, I discovered something rarely mentioned in conventional emergency management literature: women have historically played disproportionately influential roles in post-disaster reconstruction, often transforming their communities in ways that extended far beyond simple recovery.

This pattern emerges consistently across diverse cultures, time periods, and disaster types—from the Women's Emergency Committee that led Little Rock's recovery from the economic devastation of school closures during desegregation, to the women-led reconstruction efforts following the 2004 Indian Ocean tsunami, to the "Women of the Storm" who fundamentally reshaped New Orleans' rebuilding after Hurricane Katrina.

These weren't isolated anomalies but examples of a persistent historical pattern where women's leadership—often operating outside traditional power structures—created recovery approaches that addressed not just physical reconstruction but deeper community resilience building. The resulting efforts typically emphasized aspects of rebuilding that official recovery programs frequently overlooked: social connection restoration, equitable resource distribution, attention to vulnerable population needs, and integration of psychological healing alongside physical reconstruction.

I've witnessed this pattern firsthand through multiple community recoveries, most notably during the extended rebuilding that followed our region's devastating ice storm. While official recovery efforts focused primarily on infrastructure restoration and economic resumption, a network of predominantly female community leaders simultaneously developed parallel initiatives addressing dimensions official programs largely ignored:

Martha, a retired school administrator, created a "community continuity" program that preserved social connections through intentional gatherings, shared meals, and structured opportunities for collective processing of the disaster experience. These efforts maintained critical relationship networks that proved essential for sustaining community cohesion throughout the extended rebuilding process.

Elena established wellness circles that addressed psychological impacts alongside physical recovery needs—creating space for trauma processing that prevented the long-term mental health deterioration many disaster-affected communities experience when emotional dimensions receive insufficient attention.

Ruth coordinated a resource matching system that connected specific household needs with appropriate community resources through relationship-based distribution rather than bureaucratic allocation—creating more responsive and personalized assistance than official programs could provide through standardized processes.

Sarah developed intergenerational support networks that specifically addressed the needs of both elderly community members and young families, two groups often inadequately served by conventional recovery programs despite their particular vulnerabilities during extended reconstruction.

These women-led initiatives operated largely in parallel to official recovery efforts rather than through them, creating complementary systems that addressed dimensions conventional approaches typically neglect. Their work didn't replace traditional reconstruction but substantially expanded it, transforming simple recovery into holistic community rebuilding that strengthened collective resilience beyond pre-disaster levels.

This pattern reflects women's historical experiences managing household and community well-being through various disruptions. The resulting expertise—maintaining social cohesion during stress, stretching limited resources through efficient allocation, addressing psychological needs alongside physical ones, integrating diverse capabilities toward common goals—creates approaches particularly suited to the complex challenges post-disaster reconstruction presents.

For my own part, witnessing women's leadership through our community's rebuilding process completely transformed my understanding of what genuine recovery requires. Before experiencing disaster firsthand, I had conceptualized community resilience primarily through material dimensions—infrastructure hardening, resource stockpiling, technical system redundancy. But our actual recovery experience demonstrated that social dimensions ultimately proved more determinative of genuine resilience than physical preparations alone.

The women leading these social reconstruction efforts rarely received official recognition or formal authority within traditional recovery structures. Their work often happened through informal networks, kitchen table meetings, and relationship-based systems operating parallel to official programs. Yet their impact extended far beyond their formal position, creating dimensions of recovery that ultimately proved essential for genuine community rehabilitation.

This historical pattern offers important insight for communities preparing for potential disasters. Effective resilience building requires developing not just physical readiness but social reconstruction capability—the capacity to rebuild relationship networks, trust systems, psychological well-being, and collective purpose when disruption inevitably affects these dimensions. This capability has traditionally developed through women's community leadership, creating resilience that extends beyond what physical preparation alone can provide.

As you consider your own community's preparedness, I encourage you to examine whether you've balanced physical readiness with social reconstruction capability. Have you identified individuals with the skills and connections to lead social rehabilitation alongside physical rebuilding? Does your community maintain relationship networks that could facilitate recovery beyond what official programs might provide? Have you developed approaches for addressing psychological impacts alongside material ones? These social dimensions often determine actual recovery outcomes more decisively than many physical preparations that receive greater attention in conventional emergency planning.

After all, as Ruth wisely observed during our own rebuilding process: "Restored power lines without restored human connections create buildings with electricity but communities still living in darkness."

Incorporating Lessons Learned into New Social Structures

The most remarkable aspect of our community's rebuilding process wasn't what we physically reconstructed but what we deliberately redesigned based on insights from the disaster experience. The conversations that began in Ruth's kitchen that snowy night eventually evolved into substantive changes in how our community organized everything from food systems to elder care, emergency response to educational approaches.

These changes didn't emerge from theoretical planning but from practical lessons revealed through disaster experience—

insights that might have remained invisible without the stress test that stripped away our illusions about how resilient our pre-disaster systems actually were. The resulting adaptations transformed vulnerability into capability through deliberate application of hard-earned wisdom rather than simple restoration of what existed before.

Several examples particularly stand out as illustrations of how disaster experiences translated into concrete community improvements. Our local food system underwent fundamental restructuring after the storm revealed dangerous vulnerabilities in centralized distribution. What began as emergency community meals evolved into a permanent cooperative arrangement between local producers and consumers, creating redundant supply chains, distributed storage systems, and production diversity that enhanced food security far beyond pre-disaster levels. This system now serves our community more effectively during normal times while maintaining substantial resilience against potential future disruptions.

Child and elder care networks developed entirely new structures based on storm experiences that demonstrated both particular vulnerabilities among these populations and potential resources that remained underutilized. The resulting intergenerational support system matches needs with capabilities across age groups, creating care redundancy that functions more effectively than previous segregated approaches while building cross-generational relationships that strengthen overall community cohesion.

Emergency response capabilities evolved from the improvised neighborhood support networks that emerged during the disaster into formal Community Emergency Response Teams with trained volunteers, established protocols, and distributed resource caches. These teams now serve both emergency functions and regular community needs, maintaining capability through consistent engagement rather than separate preparation activities.

Housing approaches incorporated lessons about both physical resilience and social sustainability, leading to development of neighborhood clusters with shared resources rather than purely individualized housing restoration. These designs intentionally balance privacy needs with community connection, creating living arrangements that enhance both daily quality of life and emergency response capability.

These adaptations represent more than simple recovery—they demonstrate genuine community learning that transformed disaster experience into improved social structures. Rather than merely rebuilding what existed before, our community deliberately incorporated insights from the disruption into new approaches that addressed previously unrecognized vulnerabilities while building on strengths that emerged during crisis.

This transformation wasn't automatic or inevitable. It required deliberate processes that facilitated collective reflection, shared learning, and intentional application of insights rather than reactive rebuilding driven primarily by restoration urgency. The communities I've observed that achieve this transformation typically develop specific approaches that support learning integration:

Structured reflection opportunities throughout rebuilding create space for identifying both vulnerabilities exposed and capabilities revealed during disaster response. These processes—community conversations, facilitated dialogues, documentation efforts—preserve critical insights that might otherwise be lost as rebuilding proceeds and memories fade.

Cross-sector integration mechanisms connect insights from different domains into coherent adaptation approaches rather than isolated improvements. These connections—task forces with diverse representation, integrated planning processes, holistic resilience frameworks—prevent the fragmented responses that often characterize recovery efforts without deliberate coordination.

Implementation pathways translate identified improvements into concrete changes rather than merely documented recommendations. These mechanisms—phased development plans, pilot projects with expansion frameworks, adaptive management approaches—create practical application rather than theoretical proposals that never achieve actual implementation.

Feedback systems monitor adaptation effectiveness and enable continued refinement based on performance rather than assuming initial redesigns will necessarily achieve intended outcomes. These evaluation processes—structured assessment, regular adaptation reviews, continuous improvement frameworks—maintain implementation quality throughout extended rebuilding processes.

These approaches transform rebuilding from simple recovery into genuine community evolution—applying disaster-revealed insights to create improved systems rather than merely restoring previous vulnerabilities. The resulting adaptations enhance resilience not just against similar future events but across diverse potential disruptions through fundamental capability enhancement rather than hazard-specific protections.

My own participation in this evolutionary process transformed not just my community but my understanding of what genuine resilience actually requires. Before experiencing disaster firsthand, I had conceptualized preparedness primarily as protective capability—measures that prevent or minimize disruption impacts. Our rebuilding experience demonstrated that adaptive capacity—the ability to evolve based on experiences—ultimately creates more sustainable resilience than protective measures alone.

This insight doesn't diminish the importance of conventional preparedness, which certainly reduces initial disaster impacts and creates foundation for effective response. But it recognizes that even the most thorough preparation cannot prevent all disruption, making adaptive capacity—the ability to learn from and evolve through experiences—an equally essential dimension of genuine resilience.

As you consider your own community's preparedness, I encourage you to examine whether you've balanced protective measures with adaptive capacity development. Have you created processes for capturing and applying insights when disruptions inevitably occur despite preparations? Does your community maintain mechanisms for translating experiences into improved systems rather than simple restoration? Have you developed approaches for integrating learning across different sectors rather than isolated domain improvements? These adaptive capabilities often determine long-term resilience more decisively than protective measures alone yet receive far less attention in conventional preparedness discussions.

The Ethics of Preparedness: Responsibility to the Wider Community

The most challenging conversation during our community's recovery process occurred not around technical rebuilding questions but ethical ones—specifically, the tension between individual preparedness and collective responsibility that emergency situations inevitably expose. This discussion began when Thomas, who had maintained extensive personal preparations, made an uncomfortable observation during a community meeting.

"I've been thinking about something that's been bothering me since the storm," he said quietly. "I had three months of food stored for my family while children two blocks away went hungry those first days. I had a generator running while someone down the street couldn't power their oxygen concentrator. My preparations kept my family comfortable while others suffered significantly. I'm not sure how to feel about that."

His honesty opened a conversation our community had needed but avoided—the complex ethical questions surrounding preparedness that extend beyond technical considerations into moral territory. What responsibilities do prepared individuals have toward their broader community? At what point does self-protection become problematic isolation? How do we balance personal readiness with collective obligation?

These questions rarely appear in conventional preparedness literature, which typically frames preparation as purely individual responsibility without examining the ethical dimensions that actual disasters inevitably reveal. Yet the answers communities develop—whether explicitly through thoughtful dialogue or implicitly through default patterns—profoundly shape both immediate disaster response and longer-term recovery trajectories.

Through multiple community recovery experiences, I've observed that the most effective approach balances individual readiness with collective responsibility through what might be called "concentric preparedness"—an expanding circle of resilience that begins with personal capability but deliberately extends outward rather than creating isolated security islands amid broader vulnerability.

This approach differs significantly from both extreme positions sometimes advocated in preparedness communities. It rejects the purely individualistic stance that sees preparation as solely personal responsibility with no obligation toward broader community resilience. But it equally avoids the completely collectivist position that eliminates individual preparation in favor of purely communal approaches.

Instead, concentric preparedness creates balanced capability through several expanding responsibility layers. Individual and household preparedness forms the foundation—developing personal capabilities that prevent prepared individuals from immediately becoming assistance burdens during initial disaster phases. This core readiness creates self-sufficiency for immediate needs while establishing capacity that can potentially extend beyond household boundaries as circumstances permit.

Neighborhood and community connection builds the second layer—developing relationship networks that facilitate resource sharing, capability exchange, and collective response when needs inevitably exceed individual capacity. These connections create mutual support systems more resilient than either isolated household preparation or centralized assistance programs alone.

Vulnerable population consideration forms the third layer—

developing specific approaches for supporting those with limited preparation capability due to resource constraints, physical limitations, or other factors beyond individual control. These deliberate support systems address ethical obligations toward those who cannot achieve full self-sufficiency regardless of individual responsibility.

Broader community integration creates the fourth layer—developing connections between prepared individuals and formal response systems that enhance collective capability rather than creating parallel isolated approaches. These integrations maximize overall community resilience through complementary rather than competing preparation strategies.

Each layer builds upon rather than replaces the previous ones, creating resilience that begins with individual responsibility but extends deliberately outward rather than creating protected enclaves amid broader vulnerability. The resulting approach acknowledges both personal preparation obligations and wider community responsibilities without sacrificing either dimension.

Here's something crucial about ethical preparedness: genuine resilience emerges not from choosing between individual readiness and collective responsibility, but from integrating these dimensions through deliberate connection. The prepared individuals who contribute most effectively to community resilience maintain personal readiness that creates capacity beyond immediate household needs rather than merely establishing isolated security regardless of surrounding conditions.

My own journey through this ethical territory has involved considerable evolution. I began my preparedness path primarily focused on household security, developing capabilities intended primarily to protect my immediate family from potential disruptions. As I experienced actual disasters and participated in community recovery processes, I gradually recognized that this approach—while certainly better than no preparation—created limitations that undermined both practical effectiveness and ethical comfort with my preparation choices.

This recognition led to fundamental shifts in my preparedness approach: I began deliberately developing surplus capacity beyond immediate household needs, creating resource margins specifically intended for sharing rather than exclusively extended personal security.

I also established connections with neighbors and community members before disasters struck, creating relationship networks through which resources could flow during disruptions rather than trying to build these connections amid crisis.

And I integrated my personal preparations with community systems rather than developing purely parallel approaches, enhancing collective capability through complementary readiness rather than isolated security.

Finally, I participated in initiatives supporting preparation among vulnerable populations, helping develop capability among those with limited personal resources rather than merely enhancing my own security regardless of surrounding conditions.

These adjustments didn't diminish my household's resilience but actually enhanced it by addressing vulnerabilities that purely individualistic preparation inevitably creates. The resulting approach created more sustainable security through balanced attention to both personal readiness and community connection, recognizing that genuine resilience requires integration rather than isolation.

As you consider your own preparedness ethics, I encourage you to examine whether you've developed appropriate balance between individual capability and community responsibility. Have you created preparation margins that allow resource sharing rather than exclusively extended personal security? Are you connected with community members through established relationships that facilitate mutual support before disasters occur? Have you integrated personal readiness with broader response systems rather than developing purely parallel approaches? These ethical considerations often determine both practical effectiveness and personal comfort with preparation choices, yet receive far less attention than technical aspects of readiness.

After all, as the measure of good preparation isn't just how well it protects you, but how it affects who you become in relation to others when they need you most.

The Final Showdown: Tactical Tim vs. Prepared Penelope

If Hollywood ever makes a disaster movie based on actual preparedness realities rather than dramatic fantasies, the climactic scene might look something like what unfolded in our community center during day fifteen of the extended power outage that followed the ice storm. The encounter perfectly captured the contrast between stereotypical prepper approaches and what actually determines effectiveness during genuine community emergencies.

On one side stood Tim, whose tactical preparation had been legendary in our community for years before any actual disaster occurred. He had invested tens of thousands in specialized equipment, maintained elaborate security systems, accumulated impressive resource stockpiles, and frequently shared (sometimes unsolicited) advice about the coming collapse that would prove his approach superior to conventional preparedness. His tactical vest alone probably cost more than most people's entire emergency kits.

On the other side was Penelope, a kindergarten teacher and grandmother whose preparation had occurred with so little fanfare that most community members had no idea she had any emergency readiness until the actual disaster struck. Her unassuming demeanor and complete lack of tactical terminology had effectively rendered her preparedness invisible within a community that often associated readiness with more dramatic approaches.

The "showdown" began when our emergency shelter faced a critical volunteer shortage for the evening shift. Community members had been operating in rotation for over two weeks, and exhaustion was creating dangerous coverage gaps for essential functions. The coordinator called for additional volunteers during the afternoon briefing, leading to the exchange that perfectly crystallized the difference between performance preparation and practical capability.

Tim immediately listed the reasons he couldn't possibly help: he needed to return to his property before dark to maintain security protocols; his extensive resources required constant monitoring; his special generator system needed regular maintenance; his perimeter required evening checking. His preparation, ironically, had created obligations that prevented him from offering assistance precisely when the community most needed capable volunteers.

Penelope quietly signed up for the evening shift—her third that week—despite having her own household to maintain.

When someone asked how she managed to continuously help while keeping her own situation stable, her response captured a fundamental preparedness truth: "I built my systems to run without constant attention so I'd have capacity to help others, not just protect myself."

The contrast couldn't have been clearer. Tim's elaborate preparation had created brittle capability that required his constant presence, effectively removing his potential contribution from the broader community precisely when experienced assistance was most needed. Penelope's unassuming but thoughtful preparation had created stable self-sufficiency that allowed her capability to extend beyond her household, precisely the approach most valuable during extended community emergencies.

As the disaster weeks extended into the slow rebuilding process, this pattern continued. Tim remained largely absent from community recovery efforts, continuously explaining that his own complex systems required his full attention. Penelope became a quiet but persistent presence throughout reconstruction, her thoughtful capability supporting numerous initiatives that gradually rebuilt not just physical infrastructure but community cohesion.

The conclusion was both undramatic and profound: when genuine disaster struck, tactical gear and elaborate systems often proved less valuable than simple preparations administered with community awareness. The most effective preparedness wasn't that which looked most impressive before the disaster but that which created stable capability that could extend beyond household boundaries when actual needs emerged.

This observation isn't meant to completely dismiss more

intensive preparation, which certainly creates valuable capability under specific circumstances. But it highlights something crucial about effectiveness during actual community disruptions: preparation that creates isolated capability often proves less valuable than more modest readiness that allows resource and assistance flow beyond individual households.

The most effective preppers I've observed through multiple disasters rarely match stereotypical prepper images. They typically maintain:

Appropriate but not excessive resource reserves that create household stability without requiring constant management or generating excessive obligation that prevents broader contribution when community needs emerge

Simple, reliable systems that maintain function without demanding continuous attention, creating personal stability while preserving capacity for assistance beyond immediate household boundaries

Strong community connections established before disasters through ongoing relationship building rather than attempted during crises when trust development becomes substantially more difficult

Balanced security approaches that address legitimate concerns without creating isolation that undermines broader resilience through reduced cooperation opportunity

Adaptive rather than rigid protocols that accommodate changing circumstances rather than requiring precise adherence regardless of emerging community needs

These characteristics rarely create impressive prepper profiles. You won't find elaborate bug-out vehicle photos or tactical gear collections from these individuals, despite their demonstrated effectiveness when actual disasters occur. Their preparation emphasizes practical function over performance display, creating capability that serves both personal and community needs rather than isolated security that often proves surprisingly brittle when genuine disruption occurs.

As our community's recovery proceeded, Tim gradually began participating more in collective efforts—a transformation I observed with both surprise and appreciation. When I eventually asked what had changed his approach, his response revealed important self-awareness: "I realized my preparation was more about proving something than actually being ready for reality. When the real thing happened, I discovered I'd built a fortress that turned me into my own prisoner."

His honest reflection captures something many preparedness enthusiasts eventually discover through actual disaster experience: the most effective readiness creates capability that integrates with community resilience rather than isolating from it. This balanced approach serves both individual and collective needs more effectively than either complete self-sufficiency or total dependence on external assistance alone.

As you continue your own preparedness journey, I encourage you to periodically examine whether your approach creates genuine capability or performance display, adaptive capacity or rigid protocols, community integration or isolated security.

These distinctions often determine actual effectiveness more decisively than specific equipment, supplies, or systems when genuine disruptions occur.

After all, as Penelope wisely noted during one community rebuilding session: "The real emergency kit is the community we build together before disaster strikes. Everything else is just supplies."

So here we stand, at the end of a book that began with survival strategies and concludes with community building—a journey that parallels my own evolution from tactical preparation to resilience weaving. The distance between those starting and ending points represents the most important insight I've gained through years of both studying and experiencing actual disasters: true preparedness isn't about surviving apart from others but creating the capacity to thrive together regardless of what challenges emerge.

This perspective doesn't diminish the value of traditional preparedness elements—the practical skills, appropriate supplies, and personal capabilities that certainly enhance resilience during various disruptions. These elements create foundation for effective response and deserve the thoughtful attention they receive throughout this book. But they achieve their greatest potential when integrated within broader understanding of community resilience rather than isolated as purely individual protection.

The women who have quietly maintained family and community function through countless historical disruptions have always understood this truth. Their approaches—emphasizing practical skill development, resource stretching, relationship building, and adaptive capacity—create resilience that extends beyond household boundaries to enhance collective capability. The resulting preparation serves both personal and community needs more effectively than approaches creating isolated security regardless of surrounding conditions.

As climate instability increases disruption frequency while political polarization decreases institutional response capability, this balanced approach becomes increasingly essential for genuine resilience. Neither complete self-sufficiency nor total dependence on external assistance alone creates sustainable security amid the complex challenges emerging in our uncertain century. The most effective preparation integrates personal readiness with community connection, creating capability that serves both individual and collective needs through whatever disruptions may come.

My hope is that you'll carry forward the practical skills shared throughout these chapters while embracing the deeper wisdom they collectively reveal: that true preparedness emerges not from separating ourselves from vulnerability but from connecting through it. The relationships we build, the capabilities we share, and the communities we create ultimately determine our resilience more decisively than any supplies we store or skills we master in isolation.

After all, survival alone has never been the point. The true measure of our preparedness isn't just whether we personally endure whatever storms may come, but whether we contribute to creating the world we actually want to live in once those storms have passed.

That creation—the patient, persistent weaving of community resilience through both calm and chaos—represents the quiet revolution in preparedness that women have been leading since time immemorial. May you find your own place within that revolution, adding your unique thread to the resilient fabric we collectively create through both preparation for and recovery from whatever challenges our uncertain future may bring.

Because ultimately, the world we build together will prove far stronger than any we might attempt to secure alone.

16

Conclusion: The Preparedness Partnership

Throughout this book, we've explored the often overlooked aspects of preparedness that have traditionally fallen within women's domain—from resource management and community building to psychological resilience and practical sustainability. We've examined how these approaches complement rather than compete with more widely recognized tactical preparation, creating comprehensive readiness when properly integrated.

The core message emerging from these chapters isn't that one approach supersedes another, but that genuine resilience requires thoughtful integration of diverse preparedness perspectives. The tactical and the practical, the individual and the communal, the defensive and the sustaining—these seemingly opposite approaches actually create their greatest value when combined rather than when advocated in isolation.

This conclusion explores how we might deliberately bridge these divides to create truly comprehensive preparedness—

not through compromise that weakens both approaches, but through thoughtful integration that strengthens all participants. The same way I think we can bridge the divides between right wing and left wing preppers. The resulting partnership creates capabilities beyond what either perspective alone could provide, addressing the full spectrum of challenges communities actually face during both acute emergencies and extended recovery.

Bridging Gender Divides for Comprehensive Emergency Readiness

The preparedness community has long suffered from an unnecessary and ultimately counterproductive divide. On one side stand the stereotypically masculine approaches emphasizing tactical skills, security considerations, and specialized equipment. On the other side exist the traditionally feminine perspectives focusing on practical sustainability, resource management, and community cohesion. Each tends to view the other with a mixture of skepticism and occasional dismissal, creating artificial separation between complementary capabilities.

This division creates dangerous vulnerability precisely when integrated strength matters most. Communities facing actual emergencies require both immediate tactical response and sustained practical recovery, both security awareness and social cohesion, both specialized capability and adaptive resilience. The artificial separation between these approaches undermines comprehensive preparedness, leaving communities with partial readiness when complete integration would serve them far better.

Bridging this divide requires moving beyond simplistic

gender stereotypes toward recognition of complementary capabilities. While certain preparedness approaches have traditionally developed through gender-typical experiences, the capabilities themselves aren't inherently masculine or feminine but simply different aspects of comprehensive readiness. Individuals of any gender can and should develop skills across this spectrum, creating balanced capability rather than domain-restricted preparation.

Several key principles facilitate this integration when deliberately applied:

Mutual respect for diverse expertise creates foundation for productive collaboration. When tactical and practical preparedness practitioners acknowledge the legitimate value each approach contributes to comprehensive readiness, cooperative rather than competitive relationships become possible. This respect isn't mere politeness but genuine recognition that different domains require specialized expertise deserving acknowledgment regardless of traditional gender associations.

Comprehensive threat assessment beyond domain-specific focus reveals the full spectrum of challenges communities actually face. When preparedness conversations incorporate both dramatic acute emergencies and extended recovery challenges, both security concerns and sustainability requirements, both individual protection and community function, the resulting preparation addresses actual emergency experiences rather than artificially limited scenarios.

Skills exchange across traditional boundaries develops capability without unnecessary limitation. When tactical experts share security considerations with practical sustainability practitioners, and when resource management specialists share system development with tactical preparedness enthusiasts, both groups enhance their capability beyond domain-limited approaches. These exchanges don't erase specialization but complement it with expanded awareness.

Joint scenario development that incorporates diverse emergency phases reveals integration opportunities typically overlooked in domain-specific planning. When preparedness discussions include both immediate response and extended recovery, both dramatic intervention and sustained adaptation, the resulting scenarios demonstrate how different capabilities serve communities at different phases rather than competing for primacy across the entire emergency spectrum.

Complementary leadership recognition creates balanced authority distribution across emergency phases. When communities acknowledge that different challenges require different leadership capabilities, preparation can develop appropriate authority transitions as situations evolve from immediate tactical response through extended practical recovery. This recognition prevents the counterproductive authority conflicts that often undermine emergency management when single leadership approaches attempt to address all phases regardless of appropriateness.

These principles transform preparedness from competing approaches into complementary partnership—creating comprehensive readiness that serves communities throughout the full emergency cycle rather than exclusively during specific phases. The resulting integration acknowledges that genuine resilience requires both traditionally masculine and traditionally feminine perspectives, both tactical and practical approaches, both protective and sustaining capabilities.

This integration doesn't require abandoning specialized expertise or erasing meaningful differences between preparedness domains. The tactical specialist need not become a sustainability generalist, nor must the community builder develop security expertise beyond basic awareness. Rather, integration creates appreciation for different capabilities while facilitating appropriate collaboration across traditional boundaries—enhancing all approaches without undermining their distinct contributions.

The communities that demonstrate the most effective emergency response and recovery typically develop exactly this integrated approach—maintaining specialized capability while creating collaborative frameworks that deploy different expertise at appropriate phases. The resulting preparedness creates comprehensive resilience through partnership rather than competition, recognizing that diverse challenges require diverse capabilities distributed across emergency phases rather than universal approaches attempting to address all situations with limited tools.

How Combined Perspectives Create Truly Resilient Communities

When tactical and practical preparedness truly integrate rather than merely coexist, communities develop comprehensive resilience across the full emergency spectrum. This integration creates specific capabilities that neither approach alone can provide:

Seamless phase transitions between immediate response and extended recovery maintain continuous function throughout emergency evolution. When communities prepare for appropriate capability deployment across different emergency phases, transitions occur through planned progression rather than disruptive reorganization. Tactical response capabilities address immediate threats while practical sustainability systems simultaneously prepare for extended operations, creating continuity that isolated approaches cannot achieve.

During a severe regional ice storm, communities with integrated preparedness transitioned smoothly from initial emergency response to extended recovery operation. Security specialists who had trained alongside sustainability practitioners understood when their particular expertise should lead or support based on evolving conditions. Resource managers who had developed awareness of security considerations maintained appropriate protection throughout extended operations. The resulting integration created continuous capability without the disruptions communities with separated approaches typically experienced.

Appropriate resource allocation across different emergency requirements prevents counterproductive competition during resource constraints. When tactical and practical preparedness develop integrated rather than parallel supply systems, communities can deploy specific resources where they create maximum value throughout emergency evolution. This allocation prevents the protective/sustaining conflicts that often emerge when separated approaches compete for limited supplies despite serving different emergency phases.

Following widespread flooding that affected multiple communities simultaneously, those with integrated resource systems maintained better overall function throughout the extended emergency. Their preparation had deliberately identified which supplies served immediate response needs versus sustained recovery requirements, creating distribution systems that allocated resources appropriate to specific phases rather than depleting critical supplies through inadequate differentiation.

Balanced authority structures appropriate to specific emergency phases prevent counterproductive leadership conflicts that undermine effective operation. When communities develop authority systems that acknowledge different phases require different leadership capabilities, transitions occur through planned progression rather than disruptive power struggles. This approach prevents the tactical/practical leadership conflicts that often emerge when single authority structures attempt to address all emergency phases regardless of appropriate expertise.

During extended wildfire evacuations affecting diverse communities, those with integrated authority structures maintained more effective operation throughout the emergency duration. Their systems had deliberately established appropriate leadership for different phases—tactical security expertise during immediate evacuation, logistical coordination during intermediate shelter operation, community building during extended displacement, psychological support during eventual return. These transitions occurred through planned progression rather than the disruptive reorganizations communities with fixed authority structures typically experienced.

Comprehensive information systems that address both tactical awareness and practical sustainability needs prevent the dangerous knowledge gaps isolated approaches typically create. When emergency communication incorporates both immediate threat assessments and extended resource management requirements, communities maintain functional awareness across diverse needs rather than developing the domain-limited understanding that undermines effective response and recovery.

Following a hurricane that created both immediate dangers and extended infrastructure disruption, communities with integrated information systems maintained better function throughout the emergency duration. Their communication incorporated both tactical security assessments and practical sustainability updates, creating comprehensive awareness that prevented the dangerous knowledge asymmetries communities with domain-limited information typically experienced.

Psychological continuity between emergency response and normal operation prevents the disruptive transitions that often undermine recovery more severely than the initial emergency. When communities develop preparedness that acknowledges both dramatic intervention and sustained adaptation, the resulting approaches maintain psychological stability throughout emergency evolution rather than creating the discontinuity that prolongs trauma beyond necessary duration.

During recovery from an extended regional power outage, communities with integrated preparedness maintained better psychological health throughout the emergency. Their approaches had deliberately incorporated both immediate safety measures and long-term adaptation strategies, creating continuity that prevented the sharp transitions communities with phase-limited preparation typically experienced. The resulting stability supported faster recovery beyond physical reconstruction alone.

These capabilities emerge through deliberate integration rather than accidental overlap. Communities that develop truly resilient preparation typically establish specific mechanisms for bridging traditional preparedness divides:

Cross-domain training programs that develop awareness across tactical and practical specialists create mutual understanding without requiring universal expertise. These initiatives—joint workshops, scenario exercises, skill exchange programs—build appreciation for different approaches while maintaining appropriate specialization, enabling collaboration without undermining domain-specific capability.

Integrated resource systems that acknowledge both security and sustainability requirements prevent counterproductive competition during actual emergencies. These approaches—comprehensive supply planning, phase-appropriate allocation, deliberate redundancy development—create resource availability appropriate to specific emergency stages rather than undefined stockpiling that serves neither immediate response nor extended recovery effectively.

Collaborative leadership structures that deploy appropriate authority based on specific emergency phases rather than fixed hierarchies regardless of circumstance. These systems—phase-specific coordination teams, expertise-based authority transitions, contextual leadership approaches—create appropriate direction throughout emergency evolution rather than attempting universal management that inevitably fails certain phases despite potentially serving others effectively.

Unified communication networks that incorporate both tactical assessment and practical sustainability information create comprehensive awareness rather than domain-limited understanding. These approaches—integrated messaging systems, comprehensive situation reports, balanced information prioritization—develop complete operational pictures that support effective decision-making across different emergency aspects.

Holistic community planning that acknowledges the full emergency spectrum rather than artificially limited scenarios based on domain-specific concerns. These processes—comprehensive vulnerability assessment, integrated preparation development, balanced capability investment—create readiness for actual emergency experiences rather than idealized scenarios that rarely match reality despite their theoretical appeal.

These mechanisms transform theoretical integration into practical capability, creating communities prepared for the full emergency spectrum rather than limited phases alone. The resulting resilience addresses both dramatic response needs and extended recovery requirements, both security concerns and sustainability challenges, both immediate intervention and sustained adaptation.

Call to Action: Specific Steps for Readers of All Genders

Moving from theoretical appreciation to practical application requires deliberate action rather than mere acknowledgment. Regardless of your gender, background, or current preparedness approach, the following specific steps will help develop more comprehensive readiness that integrates diverse perspectives:

1. *Conduct an honest self-assessment of your current preparedness balance.* Examine whether you've invested disproportionately in either tactical or practical aspects, either security or sustainability domains, either immediate response or extended recovery capability. This assessment requires genuine self-awareness rather than defensive justification, acknowledging potential imbalances despite their discomfort. Specific questions to consider include:

- *Have you developed security measures without corresponding sustainability systems?*
  - *Does your preparation address immediate response while neglecting extended recovery?*
  - *Are your resources primarily protective rather than sustaining, or vice versa?*
  - *Does your knowledge focus predominantly on either tactical or practical domains?*
  - *Have you developed individual capability without corresponding community connection?*

This assessment isn't about abandoning your current approach but identifying potential integration opportunities that would enhance comprehensive readiness through balanced preparation.

2. *Deliberately seek knowledge beyond your comfort domains.* If you've focused primarily on tactical preparation, explore practical sustainability resources that complement your existing knowledge. If you've emphasized community building approaches, examine security considerations that enhance rather than contradict your current perspective. This expansion doesn't require abandoning specialization but developing sufficient cross-domain awareness to facilitate effective collaboration. Specific actions might include:

- *Reading resources from preparedness domains you've previously neglected*
- *Attending workshops or training in complementary rather than familiar areas*
- *Engaging respectfully with practitioners from different preparedness perspectives*
- *Exploring how different approaches might address identical scenarios*
- *Identifying integration opportunities where diverse capabilities can thrive*

This knowledge development builds foundation for integration without requiring universal expertise across all preparedness domains.

3. Establish connections with preparedness practitioners from different perspectives.** Develop respectful relationships with individuals whose approaches differ from your own, seeking understanding rather than conversion. These connections create collaboration opportunities beyond what isolated preparation could achieve, developing networks that deploy diverse capabilities when actual emergencies require comprehensive response. Specific approaches include:

- *Participating in community preparedness initiatives that attract diverse practitioners*
- *Engaging in scenario exercises that incorporate different response and recovery phases*
- *Creating skill exchange opportunities where diverse expertise is recognized*
- *Developing mutual assistance frameworks that acknowledge different capabilities*
- *Building communication channels that function across traditional prepper boundaries*

These connections transform theoretical integration into practical collaboration capability, establishing networks that function during actual emergencies rather than merely discussing potential cooperation.

4. *Develop specific preparedness elements that complement your existing approach.* Based on your self-assessment, identify and implement particular capabilities that address current imbalances without abandoning existing strengths. This development creates comprehensive readiness through complementary additions rather than wholesale replacement, maintaining specialized expertise while expanding overall capability. Specific developments might include:

- If tactically focused, establish sustainability systems that extend response capability beyond immediate intervention
   - If practically oriented, develop security awareness that protects sustainability systems without compromising community connection
   - If individually prepared, create community integration approaches that extend personal capability beyond household boundaries
   - If community-focused, establish household readiness that prevents becoming a resource burden during initial response phases
   - If response-oriented, develop recovery capability that maintains function beyond immediate emergency resolution

These specific additions create balanced preparation without requiring fundamental replacement of existing approaches, enhancing rather than undermining current capabilities.

5. *Practice integrated preparedness through comprehensive scenarios.* Develop and regularly implement exercises that incorporate the full emergency spectrum rather than artificially limited phases alone. These scenarios reveal integration opportunities typically overlooked during domain-specific preparation, creating practical experience with comprehensive emergencies before actual situations require effective response. Specific approaches include:

- Creating scenarios that extend from immediate response through extended recovery
   - Implementing exercises that require both tactical intervention and practical sustainability

- Developing situations that necessitate appropriate authority transitions
   - Establishing problems that require diverse capabilities rather than single-domain solutions
   - Designing challenges for integration opportunities across traditional prepper boundaries

These practice experiences develop practical integration capability beyond theoretical understanding alone, creating functional readiness for actual emergencies that inevitably require comprehensive rather than limited approaches.

6. *Contribute to community preparedness initiatives that incorporate diverse perspectives.* Participate in collective readiness development that acknowledges the full emergency spectrum rather than domain-limited preparation alone. These contributions create comprehensive community capability while establishing networks that function during actual emergencies rather than theoretical discussions alone. Specific contributions might include:

- Supporting balanced resource development that serves both response and recovery needs
   - Participating in training that incorporates diverse preparedness perspectives
   - Helping establish communication systems that function across traditional boundaries
   - Contributing to leadership development that acknowledges different phases require different capabilities
   - Assisting with planning processes that address the full emergency spectrum rather than limited phases alone

These contributions develop community capability beyond what individual preparation alone could achieve, creating collective resilience through integrated rather than isolated approaches.

7. *Advocate for balanced preparedness within your existing communities.* Promote comprehensive readiness that incorporates diverse perspectives rather than domain-limited approaches alone. This advocacy creates awareness beyond current limitations without requiring confrontational challenges to existing methods, developing appreciation for integration opportunities that enhance rather than undermine current capabilities. Specific advocacy might include:

- *Sharing resources from complementary preparedness domains*
- *Highlighting successful integration examples from actual emergency experiences*
- *Facilitating respectful dialogue between different preparedness perspectives*
- *Emphasizing how diverse approaches serve different emergency phases*
- *Demonstrating specific capabilities that emerge through integration rather than isolation*

This advocacy transforms preparation from competing approaches into complementary partnerships, creating comprehensive readiness through collaboration rather than unnecessary competition.

These specific actions create practical integration beyond theoretical appreciation alone, developing comprehensive preparedness regardless of your starting perspective. The resulting capability addresses the full emergency spectrum rather than limited phases alone, creating genuine resilience through balanced readiness that serves communities throughout actual emergency experiences rather than idealized scenarios.

Final Thoughts on Balancing Practical Preparation with Maintaining Humanity

Throughout this book, we've explored how traditionally feminine and masculine preparedness approaches create their greatest value through integration rather than isolation. This partnership doesn't just enhance practical effectiveness—it maintains essential humanity throughout both preparation and response, creating resilience that sustains not just survival but civilization itself through whatever challenges emerge.

This balance addresses a danger rarely acknowledged in conventional preparedness discussions: that preparation focused exclusively on survival without corresponding attention to human connection can inadvertently damage the very humanity it supposedly protects. The most tragic preparation failure isn't insufficient supplies or inadequate skills, but losing our fundamental humanity while supposedly safeguarding it against external threats.

The integration of diverse preparedness perspectives provides protection against this subtle but profound vulnerability. When tactical approaches complement rather than dominate practical sustainability, when security considerations enhance rather than replace community connection, when individual readiness supports rather than isolates from collective resilience, preparation strengthens our humanity rather than inadvertently undermining it through imbalanced focus.

This protection emerges through several specific mechanisms worth acknowledging:

Balanced preparedness maintains ethical frameworks that might otherwise deteriorate under excessive security emphasis. When practical community approaches complement tactical protection, preparation incorporates moral considerations alongside security requirements—preserving the ethical systems that distinguish civilization from mere survival. This balance prevents the gradual moral erosion that can accompany security-dominated preparation, maintaining the humanity supposedly being protected through increasingly extreme measures.

Integrated approaches preserve social connection that isolated preparation often inadvertently damages. When community resilience receives appropriate attention alongside individual readiness, preparation strengthens rather than weakens the human relationships essential for both practical survival and meaningful existence. This connection prevents the isolation that security-focused approaches sometimes create despite their supposed protection purpose, maintaining the social fabric that ultimately determines whether survival itself holds genuine value.

Comprehensive preparation acknowledges psychological needs beyond mere physical requirements. When emotional and social dimensions receive appropriate consideration alongside material provisions, readiness addresses the full spectrum of human requirements rather than reducing existence to mere biological continuation. This completeness prevents the dehumanizing reduction that sometimes accompanies exclusively physical preparation, maintaining the psychological wholeness essential for genuine resilience.

Balanced approaches recognize that meaningful survival extends beyond mere continuation. When preparation acknowledges that human existence requires purpose beyond simple persistence, readiness creates capability that preserves rather than sacrifices what makes survival worthwhile. This recognition prevents the purpose erosion that can accompany exclusively protection-focused approaches, maintaining the meaning that ultimately determines whether survival itself holds genuine value.

Achieving this balance requires constant vigilance rather than one-time adjustments. The understandable fear that often motivates preparedness can gradually distort initially balanced approaches, creating security emphasis that incrementally displaces the humanity supposedly being protected. This distortion rarely occurs through dramatic shifts but through subtle adjustments that collectively transform preparation from balanced readiness into protection that inadvertently damages what it intended to preserve.

Maintaining healthy balance requires regular reassessment through specific questions worth periodically examining:

- Does your preparation strengthen or weaken community connections?

- Do your security measures enhance or isolate you from meaningful human relationships?

- Does your readiness create capabilities you would willingly share or resources you feel compelled to protect at all costs?

- Has your preparation increased or decreased your compassion toward those less prepared?

- Do you find yourself viewing other people primarily as potential threats or potential partners?

- Has your readiness enhanced or diminished your appreciation for everyday human experiences?

These questions aren't comfortable, particularly when preparation has gradually drifted toward excessive security emphasis. But their honest examination provides essential correction opportunities, revealing imbalances before they transform readiness from humanity protection into inadvertent humanity damage despite supposedly noble intentions.

The most resilient preparation ultimately emerges not from choosing between security and community, between protection and connection, between individual readiness and collective resilience, but from thoughtful integration that acknowledges all these dimensions as essential aspects of comprehensive preparedness. This balance creates readiness that preserves rather than sacrifices our fundamental humanity, maintaining not just survival capability but civilization itself through whatever challenges may emerge.

As you continue your preparedness journey beyond this book, I encourage you to pursue this balanced integration—not through compromise that weakens both perspectives, but through partnership that strengthens all participants. Develop tactical capability alongside practical sustainability, security awareness alongside community connection, individual readiness alongside collective resilience. The resulting

CONCLUSION: THE PREPAREDNESS PARTNERSHIP

preparation will serve you far better through actual emergencies than any isolated approach alone, creating resilience that maintains our essential humanity rather than inadvertently damaging it through imbalanced protection despite supposedly noble intentions.

After all, genuine preparedness isn't about surviving at any cost, but about preserving what makes survival itself worthwhile—the human connections, compassionate capabilities, and meaningful purposes that distinguish civilization from mere existence. By integrating diverse perspectives rather than elevating single approaches, we create readiness that protects our full humanity rather than sacrificing essential aspects in supposed service to physical continuation alone.

That balanced integration—the preparedness partnership this book advocates—offers our best hope for navigating whatever challenges may come while preserving rather than inadvertently damaging the humanity we supposedly prepare to protect.

Keep it together, *together!*

About the Author

Riki Springwell has spent over forty years living in the northernmost reaches of Maine, where preparedness isn't a hobby but a way of life. A certified Wilderness First Responder with extensive training in emergency management, Riki has weathered countless blizzards, ice storms, and extended power outages while maintaining her small homestead near the Canadian border.

As a community preparedness coordinator, she has developed regional emergency response programs, taught practical survival skills to hundreds of students, and served as a shelter manager during numerous regional disasters. Her approach to preparedness combines traditional homesteading knowledge passed down through generations of women in her family with modern scientific understanding and a healthy dose of practical wisdom.

When not writing or teaching, Riki tends her extensive gardens, preserves food using methods both ancient and modern, and maintains a mutual aid network with neighbors across three counties. Her preparedness philosophy emphasizes community resilience, practical skill development, and the too-often overlooked contributions of women to survival throughout history.

Riki shares her home with an ancient shotgun named Mabel, an opinionated Maine Coon cat also named Mabel, and enough home-canned goods to weather any apocalypse in style and comfort.

www.ingramcontent.com/pod-product-compliance
Lightning Source LLC
Chambersburg PA
CBHW070539080426
42453CB00030B/2076